Palestinian Refugees

Palestinian Refugees

Challenges of Repatriation and
Development

Edited by
Rex Brynen and Roula El-Rifai

International Development Research Centre
Ottawa · Cairo · Dakar · Montevideo · Nairobi · New Delhi · Singapore

Published in 2007 by I.B. Tauris & Co Ltd and the
International Development Research Centre

6 Salem Road, London W2 4BU
175 Fifth Avenue, New York NY 10010
www.ibtauris.com

International Development Research Centre
PO Box 8500
Ottawa, ON KIG 3H9
Canada

info@idrc.ca/www.idrc.ca
ISBN (e-book) 978-1-55250-231-0

In the United States of America and Canada distributed by
Palgrave Macmillan a division of St. Martin's Press
175 Fifth Avenue, New York NY 10010

ISBN 978 1 84511 311 7

A full CIP record for this book is available from the British Library
A full CIP record is available from the Library of Congress

Library of Congress Catalog Card Number: available

Typeset by Jayvee, Trivandrum, India
Printed and bound in India by
Replika Press Pvt. Ltd

Contents

Figures and tables

Tables

Contributors

Dr Hassan Abu-Libdeh

Dr Hassan Abu-Libdeh served as Minister of Labor and Social Affairs with the Palestinian National Authority. An expert in socio-demographic statistics, Dr Abu-Libdeh was previously Founder and President of the Palestinian Central Bureau of Statistics (PCBS). He received his B.Sc. in Mathematics from Birzeit University in 1979, his M.Sc. in Mathematical Statistics from Stanford University (1981), his M.Sc. in Applied Statistics and a Ph.D. in Biostatistics from Cornell University (1988). He also served as a member of the Board of Governors and Deputy Managing Director of the Palestinian Economic Council for Development and Reconstruction (PEC-DAR), a board member Al-Quds Open University, the Palestinian Economic Policy Research Institute, the Policy Research Initiative for Palestine, the Council for Higher Education, and the Higher Council for Children and Motherhood. He served as a member of the Central Election Commission (CEC), in charge of planning and implementing the first ever general and political elections in the West Bank and Gaza Strip (January 1996). He is currently a member of the Palestinian National Council (1996). Since the beginning of the peace process with the Madrid conference in 1991, he was appointed to several dele-gations to bilateral negotiations and multilateral working groups.

Dr Rachelle Alterman

Professor Rachelle Alterman is an urban planner and lawyer who holds the David Azrieli Chair in Town Planning/Architecture at the

Technion – Israel Institute of Technology. She holds degrees in social science and city planning from the University of Manitoba, a Ph.D. in planning from the Technion, and a law degree from Tel-Aviv University. Dr Alterman is internationally known for her cross-country comparative research on planning law and property rights, urban and housing policy, and planning theory. She has published extensively in international academic journals and is the author of many books, among them *Planning in the Face of Crisis: Land Use, Housing, and Mass Immigration in Israel* (Routledge, 2002), and *National-Level Planning in Democratic Countries*, (Liverpool University Press, 2001). Dr Alterman has been invited as a visiting professor at leading American and Dutch graduate planning programmes and has served as consultant to the World Bank and the UNDP. Professor Alterman is in the process of founding the world's first international academic association of Planning and Law.

Geoffrey Aronson

Geoffrey Aronson is Director of the Foundation for Middle East Peace in Washington, DC and Editor of the Foundation's bi-monthly *Report on Israeli Settlement in the Occupied Territories*. He is author of *From Sideshow to Center Stage: US Policy towards Egypt and Israel* (Lynne Rienner, 1986) and *Israel, Palestinians and the Intifada: Creating Facts on the West Bank* (Routledge, 1990) as well as numerous newspaper, magazine, and journal articles on a wide range of Middle East issues. He writes regularly in the USA, the Arab world, and for European publications, and has consulted for both the World Bank and the UN.

Dr Rex Brynen

Dr Rex Brynen is Professor of Political Science at McGill University in Canada. He is author, editor, or coeditor of eight books on Middle East politics including *A Very Political Economy: Peacebuilding and Foreign Aid in the West Bank and Gaza* (USIP Press, 2000) and *Sanctuary and Survival: The PLO in Lebanon* (Westview, 1990). Professor Brynen has served as a member of the Policy Staff of Foreign Affairs Canada, and as a consultant to the Canadian International Development Agency, the International Development Research Centre, and the World Bank.

He is also coordinator of the Palestinian Refugee ResearchNet (<http://www.prrn.org>).

Dr Michael Dumper

Dr Michael (Mick) Dumper is Reader in Middle East Politics, Department of Politics, University of Exeter, UK. Prior to his academic career at Exeter University, Dr Mick Dumper worked for several NGOs in the Middle East. His PhD thesis was on the *waqf* in Israel and the occupied Palestinian territories and he has published two books on Jerusalem, *The Politics of Jerusalem since 1967* (Columbia University Press, 1997) and *The Politics of Sacred Space: the Old City of Jerusalem and the Middle East Conflict* (Lynne Rienner, 2003). He is currently researching on comparative perspectives on refugee repatriation programmes and has edited a volume entitled *Palestinian Refugee Repatriation: Global Perspectives* (Routledge, 2006).

Roula El-Rifai

Roula El-Rifai is a Senior Program Specialist with the International Development Research Centre in Ottawa, Canada. She currently manages the Middle East Unit (MEU) which consists of three programmes: the Expert and Advisory Services Fund (EASF), which supports policy-oriented research on the Palestinian refugee issue; the Middle East Good Governance Fund (MEGGF) which aims to increase policy-relevant knowledge that is useful to promote good governance in the Middle East region, particularly Iraq; and the Scholarship Fund for Palestinian Refugee Women in Lebanon. Roula has a Master's degree in International Relations from the University of Kent in Canterbury in the UK, and a Master's degree in Rural Planning and Development from the University of Guelph in Canada. She did her Bachelor's degree in Political Science at the American University of Beirut in Lebanon.

Ann Elwan

Ann Elwan consults for the World Bank, and others, particularly in housing and infrastructure. She worked for the World Bank for 22 years, during which time she worked on infrastructure and housing projects in the Middle East and North Africa, and the Europe and

Central Asia Regions. Also, while at the Bank, she worked on several post-conflict reconstruction projects and the Bank's post-conflict reconstruction policy paper. She is also working on a consulting assignment on a global housing finance facility for UN HABITAT.

Dr Sari Hanafi

Dr Sari Hanafi is Visiting Associate Professor at the American University of Beirut teaching Sociology. A sociologist holding a Ph.D. from EHESS-Paris (1994), Dr Sari Hanafi was formerly the Director of the Palestinian Refugee and Diaspora Centre, Shaml. He is the author of numerous journal articles and book chapters on economic sociology and network analysis of the Palestinian diaspora; relationships between diaspora and centre; political sociology and sociology of migration (mainly about the Palestinian refugees); sociology of the new actors in international relations (NGOs and international NGOs). Among his books are *Here and There: Towards an Analysis of the Relationship between the Palestinian Diaspora and the Center* (In Arabic, 2001); *Between Two Worlds: Palestinian Businessmen in the Diaspora and the Construction of a Palestinian Entity* (in Arabic and in French, 1997); *La Syrie des ingénieurs: Perspective comparée avec l'Egypte*, (1997). He is editing three books on the Arab NGOs (2002; 2004) and *Palestinian Sociology of Return* (forthcoming). His last book, with Linda Taber, is *The Emergence of Palestinian Globalized Elite: Donors, International Organizations and Local NGOs* (in English, Washington: Institute of Palestine Studies and Muwatin, 2005; in Arabic, Ramallah: Muwatin, 2006).

Dr Jon Hanssen-Bauer

Jon Hanssen-Bauer is Senior Adviser in the Norwegian Ministry of Foreign Relations on research within the area of peace and reconciliation. He is on leave from his position as managing director for the Fafo Institute for Applied International Studies based in Oslo, Norway, a position he held at the time of writing his chapter contribution. He is trained as a social anthropologist, and since 1993 has been involved in the Oslo process. He managed the Palestinian–Israeli People-to-People Programme financed by Norway, and has co-ordinated Fafo's studies of the Palestine refugee issue in all the host countries in the region. He managed the Fafo study on living conditions in the Hashemite Kingdom of Jordan.

Laurie Blome Jacobsen

Laurie Blome Jacobsen is a researcher with the Fafo Institute for Applied International Studies, Norway. Ms. Jacobsen's background is in Middle East Studies and International Public Administration. Her professional background includes consultant work in Egypt with the International Finance Corporation and various international non-profit organizations associated with USAID. Subsequently, she has worked as a researcher for Fafo in Oslo for the past five years with a focus on Palestinian refugees and the Middle East.

Jan de Jong

Jan de Jong is a Strategic Planning Consultant working for the Palestinian Negotiations Support Unit in Ramallah and a researcher for Israeli and Palestinian organizations analyzing the impacts of Israeli planning policies on Palestinian communities in the West Bank and in Gaza. He is a freelance consultant for land use planning and documentation targeted toward developing client-oriented decision support systems for institutions, local communities and developmental agencies. He taught history and specialized in historical geography and worked as a geographic editor, authoring a number of Arabic Studies related Map documents for the Dutch Encyclopedia of Islam. In 1982 he authored an illustrated documentary record, titled 'Palestine, Palestinians' for the Dutch Developmental Agency 'Novib'. From 1989 to 1993, he worked in the 'Palestine Geographic Research and Information Center' where he collected and compiled vital data and information on land use planning policies in the Palestinian territories, particularly in Jerusalem. His work in the form of reports, maps and articles, was widely published in the Hebrew, Palestinian and international press (*Ha'aretz, Ma'ariv, An Nahar, Al Fajr, Sunday Times, Tageszeitung, Le Meridien, Le Monde Diplomatique*). As a consultant in land use planning, he published a number of reports on the Palestinian territories, in particular on Metropolitan Jerusalem (*Le Monde Diplomatique, Manière de Voir, Le Meridien, Die Tageszeitung*, Foundation for Middle East Peace). He has authored chapters in books that were published in the UK and Holland and Belgium in 1996 and 1997. One report, summarizing his analysis on the current perspective of the Palestinian Territories was published in the anthology *After Oslo: New Realities, Old Problems*, published by Pluto Press, London in 1998.

Nicholas Krafft

Mr Nicholas Krafft is Operations Director, Human Development Network, World Bank. He has a post-graduate degree in economics from the London School of Economics. Prior to his current position, and while on sabbatical from the World Bank, he worked as Advisor to the Minister of Agriculture and Land Affairs in South Africa (1996–1998), as South Africa made the transition from a government that only served the white farming sector to one which aimed to include the previously disadvantaged. From 1979–1992, Mr Krafft held several positions at the World Bank working on Latin America and the Caribbean, Eastern Europe, Eastern Africa, South Asia, and the Middle East and North Africa. Prior to joining the Bank, he worked as a volunteer teaching in India for a number of years.

Khalil Nijem

Khalil Nijem is the Director General for Strategic Planning within the Palestinian Ministry of Planning. He is a planner with a rural planning/engineering background and for over 24 years has been working in community development, institutional building, and planning. Professionally, his engagement with the issue of Palestinian refugees goes back to his earlier career, in 1983, when he served as a Planning Engineer at UNRWA in Jerusalem. Since then, his involvement has continued both as a researcher and as a development planner. Further, and with the establishment of the Ministry in 1995, his involvement with the issue of refugees increased both in developing various national plans and in providing technical assistance to the Palestinian negotiators. Mr Nijjem has represented the Ministry in the Refugee Coordination Group, a body that coordinates the work of relevant Palestinian public institutions for the purpose of providing technical support and assistance to the negotiation team.

Preface and acknowledgements

There are few challenges more daunting than that of bringing about
an end to the conflict between Israel and the Palestinians. Central to
the conflict and any possible resolution is the complex issue of
Palestinian refugees. This issue is very emotional, even existential, to
the millions of refugees who are waiting – 58 years later – for a resolution to their plight. But the emotion-laden refugee issue is also a
very technical one. This book attempts to deal with the complicated
issue of how to plan for the absorption and integration of
Palestinian refugees into a new Palestinian state.

It is based on the proceedings of a conference organized
by the International Development Research Centre (IDRC)
(<http://www.idrc.ca>) in June 2003, the Stocktaking II Conference
on Palestinian Refugee Research. Its aim, by definition, was to take
stock of what research had been undertaken on the Palestinian
Refugee issue over the previous five years. The conference also sought
to bring much of the research into the public arena and, most importantly, to identify gaps in knowledge and priorities of future research.
The first Stocktaking Conference was hosted in Ottawa in 1997 by
IDRC and the Palestinian Refugee ResearchNet based at McGill
University (<http://www.arts.mcgill.ca/mepp/new_prrn>).

At the June 2003 conference, more than 100 researchers and policymakers discussed the issues of data collection, legal and international law perspectives, political processes, public opinion, the
absorptive process, compensation and mechanisms. The discussions
were in equal measure emotional, partisan and technical. But they

were also conducive to serious dialogue at a difficult time in the peace process. The discussions certainly highlighted the enormous challenges involved in resolving the refugee issue and the need for long-term planning and preparation. The conference agenda, papers, list of participants and other details can be accessed at the following site: <http://web.idrc.ca/en/ev-32583–201–1-DO_TOPIC.html>.

This conference was an activity of the Expert and Advisory Services Fund (EASF), a project funded by the Canadian International Development Agency (CIDA). It is managed by IDRC and has worked to support Canada's role as Gavel of the Refugee Working Group in the multilateral negotiations track of the Middle East peace process, and assists the Special Coordinator for the Middle East Peace Process in Foreign Affairs Canada.

The EASF has been in operation since 1992 and over time has evolved to focus its work on generating research and knowledge and to building capacity on the refugee issue; this work that has the potential to benefit researchers, academics, non-governmental organization (NGOs), negotiators and policymakers as they grapple with various complex aspects of the refugee question. Currently, the EASF is paying particular attention to three themes: (i) compensation; (ii) plan-ning for demographic change; and (iii) the importance of gauging and engaging public opinion.

These three themes were all featured in the 2003 conference agenda. One of those themes, the developmental challenges of absorbing returnees into a Palestinian state, is the primary focus of this book. The book presents data on the refugees and their living conditions in the West Bank and Gaza and host countries, examines sociological factors influencing the process of return migration and looks at the evolution of European policy analysis of the issue of absorption. The book also tackles the technical planning aspects of the absorption and integration of returnees into the West Bank and Gaza as developed by Palestinian planners and the World Bank. It also presents some of the lessons learned from Israel's experience in absorption of immigrants over the last five decades and finally provides a preliminary analysis of the potential of evacuated settlements to absorb refugees into a new state.

It is hoped that additional volumes dealing with the other important themes of the Stocktaking Conference will be published in future.

The conference was funded primarily by CIDA through the EASF. We would also like to acknowledge the support of the Human Security Division at Foreign Affairs Canada and that of IDRC. Special thanks go to Maureen O'Neil (President of IDRC), Michael Molloy (then Canada's Special Coordinator for the Middle East Peace Process) and Mario Renaud (then Regional Director for the Middle East and North Africa at CIDA) for their valuable support and advice. Rex Brynen would like to thank the Social Science and Humanities Research Council and the United States Institute of Peace for their funding of his broader research work on Palestinian refugees, Palestinian economic development, and the peace process.

We would also like to thank all those who contributed to the conference, the participants, the organizers, and all those who made this book possible, most notably the authors of the papers you are about to read. Special gratitude is due to Megan Bradley and Alex Brynen for their meticulous editing work, to Jill Tansley and Maurizio Iellina for their contribution and Bill Carman of IDRC Publications for his advice and continuous support to make this publication a reality.

One of the main conclusions of the Stocktaking II conference was that while we now have a much greater knowledge base on the refugee issue compared to 1997 and while the number of researchers specializing on the refugee issue has increased tremendously, we really have only touched the tip of the iceberg. Much more remains to be done by historians, economists, sociologists, planners and many others, including the politicians whose will is essential to move the process closer to resolution. We hope this book will contribute to the body of knowledge on such a key issue and we hope the papers will stimulate thinking, lead to further research and analysis and facilitate efforts by policymakers, NGOs, donor agencies and most importantly, Palestinian planners and refugees themselves.

Rex Brynen and Roula El-Rifai

Glossary

APIC	Arab Palestinian Investment Company
CEC	Central Election Commission
CFSP	Common Foreign and Security Policy
CIDA	Canadian International Development Agency
CIP	Community Infrastructure Program
CPAL	Commission for the Preservation of Agricultural Land
DOP	Declaration of Principles
DORA	Department of Refugee Affairs
DOS	Department of Statistics
DP	Displaced Person
EASF	Expert and Advisory Services Fund
EC	European Community
ECHO	European Commission Humanitarian Office
EHESS	L'École des Hautes Études en Sciences Sociales
EMP	Euro-Mediterranean Partnership
EU	European Union
EUSE	European Union Special Envoy
Fafo	Institute for Applied International Studies
GDP	Gross Domestic Product
GNP	Gross National Product
GTZ	German Technical Cooperation Agency
HCC	Housing Construction Commission
hu	housing units
IDRC	International Development Research Centre
IMR	Infant Mortality Rates
IOM	International Organization for Migration

MEFTA	Mediterranean Free Trade Area
MEGGF	Middle East Good Governance Fund
MENA	Middle East and North Africa
MEPP	Middle East Peace Process
MEU	Middle East Unit
MOH	Ministry of Housing
MOP	Ministry of Planning
MOPIC	Ministry of Planning and International Cooperation
NAD	Negotiations Affairs Department
NATO	North Atlantic Treaty Organization
NGO	Non-governmental organization
OPT	Occupied Palestinian Territories
PA	Palestinian Authority
PADICO	Palestine and Development Limited
PCBS	Palestine Central Bureau of Statistics
pd	Persons per dunam
PECDAR	Palestinian Economic Council for Development and Reconstruction
PIP	Peace Implementation Programme
PLO	Palestine Liberation Organization
PMHC	Palestine Mortgage and Housing Corporation
PPIs	Physical Planning Initiatives
PSR	Policy and Survey Research
PSS	Palestinian Statistical System
PUF	Public Use Files
REDWG	Regional Economic Development Working Group
RTF	Refugee Task Force
RWG	Refugee Working Group
SMS	Short Messenger Service
TFR	Total Fertility Rates
TOKTEN	Transfer of Knowledge Through Expatriates Nationals
UNDP	United Nations Development Programme
UNHCR	United Nations High Commissioner for Refugees
UNRWA	United Nations Relief and Works Agency
USAID	United States Agency for International Development
WBG	West Bank and Gaza
WHO	World Health Organization

CHAPTER 1

Introduction: Refugee repatriation, development, and the challenges of Palestinian state-building

Rex Brynen, McGill University, Montreal, Canada
Roula El-Rifai, International Development Research Centre, Ottawa, Canada

PALESTINIAN REFUGEES SUFFER the twin misfortunes of being both the largest refugee population in the world, and one of the oldest. The refugee issue traces its origins to the establishment of the state of Israel in 1948, an event that was accompanied by the forced displacement of some three quarters of a million of Palestinian Arabs from their homes within what had become the territory of the new Jewish state. The refugees fled to the then Jordanian-controlled West Bank, Egyptian-administered Gaza Strip, the east bank of the Jordan River, Syria, Lebanon, and further afield. The homes and properties that they left behind were seized by the Israeli government. Most refugees were barred from returning. In 1967, the Israeli occupation of the West Bank and Gaza (WBG) saw a further three hundred thousand or so Palestinians flee from those areas, mostly to Jordan. With the natural growth of this population and the passage of more than two generations of time, over four million Palestinian refugees are today registered with the United Nations Relief and Works Agency (UNRWA), and a majority of Palestinians live in exile in the diaspora.

It has long been recognized that a fair and mutually acceptable solution to the Palestinian refugee issue is an essential component of achieving a just and lasting peace between Israelis and Palestinians. What such an agreement might look like, of course, is far less clear. To what extent, if at all, would Israel recognize the refugees' 'right of return' or accept the return of some or any Palestinians to their original homes within Israel? What formula could be found to reconcile refugee rights and present realities? What forms and levels of compensation might be offered to refugees for their losses? How would host countries respond to a peace agreement, and what would be the fate of refugees resident there? Would any third countries offer to resettle any refugees, and if so how many and under what conditions? What resources and mechanisms would be available to implement a refugee agreement, and over what time frames? The issues are highly contentious, and outcomes are uncertain.

Despite this uncertainty, however, two things are clear. First, whatever the precise contours of any future refugee agreement, a significant number of diaspora Palestinians may choose to reside in a Palestinian state in the West Bank and Gaza. Second, it is also certain that many Palestinian refugees already resident in the WBG may choose to stay, regardless of whatever other residential options may or may not be offered to them.

Given this, it is only prudent that those concerned with the well-being of a future Palestinian state and its citizens address the challenges of refugee absorption and sustainable development. Undoubtedly, such absorption will pose a number of social, economic, and environmental challenges. Palestinian labour markets, land and housing markets, infrastructure, social services, and natural resources will find themselves under growing pressure, in addition to the significant pressures that they face from the already high rate of natural population increase in the WBG. On the other hand, returnees are likely to bring with them a varied mix of skills, capital, and enthusiasm, all of which could represent substantial assets for the new state.

This book is about precisely these sorts of questions: the social and economic effects that might be anticipated from refugee repatriation and absorption, and the various policy options that could be adopted to deal with these. It emerges from papers presented on this and other Palestinian refugee issues at the 'Stocktaking II' conference, hosted in Ottawa in June 2003 by the International Development Research Centre, as well as from other work done under the auspices of the Palestinian Refugee ResearchNet (<http://www.prrn.org>). It is our hope that, by disseminating such research more widely, we might promote further dialogue and analysis on such key issues, facilitating the efforts and reflections of non-governmental organizations, donor agencies, Palestinian planners, decision-makers, and especially refugee stakeholders themselves.

In addressing absorption policies for a future Palestinian state, we are well aware of the sensitivity of the topic. Some refugee advocates might prefer that the issue not be explored at this stage, for fear that it could detract attention from demands for the refugees' right of return to their original homes within Israel. While understanding their concerns, the editors see no such linkage. Rights are rights, regardless of development planning. As will be discussed later, Palestinian planners and others have long recognized that a future Palestinian state will face absorption challenges, regardless of whether refugees also return to Israel. The path to long-term sustainable development in Palestine will require that such future demographic realities be addressed.

On the other side, there are undoubtedly some who would prefer that no refugees return to either Israel or the West Bank and Gaza, and still others who continue to oppose the very establishment of a Palestinian state. It is clear, however, that such thinking is confined only to a small minority: the need for a two-state solution to the Palestinian–Israeli conflict is widely accepted within Israel, and almost unanimously within the international community. An independent Palestinian state, in full control of its international borders, will have every sovereign right to control its own absorption policy. It will almost inevitably welcome refugees and others in the diaspora to come and join in the task of building Palestine.

We also recognize that the terminology of the Palestinian refugee issue can be confusing. As has become standard usage, most of the authors in this book use the term '1948 refugees' to refer to those Palestinians who fled in 1947–1949 from their homes within what became the state of Israel, together with their descendants. By contrast, the term 'displaced persons' is used to refer to those who fled from the West Bank and Gaza upon or after the Israeli occupation of these territories in 1967, as well as West Bankers and Gazans who found themselves outside the occupied territories and were refused permission to return. Of course, many displaced persons were also 1948 refugees, having first fled to the WBG and then further afield. The generic term 'refugees' usually refers to 1948 refugees and 1967 displaced persons alike. 'Return' is usually used to refer to the return of 1948 refugees to their home areas within what is now Israel. By contrast, 'repatriation' – the focus of this study – is used to refer to the movement of refugees and displaced persons to the territory of a future Palestinian state. Somewhat confusingly, perhaps, both we and most of the contributors use the term 'returnees' to refer both to refugees returning to 1948 areas, and/or refugees and displaced persons repatriating to a Palestinian state.

Understood in this way, all of these terms generally reflect the way they have been used by Palestinian and Israeli negotiators themselves in the period since the signing of the 1993 Declaration of Principles ('Oslo Accord').

FINAL STATUS NEGOTIATIONS AND REFUGEE REPATRIATION

The idea that remaining in, or repatriating to, a future Palestinian state would be one of the major options presented to refugees was reflected in the permanent status negotiations between Israel and the Palestinian Authority (PA)/Palestine Liberation Organization (PLO) that took place in 2000–2001. In particular, in the 'Clinton Parameters' of December 2000, then US President Bill Clinton listed 'five possible final homes for the refugees', namely:

1　The state of Palestine;
2　Areas in Israel being transferred to Palestine in the land swap;
3　Rehabilitation in a host country;
4　Resettlement in a third country;
5　Admission to Israel.

Moreover, while 'rehabilitation in host countries, resettlement in third countries and absorption into Israel will depend upon the policies of those countries', President Clinton stressed that 'the agreement will make clear that the return to the West Bank, Gaza Strip, and the areas acquired in the land swap would be a right to all Palestinian refugees' (Clinton 2000). The Clinton Proposals were accepted by Israel, and welcomed but not unequivocally accepted by the

Palestinians. With regard to the question of residential choice, the Palestinian side concurred with the principle, but felt that some sort of recognition of the refugees' 'right of return' to their original homes (in Israel) needed to be included. However, they also emphasized that they were

> prepared to think flexibly and creatively about the mechanisms for implementing the right of return. In many discussions with Israel, mechanisms for implementing this right in such a way so as to end the refugee status and refugee problem, as well as to otherwise accommodate Israeli concerns, have been identified and elaborated in some detail.

(PLO NAD 2001)

At the Taba negotiations in January 2001, the initial Palestinian position did not frame residential choices in the same way, being largely focused instead on modalities for the right of return (PA/PLO 2001). However, the Israeli 'private response' of 23 January 2001 – which, in practice, reflected positions to which both sides were tending – did once more emphasize the same five sets of options that Clinton had outlined (ISRAEL 2001). The draft working paper on implementation mechanisms drawn up jointly by the two sides called for the establishment of a 'return, repatriation, and relocation committee' – charged, it can safely be assumed, with the return of refugees to Israel, their repatriation to the Palestinian state, or their relocation to third countries should they not remain in present host countries (PA/PLO/ISRAEL 2001).

The Taba negotiations ended without agreement, and the failure of the parties to reach a deal on the refugee issue has sometimes been cited as a primary reason for this. There is little evidence for this view. Indeed, members of both negotiating teams have affirmed explicitly to the editors that the two sides were serious, creative, and positive in trying to reach an agreement that would be fair and acceptable to both sides. The failure to resolve the refugee issue fully, they suggested, was a product of time constraints rather than inability to make progress.

A similar approach was also reflected in the unofficial 'Geneva Accord', produced by prominent Israel and Palestinian figures and published in December 2003 (see Geneva Accord 2003.) This too identified five residential options: the Palestinian state; former Israeli territories swapped to Palestine; Israel itself; third countries; and present host countries. Since admission into Israel would be at Israel's 'sovereign discretion' (although loosely related to offers of refugee resettlement by third countries), the number of refugees allowed to return would likely be very small. Consequently, the Geneva Accord, like the Taba negotiations and the Clinton Parameters before it, presumed that the Palestinian state itself would be a major destination of Palestinians wishing to return to their homeland.

REPATRIATION, DEVELOPMENT AND STATE-BUILDING

A critical first step in any thinking about refugee absorption is to examine the possible population that might choose to repatriate to a Palestinian state, as well as the existing refugee population in the West Bank and Gaza that would likely remain there. According to UNRWA, there were almost 4.2 million refugees registered with the Agency as of mid-2004 (see Table 1.1).

Such figures, however, do not necessarily reflect the actual number of refugees. Some have suggested that refugees, and hence the Agency, may under-report deaths, and hence the figures may be slightly exaggerated. On the other hand, UNRWA only registers refugees in its areas of operation, and hence does not include non-refugees in these areas (including those who failed to register in the 1950s), nor Palestinians outside these areas in the broader diaspora (such as the approximately 50,000 Palestinians in Egypt). Many refugees registered in one area with the Agency may actually be living and working elsewhere. This is particularly true in the case of Lebanon, where as little as half of the refugees registered there with UNRWA may actually be resident in the country.

Estimates by the PLO Department of Refugee Affairs (2001, cited in Table 2.1 in Chapter 2 of this book), for example, suggest that there are some five million refugees worldwide. The BADIL Resource Center for Palestinian Residency and Refugee Rights has suggested that there were seven million or more refugees and displaced persons as of 2003, including four million registered with

UNRWA, approximately 1.5 million unregistered 1948 refugees, over 750,000 1967 displaced persons, plus those Palestinians who were internally displaced in Israel in 1948, or in the West Bank and Gaza in 1967 (BADIL 2004). For its purposes, the PA Ministry of Planning uses a figure of some 9.3 million Palestinians worldwide in 2002, of which 4.7 million reside in the diaspora, outside the borders of historic Palestine (see Chapter 7).

Table 1.1: *UNRWA-Registered Refugees (mid-2003)*

	West Bank	Gaza	Jordan	Syria	Lebanon
Registered refugees	675,670	938,531	1,758,274	417,346	396,890
Refugees in camps	177,920	464,075	281,211	110,450	192,557
% of refugees in camps	26%	49%	16%	26%	49%

Source: UNRWA in Figures, 30 June 2004.

Quite apart from the numbers of refugees and diaspora Palestinians, there is the question of their demographic and socio-economic characteristics. Effective repatriation policies should be informed by a sense of local conditions for existing refugees in the WBG, as well as by the possible age distribution, educational profile, labour force skills, capital assets, and past living conditions of those who might choose to repatriate.

In this book, Abu-Libdeh, Hanssen-Bauer and Jacobsen, and Hanafi all offer valuable insights into the central question 'who are the refugees'. Hasan Abu-Libdeh highlights the contribution of statistical data in addressing the refugee issue. Following an account of the development of Palestinian statistical capacity in the form of the Palestinian Central Bureau of Statistics, he offers an overview of the socio-economic characteristics of refugees in the West Bank and Gaza as well as opinion survey data on refugee attitudes towards a possible resolution of the refugee issue. He also identifies important gaps in our existing information on the refugees and their circumstances, suggesting the need for further research on Palestinian absorption capacities, the profile of refugees in host countries, and potential returnees.

Jon Hanssen-Bauer and Laurie Blome Jacobsen focus on precisely this issue, examining the conditions of refugees in host countries as revealed through a series of living condition surveys undertaken by Fafo, the Norwegian Institute for Applied Social Science, and local partners. These findings suggest that, in general, there is little difference between the conditions of refugees and those of host country populations. The situation of refugees in camps is somewhat poorer, although not all camp populations have homogenously poor conditions. The major reason for these generally positive findings, they suggest, is the array of health, education, and other services provided by UNRWA. Among host countries, Hanssen-Bauer and Jacobsen find the situation in Lebanon to be the most pressing, especially in the camps where poverty is particularly high.

Sari Hanafi examines the range of factors that may shape the repatriation and return decisions of refugees. These include the social and economic conditions of refugee populations, the nature of social kinship networks, the 'migration culture' of many refugees, and the situation of 'camp' and 'noncamp' refugees. Investment and labour market opportunities, he stresses, are shaped not only by economic realities, but also by familial and other social networks – a fact that might facilitate refugee absorption through diaspora investments in the WBG. Moreover, his work suggests that repatriation and return need not be thought of as dichotomous – some Palestinians may well maintain transnational lives, with residences and/or investments in multiple locations, with strong social relations to all of them. Finally, Hanafi suggests a number of possible return, repatriation and resettlement scenarios, based on differing assumptions about Israel's willingness to accept the return of some refugees to 1948 areas.

Local and international policy analysis on refugees, refugee repatriation, and absorption, is explored in detail in the chapters by Dumper, Brynen, Elwan and Krafft, Nijim, Alterman, and Aronson. Here, all of the authors reflect on what sorts of policies might best serve both the refugees and a future Palestinian state. Although there are some differences of opinion, many more areas of convergence are apparent.

Mick Dumper explores the evolution of European Union (EU) policy thinking on the refugee issue, focusing on consultant studies prepared for the EU Refugee Task Force in 1999 and 2001. As lead researcher for the latter, he is able to point to a number of key issues that emerged in the course of the study. In particular he points to the challenges posed by uncertainty as to possible repatriation numbers, Palestinian development prospects, and the fiscal health of the PA and a future Palestinian state. He highlights debates among Palestinian planners as to whether a future Palestinian state should adopt an expansive (and expensive) 'big bang' approach to repatriation through the construction of new cities for returnees in less populated areas, or whether instead an 'incrementalist' approach of building on existing capacities might be preferable. Dumper raises the question of the future of UNRWA, and whether the Agency should be transformed after a peace agreement to take a lead role in refugee absorption ('UNRWA plus'), or whether other institutions are better suited to this ('UNRWA minus'). He summarizes the key policy recommendations of his study. Finally, he highlights the difficulty of assessing policy impact, given the opacity of the EU policy process as well as the eruption of the second *intifada* and the consequent diversion of European attention to more immediate and pressing concerns of humanitarian assistance.

Rex Brynen offers an overview of a dozen policy lessons that, in his view, emerge from work by the World Bank and others in the area of refugee repatriation and development. These include the need for repatriation to be voluntary; the need to avoid bureaucratic impediments and other perverse incentives that might distort population flows; the limited utility of any concept of 'absorptive capacity'; the need to integrate repatriation/absorption strategies into broader demographic policy planning; the dangers of large-scale public housing programmes for refugees; the unlikelihood that refugee camp populations could ever be relocated or rehoused *en masse*; the limits of using evacuated Israeli settlements for refugee housing; the need to reduce the transaction costs of relocation for refugees; the importance of addressing housing issues within the framework of a larger Palestinian national housing strategy; the importance of housing finance initiatives; the likely limits of donor resources; and the importance of (Israeli) compensation payments to refugees as part of the broader absorption, repatriation, and development equation.

One key aspect of previously unpublished work by the World Bank – housing and infrastructure programmes for refugees – is discussed in much greater detail by Ann Elwan and Nick Krafft. In particular, they summarize analytical work that has been done, in two phases, on the potential public and private infrastructure costs of upgrading existing refugee camps, the expansion of existing urban areas to accommodate returnees, and the construction of new towns and cities. Their chapter also emphasizes the importance of broader housing policy reform. In the end, they suggest four key 'baskets' for a repatriation programme: status-based benefits to refugees (as refugees), intended to mitigate past losses; needs-based housing assistance for both returnees and existing WBG residents; housing finance programmes to assist all low-income households; and direct public investment in both general infrastructure (roads, sewage, and sanitation, as well as health, education and other social services) and sites-and-services programmes for new residential areas. In terms of future analytical work, they point to the value of extending their earlier work to other possible residential sites in the WBG; planning pilot projects so as to help further identify the policies, procedures, and actions that would be required; and investigating how private land could be brought into use for housing on a larger scale. They also emphasize the need to examine how incentives might be used to encourage municipalities to attract returnees; the potential role of public and private infrastructure construction; and the ways in which implicit and explicit subsidies can encourage absorption yet remain within the constraints of likely available resources.

Khalil Nijim outlines Palestinian Authority policy planning on the issue of refugee absorption. As he notes, PA planning for future refugee absorption has been complicated by the uncertainty regarding other relevant aspects of a peace agreement, notably with regard to territorial, economic, and natural resource issues. He also highlights the extent to which planning for refugee-specific issues – compensation, absorption, the future of refugee camps, and the future of UNRWA – are intimately linked to the broader challenges of development planning for a Palestinian state. In preliminary planning, the PA assumed the repatriation of some 760,000 Palestinians to the WBG by 2015, resulting in a one-third increase in the WBG population growth rate. Such migration, it was assumed, would be free and unencumbered by regulation. PA planners have then sought to examine the push- and pull-factors that might shape migration, the possible profile of returnees, their associated needs (for housing, services, and employment), the human potential of the returnee population, and the development and financial implications of all of these factors. Particular, if preliminary, work has been done on issues of residential options, such as the construction of new towns or the expansion of existing urban areas in the West Bank.

Given its history of absorbing large numbers of Jewish immigrants, the Israeli experience may hold valuable lessons for a future Palestinian government in terms of what absorption policies might work best. The chapter by Rachelle Alterman offers precisely this perspective, reviewing the strengths and weaknesses of Israeli absorption policy over more than half a century. As Alterman notes, not only has Israel faced very different levels and types of Jewish immigration over the years, but also it has adopted very different policies for dealing with these immigrants at different points in its history: highly centralized and statist policies of direct allocation of public land and state construction of housing in new or existing residential areas; more market-oriented systems of land allocation, decoupled from absorption policy; below-market-value provision of land to private developers; and various forms of housing grants, subsidies, and housing finance/mortgage subsidy programmes. Throughout her study she highlights the Israeli government's mistakes as well as its successes, and the importance of learning from both. While recognizing the very different circumstances of Israel and a future Palestinian state, Alterman is nonetheless able to offer some policy suggestions, most of which are rooted in what she sees as the successes of Israeli absorption policy in the 1990s. This policy saw some government construction of emergency housing, but largely relied on private housing investment fortified by an array of carefully designed subsidy, incentive, and guarantee programmes. Moreover, all of this took place – in contrast to the early 1950s – in a context of 'direct absorption'. Immigrants were expected to find their own housing solutions, while the state focused on the provision of transitional direct grants (rental allowances) to immigrants, and appropriate housing finance mechanisms, as well as those subsidies and incentives needed to stimulate construction and housing supply.

Geoffrey Aronson and Jan de Jong examine the extent to which the evacuation of Israeli settlements might contribute to the absorption of refugees (whether camp dwellers or returnees) in the WBG by increasing the land and housing resources available to the new Palestinian state. This issue has grown in importance in recent years with Israel's decision to disengage from Gaza and evacuate its settlers and settlements there. They argue that in both the immediate term (Gaza withdrawal) and long term (an eventual peace agreement), ex-settler housing stock is unlikely to make a significant contribution to Palestinian housing needs, even assuming that Israel chooses to leave it intact. Part of the reason for this, they argue, is that Israel is likely to retain permanent control of most of the largest and most densely populated settlement blocs, as was envisaged in the Camp David and Taba negotiations. It is far from clear, moreover, that existing settler housing and existing settlement land uses are optimal for Palestinian needs. What is likely to be of greater utility to the Palestinians, Aronson and De Jong suggest, is the underlying infrastructure investments (roads, electricity, water, sanitation, communications) in evacuated settlements and the contributions that these assets might make to future Palestinian housing and broader Palestinian development efforts.

CONCLUSION

In 2004 to 2005, a combination of Israel's Gaza disengagement plan and a transition in Palestinian leadership spurred hopes for a reinvigorated peace process. Many expressed the desire that this would lead to the timely implementation of the Quartet 'roadmap', the establishment of an interim Palestinian state, and renewed negotiations on full statehood and a permanent peace agreement. In 2006, Israeli unilateralism, the election of a Hamas-led Islamist Government in Palestine and an escalating cycle of violence, all seemed to darken any hope for a return to meaningful peace negotiations, let alone peace itself.

As we noted at the outset of this introductory chapter, a mutually acceptable resolution of the refugee issue must be a central part of any just and lasting Palestinian–Israeli peace agreement – regardless of when, and how, such an agreement might come about. It is also clear that, when and if a Palestinian state is established in the West Bank and Gaza, it will be the destination of choice for many Palestinians in the diaspora. Repatriation and the absorption of returnees will thus pose a substantial challenge to both Palestinian development planners and their partners in the international community.

This in turn underscores the need for continued research, analysis, and dialogue on the refugee issue in all its dimensions. This book is a modest step in that direction. However, as so many of our contributors make clear, there is a great deal more still to do.

BIBLIOGRAPHY

Badil (2004) *Facts and Figures*, Bethlehem: BADIL; available from <http://www.badil.org/Refugees/facts&figures.htm>.

Clinton, B. (2000) *The Clinton Parameters*, Washington DC: White House.

Geneva Accord (2003); available from <http://www.heskem.org.il/Heskem_en.asp>.

Palestine Liberation Organization Negotiations Affairs Department (PLO NAD) (2001) *Remarks and Questions from the Palestinian Negotiating Team Regarding the United States Proposal*, Ramallah: PLO NAD; available from <http://www.nad-plo.org/nclinton2.php>.

Palestinian Authority/Palestine Liberation Organization (PA/PLO) (2001) *Palestinian Statement on Refugees*, Taba: Palestinian Authority; available from <http://www.monde-diplomatique.fr/cahier/proche-orient/refugeespal-en>.

Israel (2001) *'Non-Paper': Private Response to the Palestinian Refugee Paper of January 22, 2001*, Taba; available from <http://www.monde-diplomatique.fr/cahier/proche-orient/israelrefugees-en>.

Palestinian Authority/Palestine Liberation Organization/Israel (PA/PLO/ISRAEL) (2001) *Refugee Mechanism Draft 2*, 25 January 2001.

United Nations Relief and Works Agency (UNRWA) (2004) *UNRWA in Figures*, Gaza City: UNRWA.

CHAPTER 2

Statistical data on Palestinian refugees: What we know and what we don't

Hasan Abu-Libdeh, Palestinian Central Bureau of Statistics, Ramallah

BACKGROUND ON THE PALESTINIAN STATISTICAL SYSTEM

After the occupation of the West Bank and Gaza Strip in 1967, the Israeli military and civil authorities became responsible for collecting various data and statistics about Palestinian society. For almost 28 years, these authorities were actively involved in collecting the statistics about fields which, there is reason to believe, served the purposes of maintaining and prolonging the Israeli military occupation of the West Bank and Gaza Strip. The absence of an official Palestinian statistical system in the Occupied Palestinian Territories (OPT) between 1967 and 1993 resulted in the inability of Palestinian planners and policymakers to undertake future planning to create realistic and objective developmental programmes.

On the eve of signing the Declaration of Principles (DOP) between the Palestine Liberation Organization (PLO) and Israel in 1993, the PLO decided to set up a Central Bureau of Statistics for Palestine. This was the first national Palestinian agency to be set up on Palestinian soil as the peace process was unfolding, and was actually the first small beginning of an administrative apparatus for a future independent Palestinian state. At the time, there was nothing – no staff, no Palestinian produced statistics, no organization, no statistical infrastructure.

Since its establishment in September 1993, the Palestinian Central Bureau of Statistics (PCBS) has endeavoured to fill the existing statistical gap in the West Bank and the Gaza Strip by compiling data in the social, economic, geographical and environmental fields in accordance with a specified priority schedule. In view of the fact that statistical priorities are numerous and urgent, and in an attempt to lay the basis for a scientific and practical Palestinian statistical system which would enjoy national and international credibility, a Master Plan for developing Palestine official statistics was articulated to fulfill the requirements and conditions of building a national statistical system capable of meeting emerging needs and joining the global statistical system without any obstacles.

In the Master Plan the general framework was established for a detailed statistical system to be developed over a period of five years, a system which would take into account the set of internal and external considerations listed above. At the internal level, the proposed plan would allow the Palestinian statistical system to collect reliable data in a cost-effective way in most areas of concern and in the least possible time. At the external level, efforts were made for the emerging Palestinian state to qualify to join the International Statistical Society and other international bodies and organizations, whose membership requires the provision of specific data and statistics through generally accepted standard ways and means.

The Master Plan set out the goals and the path. Everyone worked diligently, demonstrating strong morale and commitment, easing the difficult task of rapidly building an institution from scratch. These kinds of attitudes may only be possible in specific periods in the history of a nation. The Master Plan advocated carrying out the first ever Palestinian Population and Housing census as a central building block and a vital strategic 'must' for the building of the Palestinian statistical system. The census was implemented four years after the creation of PCBS, in December 1997, using long forms of 77 questions for all Palestinians living in OPT. Using the long form, most of the attributes of the Palestinian social fabric were captured, including those of Palestinian refugees living in the OPT.

This census represented a turning point in Palestinian efforts to set up an effective official statistical system for Palestine. It gave the Palestinian government a real opportunity to pursue nation-building based on rigorous and sound information, which is essential for development planning. Moreover, the small area statistics that have emerged from the census have empowered Palestinian communities, making it possible for them to draft sound policies based on solid information about their communities.

Now, almost ten years after its launch, the PCBS is the main supplier of statistical data on the Palestinian population of the Occupied Territories, and assumes its functions in accordance with recognized norms for statistical production, as stipulated by the UN Statistics Commission and the international community. The Palestinian statistical system, while suffering temporarily due to the difficult conditions on the ground, supplies statistics on a routine basis in more than 30 fields covering households and individuals, economic establishments and economic activities, and land-related activities. Where possible, data on standard characteristics, such as refugee status, gender, education and economic activity, are routinely collected through various censuses and sample surveys.

DATA SOURCES ON PALESTINIAN REFUGEES

Palestinian refugees (registered and unregistered) are scattered in many countries of the world. According to the PLO Department of Refugee Affairs, almost 83 per cent of Palestinian refugees reside in historic Palestine and bordering countries, 10 per cent reside in the rest of the Arab World, and 7 per cent in the rest of the world. Estimates of the size of the Palestinian refugee population, as well as their percentage distribution in countries of residence, vary according to the source of the data. Several agencies have tried to capture the size of the Palestinian refugee population its and socio-demographic attributes in an effort to generate a reliable estimate of the size of the population.

Apart from the statistical infrastructure currently in place through PCBS for the Palestinian refugees of the Occupied Territories, the statistics on Palestinian refugees elsewhere rely heavily on secondary sources. Statistics compiled from primary sources are derived mostly from administrative records and scant sample surveys. Sources of primary and secondary data include the United Nations Relief and Works Agency (UNRWA), Fafo, an independent Norwegian research foundation, the Damascus-based

Table 2.1: *Estimated Palestinian refugee population by country of residence, 1998*

Country of current residence	Total no. of refugees	Percentage
West Bank, including Jerusalem	593,724	11.6
Gaza Strip	797,449	15.6
Israel	219,325	4.3
Jordan	1,766,057	34.5
Lebanon	382,594	7.5
Syria	431,986	8.4
Egypt	40,468	0.8
Total no. of refugees in Palestine and bordering countries	**4,231,603**	**82.7**
Saudi Arabia	274,762	5.4
Other Gulf countries	139,948	2.7
Iraq and Libya	73,284	1.4
Other Arab countries	5,544	0.1
Total no. of refugees in other Arab countries	**493,538**	**9.6**
Rest of the world	**393,411**	**7.7**
Total	**5,118,552**	**100.0**

Source: PLO Department of Refugee Affairs, 2001.

Palestinian Central Bureau of Statistics and Natural Resources[1], the Palestinian Right to Return Coalition (Al-Awda), the Palestinian Diaspora and Refugee Center (Shaml), Resource Center for Palestinian Residency and Refugee Rights (BADIL), the United Nations High Commissioner for Refugees (UNHCR), and the PLO Department of Negotiation Affairs.

Statistics issued from each of these sources, however, suffer from various deficiencies in the data such as coverage, timeliness, representation of samples to targets, and reliability. Data from UNRWA, for example, suffer from a lack of coverage of unregistered refugees; failure to capture data on refugees living outside camps; and a lack of systematic, robust, up-to-date methods to capture socio-demographic changes. Data coming from Fafo sample surveys are subject to incomplete frames in the case of Lebanon and Syria, and are subject to sampling errors in Jordan. Other sources use demographic models and UNRWA figures in arriving at the statistics produced.

Basic socio-economic characteristics of Palestinian refugees living in the Occupied Palestinian Territories have been captured by the Population and Housing census of 1997, and are routinely updated. In fact, both refugee status as well as residency in refugee camps are explicitly identified as primary identifiers in the master sampling frame, which is often used in drawing random samples for PCBS surveys. Census data and most of the sample survey data collected by PCBS are usually made public in the form of Public Use Files (PUF). These micro data represent an invaluable tool for research on the socio-economic conditions of refugees living in the Occupied Territories. Table 2.2 shows the available data, which can be used for analysis and forecasting.

Table 2.2: *Schedule of censuses and sample surveys at PCBS*

Census/Survey	Periodicity (every)	First round	Last round	Next round
Population and Housing Census[2]	10 years	1997		2007
Demographic Survey[3]	5 years	1995		2005
Demographic and Health Survey	4 years	1996	2000	2004
Labour Force Survey	Quarter	Q3, 1995		Continuous
Consumption and Expenditure Survey[4]	3 years	1996	2001	2005
Impact of Israeli Measures on Children and Women[5]		2001		2003
Impact of Israeli Measures on Household Economy	Quarter	Q2, 2001	Q2, 2003	Q3, 2003
Jerusalem Socio-Economic Survey[6]	2 years	2003		2005
Time Use Survey	10 years	2000		2010
Computer-Internet Use	3 years	2000		2003

SOCIO-ECONOMIC CHARACTERISTICS OF REFUGEES IN OPT

The end-of-year Palestinian population of the Occupied Palestinian Territories for 2002 is estimated at 3.6 million inhabitants, with 2.3 million living in West Bank including Jerusalem and 1.3 million living in the Gaza Strip. The population is fairly young, with almost 53 per cent younger than 18 years of age. Among the *de facto* population, the most recent statistics indicate that 42.8 per cent are refugees, as shown by Table 2.3.

Table 2.3: *Percentage distribution of the Palestinian population in the OPT by refugee status and region, mid-2002*

| Refugee status | Region | | | | | |
| | West Bank, incl. Jerusalem | | Gaza Strip | | Palestinian Territories | |
	Number	%	Number	%	Number	%
Refugee	596,368	27.1	886,244	70.2	1,482,612	42.8
Non-refugee	1,606,273	72.9	375,665	29.8	1,981,938	57.2
Total	**2,202,641**	**100.0**	**1,261,909**	**100.0**	**3,464,550**	**100.0**

Almost all residents of refugee camps are refugees (96.5 per cent), while refugees represent 36.5 per cent of Palestinians living in urban areas and 20.5 per cent of those living in rural areas. On the other hand, almost half of Palestinian refugees live in refugee camps (46 per cent), compared to 36.2 per cent living in urban areas and 17.8 per cent living in rural areas.

The refugee population in the Occupied Palestinian Territories is slightly younger than the rest of the population. However, the population pyramid for Palestinian refugees does not differ in a statistically significant way from that of the remaining population in the Occupied Palestinian Territories. While 46.4 per cent of the population as a whole is less than 15 years of age, 47.4 per cent of the refugees are in the same age category as compared to 45.6 per cent for the non-refugees. The age pyramid shows also some difference between the two groups at the upper end, where 3.3 per cent of non-refugees are over 65 years, compared to 3.1 per cent among refugees. Overall, however, the sex ratios are almost identical for both groups. The marginal difference between the two groups is also apparent from the statistics on Total Fertility Rates (TFR) (5.97 for refugees and 5.9 for non-refugees) and Infant Mortality Rates (IMR) (24.9 against 25.9 per 1000 live births). All these demographic indicators, which influence population growth, are suggestive of rapid population increase in the next few years. Assuming continuation of the status quo in terms of migration rates, and a steady decline in the other two components for population growth (TFR and IMR by 50 per cent in the next two decades), the refugee population of the Occupied Palestinian Territories is expected to reach 1.94 million in seven years. These forecasts are suggestive of a net growth of more than one third of the refugee population as a whole. These figures should attract attention to the growing challenges of a prolonged status quo on the question of refugees.

Palestinian households are known to be large due to high fertility rates, with significant differences between the West Bank and the Gaza Strip, and with refugee households being larger than those of non-refugees. The most recent statistics show that the average household size for 2002 was 6.4 persons, with 6.5 persons for refugee households and 6.2 for non-refugees. Table 2.4 shows that one in

Table 2.4: *Percentage distribution of households in the OPT by size and refugee status, 2002*

| Household size | Refugee status | | Overall |
	Refugees	Non-refugees	
1	4.2	3.8	3.9
2	7.1	7.9	7.6
3	6.6	6.7	6.7
4	8.5	9.4	9.0
5	12.3	11.7	12.0
6	12.6	15.3	14.2
7	12.2	13.9	13.2
8	11.5	11.2	11.3
9	9.4	7.9	8.5
10+	15.6	12.2	13.6
Total	**100**	**100**	**100**
Average household size	**6.5**	**6.2**	**6.4**

four refugee households has more than eight persons compared to one in five for non-refugee households.

Education has long been seen as a valuable asset for refugees. Statistics on enrolment rates show that 42.7 per cent of refugees of six years of age or more have been enrolled compared to 40.6 per cent for non-refugees. The difference is more striking when comparing the two groups in terms of those possessing a university degree, where 4.9 per cent of refugees have a degree compared of 4.1 per cent among non-refugees.

Various indicators relating to economic well-being show that non-refugee households are better off than those of refugees. For example, the unemployment rate in 2002 for refugees reached 35.2 per cent compared to 28.7 per cent for non-refugees. Among the employed for the same year, one in three refugees assumed a professional occupation compared to almost one in four for non-refugees. On the other hand 67.2 per cent of employed refugees are wage earners compared to 54.5 per cent for non-refugees.

Table 2.5: *Percentage distribution of employed persons (15+ years) by status and occupation, 2002*

Refugee status	Occupation							Total
	Legislators, senior officials and managers	Professionals technicians, associates, clerks	Services, shop and market workers	Skilled agricultural and fishery workers	Crafts and related workers	Plant, machine operators and assemblers	Elementary occupations	
Refugee	3.6	28.4	21.4	7.0	15.8	8.0	15.8	**100.0**
Non-refugee	5.0	21.1	17.3	16.0	18.5	8.8	13.3	**100.0**
OPT	4.5	23.8	18.9	12.6	17.5	8.5	14.2	**100.0**

Table 2.6: *Percentage distribution of persons (15+ years) by employment status and refugee status, 2002*

Refugee status	Employment status				Total
	Employer	Self-employed	Wage employee	Unpaid family member	
Refugee	2.8	23.0	67.2	7.0	100.0
Non-refugee	4.2	29.0	54.5	12.3	100.0
OPT	**3.7**	**26.8**	**59.2**	**10.3**	**100.0**

Since January 2001, there has been serious deterioration in the livelihoods of Palestinians in the Occupied Territories. The 2002 estimates of income poverty show that two of three households live below the poverty line.[7] The Gaza Strip, where two thirds of households are those of refugees, has suffered most. As for refugees, the statistics show that three in four households lived under the poverty line in 2002, compared to two thirds of non-refugee households. Discrepancies between refugees and non-refugees are also apparent through comparison of availability of durable goods in households.

MONITORING ATTITUDES REGARDING A SETTLEMENT OF THE REFUGEE QUESTION

The attitudes and positions of the Palestinian population of the Occupied Territories on rights, preferences, and expectations regarding the application of right of return, have been surveyed several times in the recent past through a series of public opinion polls. However, the findings of some of these polls should be viewed with caution due to apparent bias in tools, sampling and methodology, and analytical approach.

Without jeopardizing the right of Palestinian refugees to exercise their right of return as stipulated by the United Nations and international declarations, it is important to establish an absorption

Table 2.7: *Households by availability of durable goods and refugee status, 2002*

Durable goods	Refugee status		OPT
	Refugee	Non-refugee	
Private car	14.4	24.1	20.3
Refrigerator	90.9	91.2	91.1
Solar boiler	75.4	74.0	74.5
Cooking stove	98.9	99.0	99.0
Washing machine	84.2	87.1	86.0
Television	93.5	92.5	92.8
Video	8.2	13.6	11.5
Satellite dish	45.9	46.6	46.3
Home library	14.6	20.9	18.4
Computer	7.7	10.7	9.5
Internet connection	2.3	3.4	3.0
Cellular phone	27.9	34.0	31.6
Phone line	32.7	38.6	36.3

index to provide the emerging Palestinian state with a continuous flow of information on the various scenarios for the settlement of the refugee question, and the degree of acceptance of each of these scenarios. The index should be able to measure the process of convergence between preferences and expectations, and should be developed with a view to providing sound information for the drafting of policies on this sensitive issue.

The question of preferences and expectations was tackled by the PCBS in a survey of 2,187 households in the Occupied Territories (1,507 in the West Bank and 680 in the Gaza Strip) between 15 and 19 May 2003. The target population was all adult persons within the households selected. During the fieldwork, fieldworkers were asked to collect observations on the receptivity of the general public to this kind of statistical activity. In general, the public was very receptive, but rather sceptical and pessimistic. The sceptics, who were mostly from Gaza, wondered about raising the issue of return when in fact 'people cannot even manage to reach their homes within Gaza'. Those who were pessimistic came from different sectors and places, and thought that there would be nothing on the horizon on this issue. It is interesting also that some of the selected individuals in the 18- to 19-year-old age group were rather ignorant about the question.

According to the survey results, while almost three quarters of the Palestinian population of the Occupied Territories prefer the return of refugees to their original homes, only 18.5 per cent expect this to happen in the case of refugees living in the Occupied Territories, and 23.1 per cent in the case of other refugees. Moreover, one in six believe that the refugees will end up settled where they are, with some improvement of their living conditions. Expectations regarding an ultimate solution vary according to whether the refugee is living in the Occupied Territories or elsewhere. As for refugees living in the Occupied Territories, 43.4 per cent of those surveyed expect continuation of their status quo, compared to 33.6 per cent for the refugees living elsewhere. Details of these findings are displayed in Tables 2.8 to 2.11.

Table 2.8: *Preferred solution of refugee issue for refugees in the OPT, by region and refugee status*

Indicator	Overall OPT	Region		Refugee status	
Preferred solution of refugee issue		West Bank	Gaza Strip	Refugee	Non-refugee
Improve housing conditions in camps	15.8	15.5	16.3	17.0	14.9
Accommodation in new localities built over the existing camps	1.2	1.1	1.2	0.5	1.6
Relocation to new localities, outside camps	2.9	3.5	1.6	2.2	3.3
Return to original villages and cities	72.6	72.3	73.4	72.4	72.8
Status quo will continue	4.3	4.2	4.6	4.4	4.3
Other solutions	0.3	0.0	4.0	0.8	0.0
Do not know	2.9	3.4	1.9	2.7	3.0
Total (%)	**100.0**	**100.0**	**100.0**	**100.0**	**100.0**

Table 2.9: *Expected solution of refugee issue for refugees in the OPT, by region and refugee status*

Indicator	Overall OPT	Region		Refugee status	
Expected solution of refugee issue		West Bank	Gaza Strip	Refugee	Non-refugee
Improve housing conditions in camps	17.2	15.6	20.4	19.2	45.8
Accommodation in new localities built over the existing camps	1.9	1.9	1.9	1.4	2.2
Relocation to new localities, outside camps	2.1	2.1	2.2	2.0	2.2
Return to their original villages and cities	18.5	15.6	24.2	20.2	17.2
Status quo will continue	43.4	47.1	36.2	41.3	44.9
Other solutions	1.3	0.1	3.5	2.1	0.6
Do not know	15.6	17.7	11.6	13.7	17.1
Total (%)	**100.0**	**100.0**	**100.0**	**100.0**	**100.0**

According to survey results, the general public is not optimistic about a solution involving the realization of return to the refugees' original homes (40 per cent v. 60 per cent), with refugees more inclined to believe that eventually a solution will be found through which camp sites will be improved for final settlement.[8]

DATA GAPS ON THE REFUGEE QUESTION

Current data on Palestinian refugees come mainly from UNRWA and the PCBS. A limited database has also been setup by Fafo using a series of one-shot sample surveys on the living conditions of Palestinian refugees in Lebanon, Syrian camps, Jordan and Jordanian camps. All other data sources depend directly or indirectly on the three sources mentioned above.

Table 2.10: *Preferred solution of refugee issue for refugees living outside the OPT, by region and refugee status*

Indicator	Overall OPT	Region		Refugee status	
Preferred solution of refugee issue		West Bank	Gaza Strip	Refugee	Non-refugee
Improve housing conditions in camps	8.2	8.3	8.1	8.9	7.7
Accommodation in new localities built over the existing camps	0.1	0.0	0.2	0.1	0.1
Relocation to new localities, outside camps	12.5	11.3	15.0	14.0	11.5
Return to their original villages and cities	74.3	75.1	72.9	71.2	76.7
Status quo will continue	3.2	3.6	2.3	3.9	2.6
Other solutions	0.2	0.0	0.6	0.2	0.2
Do not know	1.5	1.7	0.9	1.7	1.3
Total (%)	**100.0**	**100.0**	**100.0**	**100.0**	**100.0**

The UNRWA databases are based mainly on data flowing from voluntary registration and administrative records resulting from the supply of services to Palestinian refugees residing within Palestine, Jordan, Syria and Lebanon. It is not clear whether systematic efforts within UNRWA are made to keep these databases current and complete. Moreover, these data are often incomplete due to the lack of systems of updating, and limited or non-existence of services outside the boundaries of refugee camps, with no clear mechanism for updating these databases.

The PCBS databases are complete and current, and can be used for extensive analysis of the socio-economic conditions of the Palestinian refugees of the Occupied Territories. These data, however, are not focused on Palestinian refugees, but cover the population as a whole, with refugees being treated as a stratum in each survey or census. Moreover, none of the PCBS surveys target

Table 2.11: *Expected solution of refugee issue for refugees living outside the OPT, by region and refugee status*

Indicator	Overall OPT	Region		Refugee status	
Expected solution of refugee issue		West Bank	Gaza Strip	Refugee	Non-refugee
Improve housing conditions in camps	15.5	15.5	15.6	16.5	14.8
Accommodation in new localities built over the existing camps	0.4	0.2	0.8	0.6	0.2
Relocation to new localities, outside camps	12.6	8.8	20.0	14.9	10.8
Return to their original villages and cities	23.1	19.3	30.3	23.5	22.8
Status quo will continue	33.6	38.0	25.1	31.6	35.1
Other solutions	0.4	0.2	0.6	0.7	0.1
Do not know	14.5	18.0	7.7	12.2	16.2
Total (%)	**100.0**	**100.0**	**100.0**	**100.0**	**100.0**

Palestinian refugees in order to conduct in-depth studies. However, PCBS data are routinely updated and easily accessible for research and analysis.

Apart from Fafo, other data sources are basically users of data, and do not deal with data as a main activity. Hence, these sources contribute very little to any credible effort to set up a current and useful database on Palestinian refugees.

The data available on Palestinian refugees suffer from a fundamental gap regarding those Palestinians living outside the mandate areas of UNRWA. According to the PLO Department of Refugees Affairs, almost 17.5 per cent of Palestinian refugees are reported to be living outside that mandate. Therefore, very little, if anything, can be known about the various indicators regarding these Palestinians, including their positions on the question of future return or settlement. As for the remaining Palestinian refugees who are currently living within the five countries of the UNRWA mandate, serious data initiatives can and should be taken to fill existing gaps, and contribute to an eventual solution of the refugee question. These initiatives may include:

- An in-depth review of various databases in terms of coverage, timeliness, conceptual basis, methodology of updates, and comparability with the international standards and recommendations. This review should aim at matching and harmonizing existing sources in order to facilitate further research using these sources.
- A review with UNRWA of their databases in terms of content, possible updates, and usefulness for statistical purposes. The review may establish pragmatic methodologies for updating these databases.
- In-depth studies using available data and specially collected data on the absorption capacity of Palestinian society and its economy and investment needs, studies which could contribute to a smooth and controlled return of Palestinian refugees. These studies may focus on the challenges of absorption, including social inclusion, infrastructure, labour, housing, health and education.
- Sample-based studies on the socio-economic conditions of refugees in host countries, and the characteristics of refugees in the diaspora using the Fafo tools. These studies may be extended to focus on the socio-economic profile of potential returnees in order to facilitate the smooth social inclusion of returnees into Palestinian society.
- It is highly recommended to provide support for setting up a regional database at PCBS on potential returnees, and for UNRWA to launch an initiative designed to update its databases.

PCBS will welcome any initiative among the various stakeholders leading to the pooling of resources and expertise to establish rigorous databases on refugees and their concerns, irrespective of their current co-ordinates. PCBS is equally eager to examine all issues or questions that might be identified in the course of progress towards a final political settlement.

CHAPTER 3

Living in provisional normality: The living conditions of Palestinian refugees in the host countries of the Middle East

Jon Hanssen-Bauer and Laurie Blome Jacobsen, Fafo Institute for Applied International Studies, Oslo, Norway

INTRODUCTION

The majority of Palestinian refugees who left Israel in 1948 as a consequence of the war found themselves in neighbouring host countries, where they and their offspring lived out their lives. Others who went to the West Bank became further displaced during the 1967 war and moved to the East Bank of the Jordan River. After living for more than 50 years as refugees, they are still awaiting a political solution to the Israeli–Arab conflict that would enable them to see their life-situation restored to normality. While these populations are still suffering from having a provisional status in which their rights to return or compensation have not yet been satisfied, our studies of their living conditions show that their livelihoods have stabilized after three generations and their basic living conditions resemble those of the host country populations.

The government of Norway has funded surveys by Fafo Institute of Applied International Studies and Fafo partners in these host countries throughout the 1990s and early 2000s (see Table 3.1). The surveys were primarily household and individual nationwide surveys covering various population groups (camp refugees, non-camp refugees, refugees living outside of camps in homogeneous settlements or 'gatherings', and some survey data on non-refugees). The Fafo surveys collected information on a wide range of health, education, labour market and housing issues, as well as other political, religious and social attitudinal information based on data collected at the individual level. Research and analysis have also included studies on the use of UNRWA services, the level and scope of UNRWA services and the UNRWA financing mechanisms.

The series of Fafo surveys has provided the most comprehensive data-set on Palestinian refugees available today, and data is directly comparable to national surveys and international standards in most cases.

Perhaps the most pertinent result of these surveys is that the data show small differentials in the main indicators of living conditions between the population of refugees living outside the camps and the host country population in these countries. There are more important variations between the countries. The purpose of these studies was to establish a better understanding of the humanitarian situation among the refugee households across the UNRWA fields of operations. By using indicators that are standard internationally, these studies allow for comparison across the fields and across different types of populations in the region. The latest of these studies, the one of refugees living in camps in Syria, is completed and published.

Table 3.1: *Fafo surveys on Palestinian refugees in the Middle East*

Location	Population	Year
Palestinian Occupied Territories	Camp refugees, non-camp refugees, non-refugees	1992, 1994
Jordan (nation-wide)	Camp refugees, non-camp refugees, non-refugees	1996, 2003
Jordan (refugees)	Camp refugees, gathering refugees	2001
Lebanon	Camp refugees, gathering refugees	1998
Syria	Camp refugees, gathering refugees	2001
UNRWA camps in Jordan, Syria, Lebanon, the West Bank and Gaza	Refugees	2003

Some shortcomings of these studies should be noted. The studies were not undertaken at the same time, and they do not always cover the total population that we, as statisticians, would have preferred. The best coverage is found in Jordan, where the Department of

Statistics (DOS) completed a survey of national coverage in 1997 that was later supplemented with an in-depth study of the camps in 1999. These surveys allow us to undertake further comparative studies because the samples used cover refugees living in camps, refugees living outside camps, as well as the host population. In the Palestinian Territories, some of the Fafo data is quite old (1992 and 1994) and needs to be updated if it is to be useful, especially in light of the sharp economic decline in the West Bank and Gaza since 2000. However, the Palestinian Central Bureau of Statistics (PCBS) has updated data for some, but not all the indicators found in a Living Conditions survey (see the chapter by Abu-Libdeh elsewhere in this volume). In Syria and Lebanon, surveys have been undertaken by Fafo and the Palestinian Central Bureau of Statistics in Damascus. Here, the studies covered only the refugee population in the camps and those living in the so-called 'gatherings' which are camp-like surroundings outside of the camps proper. Little is known in both countries about the refugees living outside the camps and the gatherings, and the available data on refugee camp population has yet to be compared to national statistics of the host country population.

Before examining the results of the surveys in detail, we will first summarize our conclusions. To the extent that we are able to determine, after 50 years of living as refugees, the living conditions of this population generally resemble those of the host countries' populations. Surveys indicate that adequate services are provided by UNRWA to cover the basic socio-economic needs of the refugees, particularly those living in camps and therefore, there are more important variations *across* the countries than *within* them.

This being said, 1.1 million refugees live in camps. These camp refugees have lower incomes and poorer health and education levels than those outside the camps. However, camp refugees have better access to basic health and education services due to UNRWA's presence. The latter point directly leads to the conclusion that the camp populations do not face *homogeneously* poor living conditions, nor do they constitute the main poverty problem in the host countries.

Living conditions in camps in general are poorer in Lebanon and in Gaza, and again the difference seems to be greater between the host countries than between host and refugee populations within the same country. In this sense, the living conditions of refugees are influenced by the local context.

There are many estimates of the size of the Palestinian refugee population, as these depend on the definition of 'refugee' used and the purpose of the estimate. Fafo has made an estimate of the population currently living in the four host countries, using a definition of refugee based on self-assignment (Table 3.2). We have used sample data and various techniques to estimate the total population. These estimates are more complicated to make regarding refugees living outside the camps in Syria and Lebanon, than for the other population segments. By mid-2002, a total 3.34 million refugees lived in these countries, assuming that all children of refugees inherit their fathers' refugee status. Some 1.1 million refugees in Syria and Lebanon are living in the camps. The out-migration from Lebanon is high, and the migration into and out of camps is relatively high in Jordan and in the West Bank and the Gaza Strip.

Table 3.2: *Fafo population projections (in thousands of refugees)*

Year	West Bank	Gaza Strip	Jordan	Lebanon (camps only)	Lebanon (incl. non-camp)	Syria (camps only)	Syria (incl. non-camp)	Total (incl. est. non-camp)
2002	585	772	1,484	106	198	159	296	3,335
2005	628	854	1,563	110	206	166	309	3,561
2010	692	996	1,681	117	218	177	330	3,918
2015	749	1,143	1,790	123	229	188	350	4,261
2020	801	1,293	1,895	129	240	198	368	4,598

As mortality rates are low and stable across all of the main refugee-hosting countries, the demographic future of the Palestinian refugee population is largely determined by fertility and migration. Fertility rates amongst Palestinian refugees are falling to the host country levels in all areas except Gaza. Migration is an important component of demographic change, but the extent of migration is largely unknown and impossible to predict. The total Palestinian refugee population is actually growing with approximately 78,000 persons a year, and will reach a total of 4.6 million in 2020 – if we assume no migration. The population growth will gradually change the distribution of the population across the countries.

When we say that livelihoods are stabilized, we actually refer to two phenomena. First, bearing in mind that refugees did not choose where to live, they nevertheless were able to create neighbourhoods consisting of social and family networks that resemble the situation of their Palestinian villages. Close kin live nearby and continue traditional patterns of intermarriage allowing larger family groups to stabilize the social space for the refugees where they live. Second, the living conditions for refugees, by and large, are similar to those of the host country population, particularly for those living outside the camps. As noted earlier, there seem to be greater differences in livelihoods between refugee populations in host countries than between host and refugee populations within the same country. As their refugee livelihoods adapt to those of the host country, it implies the livelihoods of refugee populations in different countries differ more from each other than from the livelihoods of host country populations.

There are more differences in livelihoods between refugees living in camps and those outside camps. Some variables indicate that living conditions are in fact worse for refugees in the camps. To some extent, however, this is compensated for by better access to infrastructure than that enjoyed in poor areas in the same country. Camps are mostly urban sites that are served by UNRWA, which actually improves refugees' access to infrastructure and services. Refugee camps also receive services from other organizations, including many non-governmental organizations (NGOs), as is the case in Lebanon. As the situation in the camps becomes more stable and comparable to host populations, because of the presence of UNRWA and other service deliverers, refugees tend to move to the camps when in need of these services and the protection of UNRWA. They move out if they can afford to do so. The net result of this demographic movement is what statisticians call a selection effect. In both camp and non-camp communities, however, the differences between people inside the group are bigger than the differences between the group and other groups.

The overall picture emerging from a comparison across the UNRWA fields shows that the indicators of living conditions generally are poorer in Lebanon and in Gaza than in other places. To illustrate this general picture, we present a number of examples. More thorough analysis of the results can be found in the various Fafo publications, and a cross-country comparison may be found in the *Finding Means* report (Blome-Jacobsen 2003).

HOUSING AND INFRASTRUCTURE

Refugee camps in Jordan, Lebanon and Syria are situated on land made available to UNRWA by the host governments to provide housing and services to refugees. Responsibility for the provision of infrastructure services such as sewage disposal, water and electricity, technically lies with the host government, although UNRWA has provided infrastructure in locations where other parties have not done so. Following the signing of the 1993 Declaration of Principles by the PLO and Israel, UNRWA launched the Peace Implementation Programme (PIP) – a programme specifically geared towards improving services and infrastructure to refugees across all fields as a means of encouraging the peace process.

The type of housing initially set up for refugee households in the camps to replace tents was 'shelters' or small single detached dwellings. Those who moved into the camps subsequent to this have mostly built their own shelters or purchased them. UNRWA does not own the original camp housing but refugees are free to use the housing so long as UNRWA is given use of the land upon which the houses are built. UNRWA's main role in shelter maintenance is the reconstruction of shelters damaged during natural or man-made disasters, and the rehabilitation and maintenance of the shelters of families that are registered as special hardship cases. Shelter modification is usually regulated by the host governments to a greater or lesser degree depending on the country and time frame. Outside the camps, UNRWA has provided monetary assistance for dwelling repair to families registered as special hardship cases. Since the initial setting up of shelters, the stock of refugee housing in the camps has changed considerably – a necessity given that the population has increased but the camp borders have not. Where they have had the means and permission, refugees have replaced, modified or built additional shelters.

The degree to which a 'housing market' exists in the refugee camps is unclear. A large proportion of camp refugees report that they own their dwelling (between 70 and 90 per cent), although there is no regulatory framework surrounding ownership, buying or selling. In addition to the issue of the lack of secure tenure, housing development has occurred under more or less physically restrictive conditions and has been largely unplanned by any central authority. The result is high camp density and inadequate infrastructure, including very narrow roads that often are not wide enough for emergency vehicles to pass. The displaced refugee population in Lebanon comprises a particularly vulnerable group who, because of the hostilities occurring in the country, have lost the basic shelters they were given initially. Although emergency programmes have helped to rebuild destroyed shelters, refugees who were not re-housed in camps often live as squatters on the periphery of camps or other urban areas.

Finally, apart from direct implications on security of tenure, housing market and housing regulation arising from the special situation of camp refugees, current practices and regulation within the host country have had significant implications in particular for refugees residing in Lebanon. Lebanese authorities refuse to allow building materials to enter into the camps, in addition, a recent amendment of the Lebanese property law was passed by Parliament giving foreigners the right to own property, whilst specifically excluding Palestinians.

Despite infrastructure problems commonly cited as complicating life in refugee camps, thanks to the effort of UNRWA and other providers, infrastructure facilities are generally better among camp refugees than in many Arab countries. Overall, infrastructure is quite good in the West Bank and Gaza Strip. In Syria, the Yarmouk refugee camp has good infrastructure services while other camps fare badly.

Camp infrastructure in Jordan is even worse while camps in Lebanon generally have poor infrastructure. Rural camps in the West Bank score more poorly on a range of indicators than camps in Gaza, such as the camps in the Hebron area.

Overall, Palestinian refugees have good access to electricity (98 per cent are connected to an electricity network), and have independent kitchens (96 per cent) and toilet facilities (95 per cent) in their residences. The availability of these three amenities varies little across groups. However, other infrastructure amenities are lacking for camp refugees and those living in gatherings outside the camps.

It is not surprising that access to basic infrastructure mostly depends on where one lives. However, other factors impacting on the resources of the household (like income and education level) also matter – although this is mostly for refugees living outside of camps. Thus, refugees living outside camps and who have the necessary resources, can locate themselves in places with better infrastructures. More than one third of camp residents across the host countries live in very crowded dwellings (three or more persons per room) with inadequate indoor environment.

Two thirds of the refugees report that they own their dwelling – which is a comparable figure to the non-refugee population. However, we think this figure masks a variety of 'property forms' that are of a more precarious nature than for non-refugees. We find that refugees own less fixed property when it comes to land, for instance. Yet, we also find few differences regarding ownership of durables.

Table 3.3: *Summary of good and poor health and infrastructure outcomes*

Good outcomes	Poor outcomes
• Urban West Bank and Gaza camps (1996) and Yarmouk camp in Syria infrastructure access: +80% have piped drinking water, electricity and sanitation	• Jordan and Lebanon camps infrastructure access: +60% lack piped drinking water and sanitation
• Non-camp refugees in Jordan similar to non-refugee households	• Camp households crowded: 30–40% with three or more persons per room, large households in camps (11 persons or more)
	• Poor indoor environment in camps
	• West Bank rural camps

MOTHER AND CHILD HEALTH

Maternal care standards among camp refugees are more similar to developed than to developing countries. More than 80 per cent of pregnant women use prenatal care and 85 per cent of the deliveries are assisted by qualified personnel. Less than 10 per cent of infants have low birth weight, and child nutrition is not a considerable health problem among refugees. However, conditions in Lebanon should cause concern, as the refugees living in the camps there have higher infant and maternal mortality than any other host country or camp. Camp and gathering refugees in Lebanon also have a two to three times higher rate of childhood chronic illness than the refugees in other host countries. Chronic childhood illness or disability is, moreover, a major contributor to illiteracy among refugee children.

Table 3.4: *Percentage of women receiving pre-natal care by a skilled attendant (doctor, nurse, trained midwife)*

Location/Population	Percentage
West Bank: camp refugees	90%
West Bank: non-camp refugees	95%
West Bank: non-refugees	94%
Gaza Strip: camp refugees	99%
Gaza Strip: non-camp refugees	99%
Gaza Strip: non-refugees	98%
Jordan: camp refugees	95%
Jordan: non-camp refugees	86%
Jordan: non-refugees	82%
Lebanon: camp refugees	95%
Lebanon: gathering refugees	95%
Lebanon: national	87%
Syria: camp refugees	96%
Syria: gathering refugees	92%

Table 3.5: *Summary of good and poor maternal and child health outcomes*

Good outcomes	Poor outcomes
• Maternal care outcomes among camp refugees more similar to developed than developing countries • Prenatal care +80% • Delivery assistance +85% • Less than 10% infants with low birth weight • Child malnutrition not a considerable health problem	• Lebanon: Higher infant mortality, higher maternal mortality (239 deaths per 100,000 live births), 2–3 times higher rate of childhood chronic illness • Syria and Lebanon: Gaps in vaccine coverage. Less than 75% fully vaccinated, poor measles coverage

ADULT HEALTH

Adult health conditions among refugees are similar to those of other middle-income countries. That is, chronic health conditions such as heart disease and diabetes have replaced infectious diseases as the main public health problems. What distinguishes the refugee community in this regard, however, is the large proportion of the camp refugee populations in Jordan and Lebanon suffering from chronic health problems.

The situation is worst in Lebanon. Over 50 per cent of adults (15 years and older) in Lebanese camps and gatherings are afflicted with a functional impairment (movement, sight, or hearing), chronic illness, other disabilities or severe psychological distress. From the perspective of the refugees themselves, twice as many adult refugees living in camps and gatherings in Lebanon report that they view their own health as 'bad' compared to refugees in the other host countries. Not only are rates of illness and disability higher in Lebanon, but there are also particularly high rates of poor health among young age groups (less than 35 years) compared to other settings.

In Jordan, there are lower rates of adult health failure than those found in Lebanon, but here we can measure a distinct difference between camp refugees and others. Nineteen per cent of camp refugees have a chronic illness or disability compared to 12 per cent of non-camp refugees and 9 per cent of non-refugees. Thus over twice as many camp refugee adults have chronic health failure compared to the non-refugee population.

In camps in Jordan, Lebanon and Syria, we also find that psychological distress is widespread among refugees. In all camps, 40 to 60 per cent of adults report that they suffer daily from three out of seven possible psychological distress symptoms.

Apart from geographical location, other factors are associated with poor health amongst Palestinian refugees. We have identified two main sub-groups of households having members with poor health which are not only related to poverty but also the lifecycle of the household. The groupings include the elderly or female-headed households with low income, and younger camp and gathering refugee households in Lebanon. Chronic illness is more often associated with the first group of households, while psychological distress and child illness are more likely to occur within the second group. However, there is a clustering of poor health indicators in both these two groups including functional impairment (sight, hearing or movement), chronic illness and low income.

EDUCATION

Literacy rates are generally high for refugees compared to non-refugees in the region. In every host country except Lebanon, the literacy rates are higher among camp refugees than others in the same field (Table 3.6). In Lebanon, however, there has been no improvement in the level of adult education for refugees in the last 30 years, and in Syria educational achievements are also deteriorating.

Education outcomes used to be high for Palestinian refugees, as the population traditionally invested in education for the children. The surveys show that refugee literacy rates are high compared to rates in the region, and that they are higher within the camps than outside them. We also find high-school enrolment rates, and girls have the same access to basic education as boys. However, there are also several alarming signals indicating that this situation may be changing.

In the camps in Lebanon, 60 per cent of the young adults (18 to 29 years of age) did not complete basic education. Here we also find high youth illiteracy, and a high rate of children repeating grades. In other areas, we find alarming levels of children dropping out of school in the camps. Some 50 per cent of camp and gathering refugee households in Lebanon have no member who has completed basic education. Households with typically good education outcomes are associated with high income and many working members. Camp refugees in Jordan fall into this group due to their relatively good adult education at the household level. Some 30 per cent of Jordanian camp households have at least one member with more than secondary education compared to 12 per cent in Syrian camps and 9 per cent in Lebanese camps.

In Syria, despite high levels of literacy, we also see many young adults not having completed the basic cycle of elementary school education (40 per cent), and lower secondary enrolment rates than in any place except Lebanon. Partly this can be explained by the fact that Lebanon is the only field where prepatory education has not been compulsory, while in Syria, the government included it into the compulsory cycle from the 2002/2003 school year. Another explanation for younger camp refugees in Syria failing to keep up with camp refugees in Jordan, the West Bank and Gaza is that we do not

Table 3.6: *Summary of good and poor education outcomes*

Good outcomes	Poor outcomes
• Refugee literacy rates high compared to region (higher in camps) • 97% of refugee children of elementary school age are enrolled in school • Refugee girls' education as good as or better than boys' (except in WBGS) • Syria camps: High education levels for both men and women in middle-age groups	• Lebanon camps: 60% of young adults (18–29 years) did not finish basic education, high youth illiteracy and grade retention rates • Syria camps: 40% of young adults (18–29 years) did not finish basic education • West Bank and Gaza camps: Girls drop out to marry or care for family, much higher illiteracy than boys • Jordan camps: Young males drop out, have higher illiteracy than previous generation

find the same level of education mobility. Educational mobility is defined as younger generations having higher educational status than their parents. There is tremendous education mobility among the camp population in Jordan, and also in the West Bank and Gaza. There are very high education levels among camp refugees in Syria in the middle-age groups, particularly amongst women. Unfortunately, these gains in educational achievement have not been sustained.

POVERTY

The refugees are not a homogeneously poor population. Using a simple poverty index, poverty ranges from 23 per cent of refugees earning less than two US dollars per person per day in Syrian camps to 35 per cent in the camps in Lebanon. Extreme poverty (those earning less than one US dollar per person and day) ranges from 5 per cent in the Syrian case to 15 per cent in the Lebanese. Poverty is also a factor that is determined by the context in which the refugees live. Refugees rely heavily on employment income, but have differing access to labour markets and to the social welfare benefits that come with employment.

Knowing poverty rates for different types of households is useful, but this does not tell us whether or not those in poverty collectively face similar situations. That is, we know households dependent on financial transfers from UNRWA are more often poor, but this includes many types of households such as the elderly and retired, or female-headed with children, or a single, disabled person with no hopes of employment. These different types of households have possibly very different coping strategies. We find that the higher poverty rates among camp refugees in particular are most closely related to a very high dependence on wage income to keep the household out of poverty.

There are three types of poor refugee households: (i) families with the main earner unable to work (poorest), (ii) elderly- or female-headed households (less poor), and (iii) families with one working member and many dependents (the largest group of the poor). Within the first category, young families with no earners are the poorest. These are households with heads in the prime-earning age group, in which no member is employed, and in which one or more members are seeking work without success.

The second group, also with no working members, the elderly and transfer-dependent households, are less often poor than the first. They are less often poor because lack of income is compensated for by private transfers. They have children and other relatives' support, preventing many from falling below the poverty line.

The third group, the working poor, is comprised of families relying on few wage earners with many dependants. These families comprise the largest group of the poor.

The refugees in Lebanon are worst off in terms of poverty because they are relatively more excluded from the formal labour market and they have poorer health. They make up the highest proportion of families with no employed member and the transfers they receive cannot compensate for their situation. The refugees in Syria are better off than those in other host countries, despite Syria being the poorest country. This is because many refugee women in Syria work, and because the education level of middle-aged working refugees in that country is higher than in other host countries, leading to relatively higher incomes. Some 20 per cent of women aged 15 to 64 years among camp and gathering refugees in Syria are employed, compared to 15 per cent in the camps in Lebanon, and only 10 per cent in the camps in Jordan.

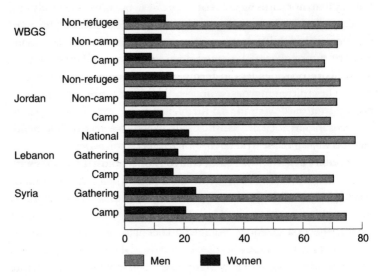

Figure 3.1 Labour force participation rates

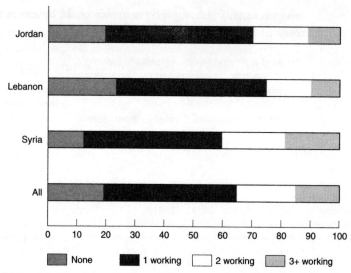

Figure 3.2 Number of household members in the labour force. Camp refugees

Our studies show that refugees in general, notably those living in camps, are somewhat more vulnerable to poverty than the host country population. This finding is reflected in the fact that although refugees are as economically active as the host country population, they earn less per invested hour. Like the host population, they have low labour force participation due to the low labour force participation of women generally. They also work in sectors of the economy where work provides less in terms of social welfare benefits. The main factor in creating their increased vulnerability, therefore, lies in their weaker relation to the labour market.

The poor are not only found among those who do not have work, but also among those who have work that does not pay enough. This vulnerability is somewhat compensated for by transfers and remittances, but more importantly by the services and relief work of UNRWA and others. In terms of poverty, unemployment in itself is not the main problem, but low productivity and few household members who work and earn a low income.

Despite the prevalence of poverty among the camp and gathering refugee populations, basic welfare outcomes among the poor and non-poor according to most indicators differ little. In the case of chronic illness prevalence among the poor, this could be either a cause or a result of poverty.

Table 3.7: *Summary of poverty rates among camp and gathering refugees*

	Syria		Lebanon		Jordan		West Bank	Gaza Strip
	ultra-poor	poor	ultra-poor	poor	ultra-poor	poor	poor	poor
% households	5	23	15	35	9	31	19	38
% persons	6	27			10	36		
Gap ratio	29	31	42	43	38	36		
Poverty gap	2	7	6	15	3	11		
Estimated population	10,590	45,850	24,343	55,182	17,480	17,480		

*Poor = less than $2/person/day; ultra-poor = less than $1/person/day. West Bank and Gaza Strip figures reflect PCBS poverty line.

The stabilization of livelihoods can be explained by the efforts made by the refugees themselves in reshaping their lives, as well as to the assistance and access to labour markets and public welfare provided by host countries. This stabilization is also due to the assistance provided by the international community, mainly through UNRWA. However, not all refugees are users of UNRWA services and assistance. The number of users varies among the different host countries from 26 per cent using UNRWA health services in Jordan (only 2 per cent of those living outside the camps) to 42 per cent in camps and gatherings in Lebanon. When we compare the population that uses UNRWA services with the population that does not, we find that women, the poor and those with low education have a higher propensity to use UNRWA services than others.

UNRWA therefore constitutes the basic security net for Palestinian refugees, supporting those who are unable to stabilize their livelihoods or make their livelihood comparable to that of the host country population – by their own means and their own labour force. Should UNRWA discontinue its assistance, the picture of a stabilized and comparable livelihood situation to that of the host country population would be severely changed into one of clearly unsatisfied basic needs that often characterize a provisional presence.

Earlier in this chapter we emphasized that there are important migratory movements among refugees. People move in and out of camps, and they leave one country to find work in another. This is particularly evident in Lebanon, but we think this may also apply to other countries where data is lacking, and where refugees may leave the country to seek work in the Gulf, in Europe or in North America. Migration may have implications on our living conditions measurements and our selection of samples. It is possible that refugees who do stay are those who did not have resources to leave, or did not find the opportunity to leave. This may cause increased unemployment, lower educational levels, and probably also poorer health among those who remained than what might otherwise have been found.

By way of conclusion, we should ask whether this picture of living in provisional normality – that is, in a stabilized livelihood situation that is comparable to conditions in the host country – is a simplified or rosy picture? Perhaps. The immediate corrective to this impression that should be made is that refugees have left their homeland, identity and property behind. They have been forced into a provisional situation where their choices are severely limited. Not being worse off than others is little relief when your situation is perceived to be unjust. The efforts of host countries and the international community have helped to avoid a humanitarian disaster, but the camps are still monuments to the suffering of millions of Palestinian refugees.

BIBLIOGRAPHY

Blome Jacobsen, L. (2003a) *Finding Means: UNRWA's Financial Crisis and the Living Conditions of Palestinian Refugees: Summary Report*, Oslo: Fafo.

—— (2003b) 'Housing and Infrastructure', in *Finding Means Volume I: Socio-economic Conditions of Palestinian Refugees in Jordan, Lebanon, Syria and the West Bank and Gaza*, Oslo: Fafo, pp. 56–78.

—— (2003c). 'Health Services', in *Finding Means Volume III: Social Service Delivery to Palestinian Refugees: UNRWA and Other Providers, UNRWA Financial and Donor Environment*, Oslo: Fafo, pp. 9–50.

Pedersen, J. (2003) 'Population Forecast of Palestinian Refugees 2000–2020', in *Finding Means Volume I: Socio-economic Conditions of Palestinian Refugees in Jordan, Lebanon, Syria and the West Bank and Gaza*, Oslo: Fafo, pp. 219–230.

CHAPTER 4

Social capital, transnational kinship and refugee repatriation process: Some elements for a Palestinian sociology of return

Sari Hanafi, Shaml, the Palestinian Diaspora and Refugee Center, Ramallah[1]

INTRODUCTION

Around the world, the experience of repatriating refugees has shown that there are few aid packages available from governments or international organizations to fully support the return process. Social capital, or the capacity of the individual to command scarce resources through adhesion to networks and broader social structures, seems to play an important role in supporting returnees, especially at the beginning of such a process. This chapter will examine the social capital from which Palestinian refugees might benefit in the event that they are allowed to exercise the right of return, and will use an analysis based on the study of economic and social transnational kinship networks of Palestinian refugees. To develop this analysis, a socioeconomic and anthropological survey was conducted in the West Bank and Gaza examining the different types of networks to which individuals have access. The survey also gave particular attention to understanding the processes by which inclusion in (or exclusion from) these networks is sustained. The survey was conducted by the Palestinian Diaspora and Refugee Center, Shaml, in Palestine and Israel, between January and October 2003. Other surveys, like Birzeit University's Survey of Households,[2] Fafo[3] surveys in Jordan and Lebanon, as well as surveys conducted by the Palestinian Center for Policy and Survey Research (PSR)[4] will also be used for comparison.

This chapter identifies some of the factors influencing patterns of return and transnationalism, and highlights the social and economic

kinship between Palestinians inside and outside the Palestinian territories, as well as the mode of entrepreneurship in the Palestinian
territories. Unlike other studies on the absorption of refugees, which
focus only on the contribution of the state and the international
community in facilitating return, I am more interested in examining
what sociological factors, such as social capital, can encourage return
or adaptation to a new economic environment. This study will focus
on the structural factors that influence the decision to return, such as
economic and social kinship networks, entrepreneurship and migration culture, as opposed to emotionally based attitudes, which
express the subject's political position but not necessarily their actual
intention to return.[5]

What pattern of return will take place? What will be the profile of
returnees? Will there be a literal mass of refugees rushing in simultaneously, or a trickle of fragmented groups? What is the motivation
for return: pure nationalism and the desire to stabilize identity/iden-
tities after the experience of exile, or something extending beyond
that? In case of an Israeli acceptance of the principle of the right of
return, would return be voluntary or coerced? What constitutes
return 'in safety and dignity'? Should refugees be required to return if
they cannot go back to their areas of origin, but must settle instead in
another part of the country? These are some of the questions that
this study attempts to address.

Examining return migration from the perspective of network
analysis will be fruitful for the objectives of this study. I will draw on
studies that consider a wide spectrum of factors affecting the possibilities and potentialities of return, including the role of kinship
networks, refugee dispersion patterns, and pre- and post-return
economic and social profiles. Other factors to be considered include
the desires of individual refugees to return to the (or *a*) homeland,
and the ways in which return is likely to be implemented (be it immediate or over an extended period of time).

ASSUMPTIONS

For this study I formulate four assumptions. The first assumption is
that *economic action is embedded in social structure*. For this reason it is very

important to study social networks and understand the economic behaviour of Palestinian returnees and local entrepreneurs at present, and in case of either their return or the intensification of transnational movement.

The second assumption concerns *the privilege of family ties over friend- ship ties*. As mentioned, I attempt to identify the different levels of social structures into which the individual, the subject of intended (return) migration, is inserted (friendship, extended family, village ties, national ties). I believe, however, that the nuclear and the extended family are major factors influencing the decision to migrate and also the system of support for the future absorption of Palestinian refugees. Therefore, one of the objectives of the field- work was to identify the different types of family ties: strong, weak or broken.

The third assumption deals with a *pattern of return that is not just definitive but also transnational*. This means that the refugees/returnees would maintain their social, economic, and political lives in both the country of return and the country in which they lived prior to return, and might even be citizens of both countries.

The last assumption of this study is political. *The project of two nation states remains popular with the majority of both Palestinians and Israelis.* What is at issue is the type of nation states that Israelis and Palestinians will develop. If Israel accepts the Palestinian right of return, Palestinian refugees' return will be subject to sociological and economic considerations. Moreover, imposed quotas will tremen- dously influence the choices made by refugees concerning their future place of residence.

COMPARING THE PALESTINIAN EXPERIENCE WITH OTHER REFUGEE EXPERIENCES

Solutions to refugee problems have traditionally been divided into three categories: voluntary repatriation, local integration in the coun- try of asylum, and resettlement from the country of asylum to a third country. The first option might be perceived as the most 'natural' option but it is also the most complicated. I prefer to call it 'return migration' to emphasize the fact that voluntary repatriation is a migration like any other migratory movement. It involves a complex legal framework and institutional arrangements as well as favourable political, economic and social conditions. In addition, the international environment is very important to enable such movement. In the optimistic environment that accompanied the end of the Cold War, a number of large repatriation operations have taken place and there was hope that lasting solutions might be found for many of the world's refugee problems.

FACTORS INFLUENCING THE MOVEMENT OF REFUGEES

Many factors influence a refugee's decision to return. Understanding patterns of return cannot be achieved through an analysis of macro processes of globalization and global markets, but should be gained through a sociological analysis of the political, social, and cultural attributes of the Palestinian people.

In this section, I focus on some elements mainly related to the economic sociology of Palestinian refugees in the host country and in the country of return (the Palestinian territories or Israel). Focusing on these elements, however, does not mean that they are the only important factors. For instance, geographical factors influence refugee decisions. Here I must highlight the importance of Salman Abu Sitta's work (2001) in opening the debate concerning the potential of geographic absorption in Israel. He demonstrates, after dividing Israel into three demographic areas (A, B and C), that 68 per cent of Israeli Jews are now concentrated in 8 per cent of Israel and that the areas in and around the former Palestinian villages remain empty and could absorb returning refugees. Abu Sitta argues that these empty rural areas correspond with the original location of the homes of the majority of Palestinian refugees. However, it is important to ask if, after 55 years of exile, these refugees, the majority of whom now dwell in cities, can still be considered peasants. They have become residents of big cites and it is pertinent to ask if they would choose to resettle in their villages of origin. Those who became urban refugees were stripped of their ecological and sociological relationships with their original homes in these rural areas. They may no longer identify with the land upon which their families worked, a phenomenon experienced by Algerian refugees after independence. Moreover, according to the 2003 survey by the Palestinian Center for Policy and Survey Research (PSR) in the Palestinian territories, the houses of half of these refugees have been destroyed, while 40 per cent of refugees have declared themselves unwilling to return if a family home no longer exists.

The ability to absorb refugees geographically is not a decisive factor in return scenarios. Irish-Americans did not return to Ireland following the end of British colonialism, few Armenians returned to Armenia after its independence, and only a small number of Lebanese returned to their country of origin following the end of the civil war. In all these cases, there was not only ample capacity, but also the political will for re-absorption.

Another important factor, which demands attention but is not addressed in this study, is the comparison between the social welfare systems in refugees' current countries of residence and the return areas. For instance, in comparison to Israel, the Palestinian territories and Jordan have inadequate health, social welfare, and educational services. This could be a factor which would encourage Palestinians to return to Israel, rather than to the Palestinian territories.[6]

Finally, the possibility of the return of Palestinian refugees is still closely connected with three elements: the right of return and its applicability; the urban situation of refugee camps; and the political position of Arab host country governments. It is worth mentioning that many studies show that refugees have low expectations about a political solution which would allow them to return to their homes of origin. The 2003 PSR survey found that some 50 per cent of the refugees believed that once a Palestinian state is established, the resolution of the refugee issue will be indefinitely postponed.

Social capital: the density of transnational social kinship ties

Because the extended family network is an important safety net for migrants, I focus on 'bonding', a form of social capital that ties people to family members who are similar in terms of their demographic characteristics. I examine how transnational kinship networks are affected by the occupation and national borders that structure, extend, and deepen the rupture of Palestinian society and ask: how should the strength of kinship ties be measured? Do close relationships link people who are similar to each other? Do weaker ties link more dissimilar people? Indeed, some forms of social capital can be used to hinder rather than help a return migrant, such as when group membership norms confer obligations to share rather than accumulate wealth or when they deny members access to services (Portes 1998).

Connectedness between different family members is based on a large spectrum of choices by individuals and families. The measurement of this feeling of connection is certainly subjective, but Shaml's survey chose a set of structural factors that may shape and ultimately limit these choices. The border predicament, the frequency of visits, phone calls, and the use of cyberspace are indicators of the (non) connectedness of the family network. They shape relations among family members and thus may influence the decision to return.

Transnationality

The Shaml survey confirmed a certain degree of transnationality among Palestinians (more among those in the Palestinian territories than those in Israel). This suggests that there will be a transnational pattern of return migration in the future, much more than a definitive return, and that the kinship networks can be used to facilitate this movement.

Among those living in the Palestinian territories, 40 per cent have close relatives[7] who live abroad, only a quarter of whom are able to visit Palestine/Israel. In contrast, among Palestinians in Israel, only 15 per cent have close relatives who live abroad of whom 13 per cent can travel to Palestine/Israel. When we broaden the picture to include second degree relatives,[8] 76 per cent of Palestinians living in the territories have second degree relatives abroad, half of whom are able to visit Palestine/Israel; more than 79 per cent of them are refugees. Social and economic ties were found to have diminished, as only 15 per cent of those interviewed have received aid from their relatives abroad; a figure that drops to 8 per cent for those who live in Israel. There are also very few business–economic relations between Palestinians abroad and those in Israel. The survey found that those who have property in the Palestinian territories tend to meet their relatives there more often. It seems that the possession of property encourages Palestinians abroad to maintain contact with their families there, at least in order to discuss the use and the future of the property.

Relations with more distant relatives are very weak. A third of those interviewed said they had no ties with these distant relatives, and only 25 per cent said they had some ties. Moreover, the overwhelming majority said they have no economic ties. This is not unusual for such a family-oriented society, but it means that the importance of ties inside the *hamula* (clan) is fading. This is perhaps due to the rapid urbanization of Palestinian society.

Place of birth plays a major role in the degree of connection that is maintained with family members abroad. For example, 79 per cent of those born in Jordan retained ties with their close relatives in Jordan, even though they no longer lived there. For those who returned to the Palestinian territories, however, their relations with Jordan diminished with time. To a large extent this may be due to the fact that they are unable to cross the border to visit each other.

Transnationality is also expressed by peoples' interest in owning property in the host countries. When asked about what they intend to do with property in the host country when they return, the overwhelming majority of the refugees living outside the Palestinian territories stated that they would keep their property and rent it. In other words, refugees do not want to sever all their ties with their countries of refuge.

Solidarity and connectedness

The duration of the exodus for Palestinians – now more than 55 years – and the impact of the restriction on movement across borders have hindered the maintenance of ties between relatives. The hypothesis that the closest ties are with family members and not with friends is confirmed by the fact that, when asked about their closest ties, only 5 per cent of Palestinians living in the West Bank mentioned friends and 8 per cent mentioned both family and friends. Men were more likely than women to declare that their best social ties are with their family. There was also a difference between different age groups: young people rank their relations with their siblings higher than with cousins and friends. However, returnees give the most importance to their relations with friends, most probably because these returnees do not have family in the Palestinian territories or because their long absence has diminished such ties.

Visits with relatives

Palestinian men interviewed in Palestine/Israel on average have lost regular contact with a third of their close relatives and meet them once every two years. In contrast, the survey found that women maintain closer contact with relatives: 29 per cent in the Palestinian territories and 14 per cent in Israel. The gender-constructed reality of ties is very important for return migration as it concerns a refugee population in which women are the most vulnerable due to early marriage and the high proportion of widowed, divorced, and single middle-aged and elderly women (Giacaman and Johnson 2002: 9. See also Isotalo 2002). This might indicate a propensity for more families who have ties to Palestine/Israel through maternal relatives, to return, than those who have ties through paternal relatives.

The survey also reveals that men have very few contacts with their step families and families-in-law. The same observation pertains to contact by phone: in the Palestinian territories men make more phone calls to their sisters than to their brothers. The more ties that women had to their relatives can be explained by their greater emotional attachment to the family.

Thus, the decision to return will be shaped by the types of relatives (nuclear or extended family) with whom the refugees have ties. Proximity of age also plays a major role in social connectivity but less in terms of economic ties. This is the case partly because the generational gap between children and their parents and elderly siblings has widened rapidly, especially in people with transnational experience. This was evident in Shaml's survey: young people who had grown up in the USA expressed a cultural conflict with their relatives who did not have the same transnational experience.

The geographical location of the interviewees is also very relevant. In the Gaza Strip, 43 per cent do not visit (or receive visits) with their close relatives outside the Strip. This percentage increases for those living in camps, as their relatives are more likely to be refugees who live outside Palestine. In Israel, 82 per cent of interviewees from big cities like Haifa have lost direct contact with close relatives. Visits decrease as people age. Whereas the economic situation seems irrelevant to the frequency of visits, better-educated people seem to visit their close relatives more often. It seems that education increases the possibility of travel to meet with transnational relatives.

The use of the phone does not seem to replace face-to-face meetings; there are very few phone calls between people who do not exchange visits. Generally speaking, most speak on the phone about once every two months. Those who have property in Palestine tend to speak and meet more often. It seems that the presence of property encourages them to maintain contact with their families.

The restrictions on movement between borders help explain the absence of face-to-face meetings. Approximately 56 per cent of the people who cannot visit Palestine/Israel have lost contact with their close relatives. The geographical location of relatives also impacts on the frequency of meetings. Palestinian refugees in Jordan and Egypt are more likely than those who live in the Gulf states to maintain contact, but even then they meet on average once every two years. It is practically impossible to meet relatives in Lebanon and Iraq. It is important to note that Palestinians living in Europe and the USA are able to meet with their Palestinian relatives in Palestine/Israel more easily than those living in Arab countries, due to the fact that travel between Arab countries and Palestine/Israel is difficult, even impossible in some cases.

In addition, the second *intifada* has sharply affected the ability of Palestinians living in the Palestinian territories to maintain face-to-face contact with one another let alone with those living abroad. The situation is especially acute in Gaza, where Israel has imposed a total closure since the beginning of the *intifada*. Majdi Malki (2003) argues that the length of time of the Israel closures and military operations intensifies local solidarity, and family ties with those living abroad become less important. Here we see a fragmentation and segmentation of Palestinian society that has a definite negative impact on establishing and maintaining ties throughout the Palestinian territories.

Telephone contact

Most calls are to sons and daughters dwelling abroad, and occur about once every two months or more. Phone calls to relatives abroad vary according to the location: they are very important in places like Bethlehem, Walaja (a suburb of Jerusalem), Ramallah, and refugee camps. They seem to be less important in places like Nablus and the Gaza Strip. Calls from Israel to abroad are very rare, except for in the village of Umm al Fahm where residents maintain contact to express solidarity with relatives in the West Bank and Jordan. In the Palestinian territories, men and women maintain phone contact with their relatives abroad at the same rate, but in Israel, women use the phone less frequently. Overall, those who are less educated tend to use the phone less often. Conversations by phone with close relatives living abroad are more important with Europe and the USA than with the Gulf states, Egypt, and Jordan. This can be explained by the cost of the call; it is cheaper to call abroad from the USA or Europe. Communication with Lebanon is very rare, as it is impossible to phone from Lebanon (and from Syria) to Israel/Palestine. One female interviewee in Lebanon said that she gave her uncle who lives in Jordan money every year to call the family in Palestine.

E-mail communication among immediate family members in Palestine/Israel is infrequent; only one third of close relatives are connected by e-mail with those who live in the Palestinian territories, and mostly those under 40 years old. In Palestine, women use e-mail less often than men, whereas in Israel it is the reverse. Several modes of communication, such as internet chatting, Short Messenger Service (SMS), and sending pictures through the internet, are used to connect people beyond the borders.

Marriage patterns

Endogamous marriage, that is, marriage within the same lineage, sect, community, group, village, or neighbourhood, is an important indicator of connectedness. Marriage between first cousins and blood-related kin is the most common form of endogamy in the Arab world (Holy 1989). Many studies show the persistence of a high rate of endogamy in the Palestinian family. The Fafo study (Pedersen *et al.* 2001: 80–84) states that 'the family, and in particular the parents, play an important role in the process of finding an appropriate marriage partner in Palestinian society'. Fafo researchers found that only 36.6 per cent of women born between 1940 and 1949 and 43 per cent of women born between 1960 and 1969 married outside of the family or the *hamula*. Marriages are often arranged, as is the case in most of the Arab world.

The Shaml survey and Riina Isotalo's work (1997, 2002) show that endogamous practices exist even at the transnational level, that is, between family members but in different countries, but much less so than when other relatives live in the same country. The small number of transnational endogamous marriages can be explained by their high cost; in contrast, local endogamous marriages are economical since dowries are smaller (Jacobsen and Deeb 2003). However, in some cases, transnational endogamous marriages are encouraged to sidestep bureaucratic and mobility problems.

Economic assistance

Social capital refers to the capacity of the individual to command scarce resources through adhesion to networks and broader social structures. These resources include economic favours, such as the reduction of price, credit without interest, and information on business conditions. These resources in themselves are not a social capital but the concept refers to the ability of individuals to mobilize support in case of need. People, especially migrants, do not need only jobs; they need companionship, emotional support, help with everyday problems, care when ill, and other forms of social support.

In terms of help between close and second-degree relatives, this study distinguishes between two forms of aid: non-mutual and reciprocal. According to the 'exchange theory', the network is much stronger when help is non-mutual. It is argued that networks characterized by non-mutual help are more connected and stable because 'in the hiatus between giving and the reciprocation of an item, obligation, trust and cooperation are created and extended among exchangers' (Uehara 1990: 524; quoted by Jacobsen and Deeb 2003: 223).

Solidarity between Palestinians in the Palestinian territories and abroad is important. A third of those interviewed in the Palestinian territories received financial and non-financial help from abroad that began before the start of the current *intifada* and is therefore not related to the increased economic hardship experienced during the *intifada*.[9] This help takes place mainly among parents, children, and siblings. It includes small gifts and the occasional major gift, such as the cost of education or health treatment. While payment for health treatment is extended to all relatives, payment for education is usually extended only to male family members. Religious holidays, such as the Eid and Christmas, are also occasions when gifts are given. This result is confirmed by the Birzeit University Survey: there is a regular financial link with 15 per cent of migrants, defined as giving or receiving money every three months or less, with 8 per cent of emigrants sending money to their families in Palestine, 6 per cent of families in Palestine sending money to their relatives abroad, and 1 per cent both sending and receiving money depending on the situation. Villagers score highest in terms of receiving money from relatives abroad (20 per cent), probably related to the higher proportion of relatives in western countries (Giacaman and Johnson 2002: 36–38).

Face-to-face contact is very important for economic transactions and especially for receiving and giving help. A Fafo study (Sletten and Pederson 2003: 47) shows that a family living in the Palestinian territories typically relies on members abroad, but that the lack of physical communication hinders transactions. The Shaml study found that half of the transfers do not go through banks but are transmitted during family visits. The study also found that money is brought as presents.

It is interesting, however, to note that about half of the financial assistance is now transferred through banks, a radical change from the 1970s and 1980s when most financial help was transferred in person. Few Palestinians in Israel receive help from their relatives abroad, probably due to their relatively good economic situation and to the weakness of transnational social ties.

Concerning reciprocal help, the survey found very few cases on the transnational level. Help not only entered the Palestinian territories but was also sent from the territories to close relatives living abroad (a third of the interviewees). However, this is not necessarily reciprocal or economically based assistance, as in the case of parents who give financial help to their daughters living abroad.

While solidarity is important at least between the Palestinian territories and abroad, economic ties based on partnerships are very problematic in the current situation (bringing an economic partner from the diaspora seems to be a hazardous enterprise). However, small entrepreneurs who are setting up their businesses receive some financial help from their relatives abroad.

It seems that help in Palestine/Israel has an altruistic motivation, such as transferring resources for general moral imperatives or solidarity with in-group needs and goals, more so than instrumental motivation which is based on the expectation of commensurate returns by beneficiaries such as a higher community status (Portes 1985). This will have an important impact on facilitating the process of return of people back home, especially in the initial period.

In brief, the findings in Shaml's survey show less social connectedness and solidarity than expected in Palestine/Israel and especially in Israel. This will make the use of kinship ties to assist return less important than generally assumed for a nation whose source of cohesion is its ongoing plight. Moreover, the restrictions on movement between borders and everyday Israeli colonial practices in the Palestinian territories have a vast negative impact on the capacity of Palestinians to maintain local and international ties.

Fractured nuclear family

Recent field research presents a profile of fractured networks inside the nuclear family in the Palestinian territories, but not in Israel (Hanafi 2001; Isotalo 2002; B'tselem and Ha'Moked 1999). Mothers and children may reside in one country, husbands and fathers may live and work in another, and grandparents and more distant relatives may live elsewhere. The fractured family experience indicates that return will not necessarily involve the whole family, especially in the first years.

This pattern is also found in other diaspora groups. Awhio Ong (1999: 20) found that cultural norms dictate the formation of business networks in the case of Chinese living abroad and were mainly led by males who possessed mobility, unlike women and children. In the Palestinian case, men tend to decide whether to relocate to Palestine/Israel or choose other migrations for the whole or a fragment of the family, based on several factors, including market structures. In particular, the person who has found suitable employment brings the family to join him/her and makes the decisions concerning the family's mobility. International migration statistics show that the percentage of females who are international migrants is increasing; currently, 47.5 per cent of international migrants are female. The decision to migrate is also based on the availability of affordable educational opportunities for children. In the Palestinian case it was evident from an electronic discussion on PALESTA (an independent internet-based network seeking to connect Palestinian professionals in the diaspora and abroad) that many discussions revolved around the existing education structure and the language of instruction for children at all levels of education.

Modes of entrepreneurship favourable to return

Returnees not only consume the resources of the place to which they return but some also bring capital and expertise sufficient to generate improvements to the country's economy. Some studies have demonstrated that the capital influx and investment that accompany the return of professionals generates investment. This type of investment is significantly different from the classical model of remittances studied in the Arab world (Hanafi 2000), which were dominated by limited economic benefits and negative effects of migration, weak investment of remittances in productive activities, and inflation provoked by the transfer of currency (Saad Al Din and Abdel Fadil 1983; Fergany 1988).

Contrary to studies that view returnees as a future burden on Palestinian society[10] and that examined the absorptive capacity of Palestinian refugees from a narrow and short-term economic perspective, other studies have shown great potential benefit from the absorption of returnees (Van Heer 1996). The Oslo transition period generated a high rate of growth in the Palestinian territories. Palestinian gross domestic product and gross national product before the *intifada* were higher than in neighbouring countries, with the exception of Israel. If this level were to be regained, the Palestinian territories would have to attract refugees from Jordan and Egypt, especially if family members were to provide support to these returnees at the initial stage. Some Palestinians might also move from the Gaza Strip to the West Bank, where income is higher. This also applies to Israel, where future government policy will determine whether Palestinian workers, engineers, and information technology professionals can assume or resume residence there.

In the era of globalization, the decision to move people or capital is subject to a complex set of factors related to both host and return country and other geographical areas. I do not assume a straightfor-ward relationship between transnationalism and global capitalism, as advocated by Basch *et al.* (1994: 22).[11] What I will show here is that the potential return of the refugees (especially the entrepreneurs and professionals) is structurally constrained and does not only represent a model of pure economic choice geared to optimal benefit. Palestinian capital inflows to the Palestinian territories can best be understood as supporting vulnerable refugees and communities. As such, these investments are more altruistic in nature and reflect more an economy of survival rather than the exercise of real political and economic power in the economy of globalization. As Grillo, Riccio, and Salih argue, 'economic dislocation in both developing and indus-trialized nations has increased migration, but made it difficult for migrants to construct secure cultural, social and economic bases within their new settings' (2000: 19).

The experience of Palestinians recruited through the UN Development Program's TOKTEN programme[12] indicates that many people came to Palestine due to their precarious situation in their host country. Accordingly, their return expresses a model in which a constrained people seeks to improve its situation and mobil-ity, rather than one in which people have a straightforward choice between the country of residence and the country of origin.

Below I will present two interconnected arguments. First, the nature of the investment and the motivations for it are driven by non-economic factors more so than by economic ones and, second, the familial mode of entrepreneurship predominates in the Palestinian territories and Israel. These two points indicate that the Palestinian economy in Palestine/Israel will be strongly affected by certain forms of refugee repatriation to these places.

Diaspora investment

During the Oslo transitional period, local and international eco-nomic links were re-established after a long period of conflict and separation. Already partially tied to their native community, the Palestinian diaspora contributed to the reshaping and the emergence of new transnational economic networks. The proportion of the investments by the Palestinian diaspora in the Palestinian territories to the volume of the Palestinian capital abroad was modest, although

it was vital for the Palestinian economy. As an indicator, according to
Palestinian economist Fadl Naqib (2003: 45), in the period 1993 to
1999, the average annual investment growth was 12.3 per cent.

To give an idea of the size of the diaspora's contribution during
'normal' times (that is before the *intifada*), one of my previous studies (Hanafi 1998b) showed that the diaspora's contribution in terms
of investment and philanthropic activities could be valued at
$408 million in 1996 (of which 74 per cent was investment) and
$410 million in 1997 (of which 76 per cent was investment). This
represented one of the main resources available to Palestinian
society and the economy. Indeed, it constituted 74 per cent of total
international assistance ($549 million) in 1996, and 95 per cent in
1997 ($432 million) (MOPIC 1998). However, this contribution
remained insufficient for a young entity ravaged by thirty years of
de-development (Roy 1995) and was well below the capacity of
Palestinian business people in the diaspora. In fact, these investments did not necessarily come from wealthy people but often from
the middle classes, especially in the Gulf, because of the familial
nature of entrepreneurship in the Palestinian territories.

Table 4.1: *Financial contribution of the Palestinian diaspora (US$ million)*

Total contribution	1996	1997
Total investment	303.8	311.1
Philanthropic and familial aid	104.2	99.1
Total contribution of the diaspora	408.0	410.2
Donors' foreign aid	549.4	432.2

Diverse sources: See Hanafi 1998b.

The impact of these contributions from the diaspora has been
both quantitative and qualitative. A holding company permits strategic and long-term investment and the creation of substantial projects
that are beyond the capacity of one entrepreneur. It is a new model
introduced into a country dominated by family-based, small or
medium enterprises. Infusing vitality into the Palestinian economy at
such an early stage is crucial to any future prospect of stability and
sustainable development. This not only relieves the economic, social,

and political tensions that are now a fact of daily life, but also initiates a catalytic process of capital accumulation in a low-resource based economy that consumes imports at a very high rate.

The most significant of these holding companies is PADICO, which was founded by 140 prominent Palestinian businessmen in the diaspora with a capital of $500 million. One of its objectives is to help channel new capital, either directly or through affiliated or subsidiary companies, towards projects that can create jobs while providing competitive financial returns to investors; in short, to attract and use investment to help rebuild the economic infrastructure in the territories.

A collective mobilization of resources has also taken place. A number of stockholding companies have been founded, chief among them the Arab Palestinian Investment Company (APIC), whose activities include the joint efforts of Palestinian business people in Israel and the territories. The Arab Palestinian Financial Foundation (*Beit Al-Mal Al-Arabi Al-Falestini*), the Palestine Bank for Investment, and the Arab Islamic Bank constitute other examples. The impact of such companies, however, has been limited when compared to PADICO.

This new pattern of big companies is not necessarily the best model for progress. Within developed countries it is clear that some challengers to corporate hegemony have appeared. Small businesses, which tended to be stereotyped as dependent, backward and low-skilled until the 1970s, have begun to increase in number again. Some of these, such as Silicon Valley and Third Italy in the USA, have been highly successful and innovative self-starters, using and developing the latest technology and design for the newest markets. Few, however, have thought of these small firms as actual or potential actors on a global stage or as nascent rivals to the international operations of the multinationals (Lever-Tracy, Ip and Tracy 1996).

The involvement of the Palestinian diaspora in the territories' economy has limits at present that are expected to carry on in the future. This is partly explained by the nature of the Palestinian diaspora's economic niches, which are mainly trade and construction. These two niches do not constitute value-added contributions to local expertise as they encouraged the diaspora to separate know-how and capital. Those who had capital teamed up with those who had expertise externally in order to start businesses in the territories or Israel. The creation of holding companies resolved this structural problem. In the Oslo period, many Palestinian citizens of Israel, who lacked the access and relationships to invest in the territories, invested through such companies.

As for their motivation, Palestinian diaspora investors said they did not expect to achieve quick profits. According to those sampled in my preliminary survey, they also felt that it would be wiser to invest in any other region in the Middle East, particularly in the industrial sector. Most decisions in favour of investment in Palestine were made for social rather than strictly economic reasons.

Transnational familial entrepreneurship

The mode of entrepreneurship is a concept that allows us to understand how capital and the know-how necessary for launching development are acquired, as well as the sustainability of any business.[13] Entrepreneurship does not imply a fixed behaviour or a kind of economic mentality, but rather is a dynamic concept. Entrepreneurship concerns not only business people but entrepreneurs in general, including the self-employed and employers (ILO 1998). According to this definition, Palestinians in the diaspora (whether refugees or not) are quite entrepreneurial. Some 20 per cent of the labour force is self-employed or employers (Khawaja and Tiltnes 2002: 99).[14] This percentage becomes 15 per cent in the Palestinian territories, according to the Palestinian Central Bureau of Stastics (PCBS) (Al Rimmawi and Bukhari 2002: 54).

The fieldwork conducted previously by myself and currently by Shaml concerning modes of entrepreneurship in Palestine/Israel and the diaspora, indicates two different types of Palestinian entrepreneurship, individualist and communitarian, both operating on a transnational level. Business people diversify their business in different fields and across geographical areas, using mainly capital transfers rather than physical re-location.

This diversification is not generally due to the orientation of business toward new markets or new methods of production designed to benefit from the economic environment in the host countries. It is rather a strategy of diversifying economic activity in new geographical areas and new sectors in order to ensure the security of capital in case one economic sector in a country should encounter difficulties. The insecurity of Palestinian economic activity in the diaspora can be perceived as stemming from a generalized anxiety in a population characterized by a psychology of transition and impermanence.

The nature of sectoral diversification and choice of place of investment by Palestinian entrepreneurs does not depend solely on the rational economic model and its complex calculations of different factors related to the size of markets, labour costs, technological performance, and the presence of infrastructures to facilitate investment. Palestinian economic diversification is also dependent on the vagaries of social and political criteria such as the impact of the Oslo peace process, the juridical status of the investor in the host and investment countries, mobility, access, and difficulties in obtaining visas. As a result of such factors in the Gulf States, for example, Palestinians were unable to convert and recycle the capital they acquired during the golden age in that region, when they migrated to North America after the Gulf crisis in 1990–1991.

If the outcome of the peace process explains the Gulf capital flow toward Palestine and Jordan, the subsequent movement toward Canada and the USA demonstrates the inability of the Middle East to absorb investment and its difficulty in keeping pace with the process of economic globalization. Since the 1980s, inter-Arab migration trade and investment has shrunk substantially when compared to general economic activity. Most economic activity and patterns of capital ownership have been confined within Arab states. The trend prevails despite exhibiting some signs of change after 1994.

Kinship networks between the Palestinian diaspora and its gravitational centre (the Palestinian territories and Israel) have assumed critical importance in diaspora economies, although the trend is not necessarily self-evident. In the Gulf countries, political instability and limited conditions for investment in the region have increased the value of economic kinship networks, while in other countries of the Palestinian diaspora, individual entrepreneurship has assumed a greater role (Hanafi 2000). While ethnic and kinship networks are not specifically necessary for the success of the investment and recycling of capital in the new receiving countries, the situation in the Palestinian territories may tend more toward entrepreneur–family rather than entrepreneur–individual relationships. Many interviewees indicated the importance of role models, such as other successful entrepreneurs in their social networks. Many family stories show that people who engaged in micro- or macro-enterprise creation have close relatives who operate businesses. The experience of many families shows a typical transnational type of entrepreneurship. Difficulties caused by diaspora life with transnational strategies are ensuring economic continuity in spite of diverse crises.

In the context of my fieldwork, transnational networks are not the expression of global capital but rather constitute strategies for survival. In many transnational experiences around the world, such as the Chinese in the USA (Ong 1999: 6), the quest to accumulate capital and social prestige in the global arena emphasizes and is regulated by practices favouring flexibility, mobility, and repositioning in relation to markets, governments, and cultural regimes. In the Palestinian case this acquisition of capital reflects a struggle for economic survival. A New York businessman may not need to spend more than a fraction of a second of his time on a million dollar transaction, thanks to the time–space compression enabled by new information technologies (Harvey 1990). However, a Palestinian transnational refugee in many countries in the Middle East will be likely to need to spend days to make a much more modest transfer, rendering the transaction cost much higher.

Shaml's socio-anthropological survey in 2003 focused on 40 entrepreneurs, mostly in Ramallah. The results show the economic importance of Palestinian refugees: half of the entrepreneurs are refugees although few live in camps. The Oslo process seems to have generated around 40 per cent of the entrepreneurial activities. The capital mobilized came mostly from inheritance or family assistance. Very few cases indicate the use of bank credit, due mainly to the conservative policies of banks in the Palestinian territories. Moreover, using family partnerships privileges a mode of trust that reduces the cost of economic transactions. Family partnerships before Oslo tended to involve the family living in the territories more than the diaspora (the transnational family). The peace process created connections between the West Bank and Gaza and encouraged many partnerships, and the locations of these partnerships went beyond the territories: a quarter of the entrepreneurs interviewed had investments abroad. The number of social familial ties that entrepreneurs maintain seemed more important than other socio-economic categories in the Shaml survey. Telephone and travel encourage such connections. However, ties with distant relatives (aunts, uncles, and their offspring) are weak. Some entrepreneurs use their relatives abroad to facilitate export and import, especially if those relatives live in Jordan. This seems important as travel restrictions and closures imposed by the Israeli occupation are a major obstacle to the development of businesses in Palestine.

Meanwhile, economic ties between Palestinians in Israel on one side, and those abroad and in the Palestinian territories on the other, are unlikely to flourish if the situation remains as it is at the time of writing this chapter. The absence of an independent Arab economy will discourage many Palestinians in the diaspora from investing in Israel as they are not willing to help the Israeli economy. The only economic ties continue to be those with members of the family. In regards to Palestinians in Israel investing their money in the Palestinian territories or the Arab world, many Palestinian entrepreneurs believe the fact that they hold Israeli nationality makes their investment risky and makes them feel vulnerable. We should note that the closures Israel enforces against Palestinians in the territories apply to those in Israel who cannot travel to cities in the territories, especially the Gaza Strip. As a result, many economic ties have been severed, as noted for example by many interviewees in Beer Sheva and Nazareth.

Comparing the Palestinian case with other return experiences is crucial. Many studies, like those of Nicholas Van Heer (1997), have provided us with very instructive conclusions drawn from several case studies about return migration. Van Heer generally found that return migration can be a generator of employment that allows an economy to flourish. The first case study was that of the 50,000 Asians who were expelled from Uganda in 1972. Van Heer found that the limited return two decades later of approximately 7,000 of them was an important factor in the recovery of the Ugandan economy. A second case study dealt with the forced exodus of 300,000 ethnic Turks from Bulgaria to Turkey in mid-1989. In this case, external assistance played a major role in facilitating the integration of the ethnic Turks in Turkey. Another case study concerned the exodus in 1991 of 350,000 Palestinians from Kuwait and other Gulf

States, most of whom went to Jordan. The mass migration from Kuwait and the Gulf region represented a 10 per cent growth in Jordan's population, increasing it to approximately 3.8 million. While the immediate consequences of the mass arrival were negative and disruptive, longer term benefits with great positive impact on the national economy became apparent within the first two years. Two important factors account for this positive impact on the economy: first, the majority of returnees were well-educated and skilled professionals who immediately entered the labour market; second, the migration was accompanied by a large influx of capital estimated at some $1.5 billion (Central Bank of Jordan 1992). The economic behaviour of these Palestinian returnees and the way they integrated in their new environment could tell us much about what to expect in the Palestinian territories. In these two latter cases, external assistance was a positive factor in integration. In comparison, the expulsion of 800,000 Yemenis from the Gulf states in the late 1990s, where no external assistance was provided, showed a negative impact on the society of origin.

Power structure: the encounter between Palestinians from the two sides of the Green Line

Palestinian sociologist Aziz Haidar observed that after the 1967 war, encounters were problematic between Palestinian refugees living in the newly occupied West Bank and Gaza Strip and their relatives within the 1948 borders. While their first meetings, after many years of separation, were warm, people quickly realized the differences between them.[15] Occupation, surveillance, and control had created a new Palestinian world inside Israel. In addition to the impact of the political system, a social class issue had also arisen. The Palestinians inside Israel had become much wealthier than their relatives who were living as refugees in the West Bank and Gaza Strip. Haidar notes that over time, the visits quickly stopped. One interviewee who lives in Haifa told me he became too upset when he accompanied people to their former homes in Wadi Salib and other parts of Haifa and had to stop doing this.

There are many explanations for this rupture between the two sides of the Green Line. The Palestinians of Israel channeled power from the hegemonic Israeli society, absorbed it and then exercised it against the Palestinians living under occupation in the West Bank and Gaza Strip. Second, the differences in their socio-economic situation created a feeling of superiority on the part of Palestinians with Israeli citizenship. The sociologist Nabil Saleh argues that the Palestinians of Israel did not worry about what the occupation meant for the West Bank and Gaza Strip. He remembered from his childhood how the Palestinians of Israel would say 'when the West Bank was *opened*' and not '*occupied*'. On their first trip to East Jerusalem, Palestinians of Israel took pictures with Israeli soldiers in their uniforms and their guns. Historian Adel Manaa considered the case of 350 Palestinian families from the north of Israel who moved to East Jerusalem to be closer to Palestinian universities and showed with a lot of subtlety the desire of these people to be close to Palestinians under occupation. This desire, however, did not prevent a number of complications arising. Some of them felt the double marginality: the marginality of a minority in a racist Israeli society and marginality with the Palestinian Jerusalemites who did not integrate them. One can argue that these prejudices among different groups are no different when a Palestinian Bedouin from Beer Sheva goes to live in Jaffa or Nazareth. In a highly segmented and tribal Palestinian society, prejudices among different groups are only aggravated by the border separation and not created by it. Nor must we underestimate how much the current Israeli politics of controlling space also hinders connections between Palestinians inside the West Bank and Gaza Strip. The result in the long term is very significant in creating mental borders. A border does not necessarily change one's national identity – everyone is Palestinian – but it changes people's everyday practices, including their willingness to move to their places of origin. Similarly the current fragmentation of the Palestinian population creates differing local identities in the population. This will not necessarily cancel the national identity, but will interact with it, sometimes harmoniously and sometimes conflictually.

Palestinian refugees in the West Bank and Gaza Strip as well as in the diaspora have a much stronger feeling of nostalgia for the land of Palestine than for the people of Palestine. The interviews I carried out illustrate that refugees insist on talking about property, land, the Mediterranean Sea, the Al Aqsa mosque, Khader tomb, and Deir

Bor'om Church. When confronted with questions about with whom and how they would live, they become evasive. Any reflection on the return of refugees should be a reflection on the society of return and not only the land of return. Palestinian refugees should not create a myth of a land without a people for refugees without land as a parody of the Zionist myth.

SCENARIOS OF REFUGEE MOVEMENT BASED ON SOCIO-ECONOMIC FACTORS

The issue of return is determined by factors that go beyond the mere right of return. But the right of return is the key for any solution as it will open up the various choices available to Palestinian refugees after more than half a century of exile.[16] Shaml's fieldwork and my studies in 13 countries of the Palestinian diaspora from 1990 to 1995 uncovered a very heterogeneous population of five million refugees, all of whom would have the right of return but might not necessarily exercise it; it seems that a smaller number are ready to return physically. The original places of birth of some of these refugees are today populated by Jewish immigrants. Among the Palestinians in Lebanon, Fafo's 2002 survey found that only 1.2 per cent were originally from the Palestinian territories whereas nearly all came from parts of historical Palestine now inside Israel. In fact, 40 per cent came from places that are now completely Jewish, such as Safad and Tiberias/Bisan (33.1 per cent and 6.3 per cent) or have a large Jewish majority, such as Acre (36.6 per cent from Akka and 9 per cent from Haifa), and only 10 per cent came from Arab cities, notably Nazareth (9.5 per cent) and southern Palestine (3.3 per cent). Although two out of five Palestinian-Lebanese were born in Palestine, very few have maintained ties with Palestinians inside Israel, according to the Shaml and Fafo surveys (Khawaja 2003).

It is difficult to imagine a single likely scenario for refugee return, due to the uncertainties of the results of negotiations and possible reactions on the part of Arab states.[17] Those uncertainties will cause any eventual number of returnees to vary tremendously. Based on a wide spectrum of factors influencing the realization of return but without taking into account patriotism as a push factor, I can propose three scenarios for eventual refugee movement. They differ in regards to the possibility of exercising the right of return and the extent of improvement in refugee camp conditions.

Scenario one: application of the right of return coupled with no improvement in refugee camp conditions

This scenario takes into account many surveys that question people about their willingness to return to their homes within the 1948 borders of Israel or in the Palestinian territories. My estimate is not based on their declarations but on the interpretation and contextualization of such declarations. For the migration movement from outside the Palestinian territories, a 'generous' quota would be provided for Palestinian refugees by third countries, a small percentage of refugee camp dwellers will choose to settle near their relatives abroad (outside the Palestinian territories), and an even smaller percentage of refugees will move outside the camps. The percentage in both cases is small if we take into account the fractured nature of the Palestinian family. This means the head of family may live temporarily in the new location until he or she finds a proper job and becomes relatively settled. As the conditions of refugee camps will not improve in this scenario, it is expected that 15 per cent of camp dwellers in the Palestinian territories will leave the camps: around 90,000 will leave to live in Palestinian cities, while the rest will stay in the camps, return home or move to a third country.

This scenario also takes into account the high percentage of Palestinian refugees in the Palestinian territories who have relatives abroad. There are about one million Palestinian refugees and displaced living abroad, who are originally from the West Bank and Gaza Strip. Taking into account the fractured nature of the Palestinian family, I expect that 20 per cent or 200,000 potential newcomers from among this group would settle in the Palestinian territories.

The number of Palestinians in Arab countries, according to an estimate of the PCBS, is around 4,017,000, of whom 402,000 reside in Lebanon.[18] Since the situation of the Palestinians in Lebanon is critical, I expect just under half of them, approximately 150,000 (mainly camp dwellers), to come to the Palestinian territories or Israel, even if they have no kinship ties. I expect Palestinian refugees resident in other Arab countries (subtracting 30 per cent from the Palestinians in Jordan and Egypt, as they are originally from the West Bank and Gaza) to come for different socio-economic reasons, push factors from the host countries, and pull factors from Israel or the Palestinian territories. A figure of 15 per cent would amount to 390,000 returnees. For Palestinians resident in western countries, I expect 3 per cent to return, totaling 15,000 migrants. Thus, around 500,000 will return in this scenario, with two-thirds going to the Palestinian territories and one third inside Israel.

Scenario two: a restricted right of return with improved refugee camp conditions

Under this scenario, an urban rehabilitation of the camps is undertaken. The major problems are infrastructure and housing rather than health and educational services, which are currently provided at a relatively acceptable level by the United Nations Relief and Works Agency (UNRWA). A key aspect of improving the camps is organizational and does not require vast financial resources. This particularly involves enhancing the representation of the camps in the local municipalities. These problems are less serious in the West Bank than in Gaza, as camp dwellers in the West Bank constitute 6.4 per cent of the population while in Gaza the figure is 31.1 per cent.

The movement of refugees is predicted as follows: I predict the return to Israel would be much less than in the first scenario, around 10 per cent or 145,000 refugees. I also expect that 3 per cent of refugee camp dwellers would choose to settle in a third country in order to be near relatives (18,000) while 2 per cent would move out of the camps (17,000). A small portion would leave the camps for social reasons as even after the physical and practical improvement of the camps, their social and political stigma will still remain. I expect 5 per cent to leave the camps (30,000). As with the first scenario, I expect 20 per cent of the Palestinians originally from the West Bank and Gaza who live abroad to settle in the Palestinian territories. This would result in 200,000 potential newcomers. As with the first scenario, 500,000 could come from abroad, with two-thirds settling in the Palestinian territories and one-third inside Israel.

Scenario three: no application of the right of return, with varying situations in refugee camps

Almost 20 per cent of West Bank and Gaza camp dwellers used to work in Israel before the second *intifada*. This work could be resumed, but people will experience a high degree of alienation due to working in one place and living in another. The movement of refugees in this scenario is predicted as follows: I anticipate that only a few individuals will return to Israel through inter-marriage (less than 10,000 from the West Bank and Gaza and 20,000 from the diaspora). I also expect 10 per cent of refugee camp dwellers to choose to settle in a third country near their relatives (60,000) and 3 per cent of refugees living outside the camps (25,000) to settle in a third country. As with the first and second scenarios, I expect 20 per cent of the Palestinian refugees who live abroad and are originally from the West Bank and Gaza to settle in the Palestinian territories. This will make 200,000 potential newcomers. As with the first and second scenarios, 600,000 might come from abroad and, as they cannot go to Israel, they will settle in the Palestinian territories.

The movement of Palestinian refugees will accordingly follow the logic of Table 4.2.

Table 4.2: *Scenarios taking into account only socio-economic factors*

	Return from Palestinian Territories to Israel	Return of refugees from abroad to Israel	Emigration from Palestinian Territories to western countries	Departures from camps	Arrivals from abroad to Palestinian Territories
First scenario	200,000	200,000	47,000	90,000	500,000
Second scenario	150,000	150,000	35,000	30,000	500,000
Third scenario	10,000	20,000	85,000	30,000–90,000	600,000

Certainly the number of those willing to return might be greater if we introduce other factors like patriotism or a strong push factor from the host countries, such as expulsion.

Potential returnees do not constitute a homogenous group. On the contrary, they represent diverse social, cultural, political, and economic strata of the refugee and diaspora population, varying from illiterate labourers to highly educated professionals and entrepreneurs.

It is hard to predict with precision the percentage of people who may return from each of the socio-economic categories and whether returnees would opt for permanent family return; individual return without the entire nuclear family; flexible return with a transnational option (i.e. being in two places and retaining the possibility of moving); investment without moving; or simply providing expertise through a short stay in the Palestinian territories. Three configurations are possible: first, in the case of a *voluntary return decision*, it is likely that a combination of patterns will emerge that will benefit the Palestinian economy, because the mode of entrepreneurship is familial and kinship ties remain strong between those in the West Bank and Gaza Strip and those living abroad. However, the possibility of investing in the Palestinian economy in Israel is less probable as there is no autonomous Palestinian economy there. Returning Palestinians will not feel loyal to the Israeli system if it maintains its Jewish character and kinship ties are weak.

The second configuration assumes *an enforced return* and posits that such refugee movements will yield bad results as they will be regulated by a centralized system thus neutralizing the capacity of the household or individual to mobilize social and economic resources in a new location. The third configuration is the optimum, and foresees refugee repatriation as *voluntary but with incentives and subsidies*. The role of the donor community and local governments (Palestinian and Israeli) is decisive in facilitating loans for housing and packages for re-installation. I agree with Rex Brynen's conclusion (2003) that the option of public housing in any absorption strategy should be eschewed in favour of employment-generation programmes and direct development of desirable locations in accordance with national planning policies. Otherwise, the process of return will perpetuate the historical injustice whereby the poor stay poor and those who can afford to compete in the global market will succeed in their move to their places of origin or third countries.

Palestinian entrepreneurs abroad meanwhile will likely invest either with capital or physical return, as they seek to enhance their social standing in their country or village of origin, even if the situation is not conducive to investment and economic stability is not ensured. I have seen similar behaviour in other post-conflict and transitional countries, for example Hungary, Romania, Armenia and Bosnia, where the diaspora elites play a role in the political arena. Extrapolating from the rate of investment and from family and other philanthropic activities of the Palestinian diaspora, I expect that the contribution would run to at least half a billion US dollars per year over the 10-year period following the independence of the Palestinian state.

As there will be two concurrent movements, one of the mass of returnees and one of select people, graduates and professionals as well as entrepreneurs, four conclusions can be drawn. First, researchers underestimate the importance of education and know-how among refugees. Many statistical indicators show that a quarter of Palestinian refugees in the Arab host countries are entrepreneurs according to the definition of the International Labor Organization (self-employed and employers). Thus, I expect that a quarter of the returnees will be able to integrate into the new Palestinian market. The return, in any case, cannot be viewed as purely a burden on the Palestinian economy. On the contrary, it could generate economic growth, thanks to the human and financial capital that refugees bring with them.

Second, the Palestinian state will have the right to adopt a policy of selectivity, as many countries in post-conflict areas have done. Historically, the policy of selecting (return) migrants has been applied by all countries that received a mass return of nationals or a like influx from another country. Even when the return is partially ideological, as with the Israeli *aliya,* selectivity was always the rule and has been kept firmly under Israeli government control. As Eliezer Kaplan, Israeli finance minister in 1949, said 'We need workers and fighters' (Segev 1986: 117).

Third, if Arab states do not compel Palestinian refugees to leave, I expect an initial pioneer group to return, to be followed, once they give a 'good report' about their situation to relatives and social networks, by larger groups. Finally, I expect a return of retired people, especially from the Gulf and western countries. This form of lengthy 'tourism' will benefit the Palestinian economy and these people will not need direct state assistance.

CONCLUSION

The most striking finding of the current research is that social ties between the Palestinians of Palestine and of Israel and their relatives abroad have been shaped more by rupture than continuity after a protracted period of conflict. The duration of the exile of the Palestinians, now more than 55 years, and the impact of the restrictions on movement across borders have lessened the intensity of ties between relatives. This is more the case for Palestinians living in Israel than those in the territories. Nevertheless, transnational kinship ties remain very important. They are often expressed by peoples' interest in maintaining social and economic links with their current place of residence. These social and family ties are often the motivation behind diaspora investment and business relations and I expect that many entrepreneurs will exercise their return in a transnational way. Moreover, I believe that these remaining types of ties will have a great potential to facilitate refugee absorption in the Palestinian territories and Israel.

In brief, Palestinian returnees should not be seen as a burden to society but rather as an asset, bringing skills and capital and having great potential to contribute to the social and economic life of the receiving country. This study is a pioneer in what I call the 'sociology of return'. I hope it will encourage more investigation and study based mainly on comparisons with other cases of refugeehood around the world.

BIBLIOGRAPHY

Abu Sitta, S. (2001) *The End of the Palestinian–Israeli Conflict: From Refugees to Citizens at Home*, London: Palestinian Land Society and Palestinian Return Center.

Al-Rimmawi, H. and Bukhari, H. (2002) 'Population Characteristics of the Palestinian Refugee Camps', *PCBS and Dissemination and Analysis of Census Findings Analytical Report Series* 3 (in Arabic).

B'Tselem and Ha'Moked (1999) *Families Torn Apart: Separation of Palestinian Families in the Occupied Territories: A joint comprehensive report of B'tselem and Ha'Moked – Center for the Defence of the Individual,* Jerusalem: B'Tselem.

Brynen, R. (2003) 'Refugees, Repatriation, and Development: Some Lessons from Recent Work', paper delivered at the Stocktaking II Conference on Palestinian Refugee Research, International Development Research Centre, Ottawa, June 2003 (and here see Chapter 5).

Charalambos, T. and Huliaras, A. (1999) *Prospects for Absorption of Returning Refugees in the West Bank and the Gaza Strip,* Institute of International Economic Relations, December (unpublished report).

Fergany, N. (1988) *Striving for Subsistance,* Beirut: Centre d'études de l'Unité arabe (in Arabic).

Giacaman, R. and Johnson, R. (eds) (2002) *Inside Palestinian Households: Initial Analysis of a Community-based Household Survey, Volume I,* Birzeit: Birzeit University.

Grillo, R., Riccio, B. and Salih, R. (2000) 'Introduction', in Falmer (ed.) *In Here or There? Contrasting Experiences of Transnationalism: Moroccans and Senegalese in Italy* (CDE Working Paper), Sussex: University of Sussex.

Hanafi, S. (1996/1997) *Between Two Worlds: Palestinian Businessmen in the Diaspora and the Construction of a Palestinian Entity,* Cairo: CEDEJ (in French).

—— (1998a) *Business Directory of Palestinians in the Diaspora,* Jerusalem: Biladi.

—— (1998b) 'Contribution de la diaspora palestinienne à l'économie des Territoires: investissement et philanthropie', *Maghreb-Machrek* 161. (in French).

—— (1999) 'Investment by the Palestinian Diaspora in the Manufacturing Sectors of the West Bank and Gaza Strip', 201–226 in ESCWA (ed.) *Proceedings of the Expert Group Meeting on the Impact of the Peace Process on Selected Sectors,* Amman: Economic and Social Commission of West Asia.

—— (2000) 'Penser le rapport diaspora, centre. La contribution de la diaspora palestinienne à l'économie des Territoires', in Hassan-Yari, H. (ed.) *Le Processus de paix au Moyen-Orient,* Paris: Harmattan (in French).

—— (2001) *Here and There: Towards an Analysis of the Relationship between the Palestinian Diaspora and the Center,* Ramallah, Muwatin and Jerusalem: Institute of Jerusalem Studies (in Arabic).

—— (2002) 'Opening the Debate on the Right of Return', *Middle East Report* 222.

—— (2004) 'Rethinking the Palestinians Abroad as a Diaspora: The Relationships between the Diaspora and the Palestinian Territories', in Levy, A. and Weingrod, A. (eds) *Homelands and Diasporas: Holy Lands and Other Places*, Stanford: Stanford University Press.

Harvey, D. (1990) *The Condition of Postmodernity*, London: Blackwell.

Holy, L. (1989) *Kinship, Honour and Solidarity: Cousin Marriage in the Middle East*, Manchester: Manchester University Press.

Husseini (2000) 'Current Socioeconomic Status of the West Bank Camp Refugees', paper delivered at the Shaml workshop 'Palestinian Return Migration: Socio-economic and Cultural Approaches', Ramallah, 2–4 March 2000.

International Labor Organization (ILO) (1998) *Resolution Concerning the Measurement of Underemployment and Inadequate Employment Situations*, The Sixteenth International Conference of Labor Statistics, Geneva: ILO.

Isotalo, R. (1997) 'Yesterday's Outsiders, Today's Returnees: Transnational Processes and Cultural Encounters in the West Bank', in Linjakumpu, A. and Virtanen, K. (eds) *Under the Olive Tree: Reconsidering Mediterranean Politics and Culture*, Tampere: European Science Foundation and Tampere Peace Research Institute.

—— (2002) 'Gendering the Palestinian Return Migration: Migrants from the Gulf and Marriage as a Transnational Practice', paper presented at the Third Mediterranean Social and Political Research Meeting, Mediterranean Programme, Robert Schuman Centre for Advanced Studies, Florence, 20–24 March 2002.

Jacobsen, L. and Deeb, M. (2003) 'Social Network', in Ugland, O.F. (ed.) *Difficult Past, Uncertain Future: Living Conditions Among Palestinian Refugees in Camps and Gatherings in Lebanon*, Fafo Report 409.

Jayyusi, L. (forthcoming) *Citizenship and National Identity: Reflections on the Palestinian Experience*, Ramallah: Muwatin.

Khawaja, M. (2003) 'Population', in Ugland, O.F. (ed.) *Difficult Past, Uncertain Future: Living Conditions Among Palestinian Refugees in Camps and Gatherings in Lebanon*, Fafo Report 409.

Khawaja, M. and Tiltnes, A. (eds) (2002) *On the Margins: Migration and Living Conditions of Palestinian Camp Refugees in Jordan*. Oslo: Fafo.

King, R.E. (1984) *Return Migration and Regional Economic Problems*, London: Croom Helm.

Lever-Tracy, C., Ip, D. and Tracy, N. (1996) *The Chinese Diaspora and Mainland China: An Emerging Economic Synergy*, London: MacMillan.

Malki, Majdi *et al.* (2004) *Towards a Sociology of Civil Resistance: Palestinian Society During the Second Intifada*, Ramallah: Muwatin (in Arabic).

Malki, Majdi, and Shalabi, Y. (2000) *Internal Migration and Palestinian Returnees in West Bank and Gaza Strip*, Ramallah: MAS.

Ministry of Planning and International Cooperation (MOPIC) (Palestinian Authority) (1998) *MOPIC's 1997 Fourth Quarterly Monitoring Report of Donor Assistance*. Available online from <http://www.pna.net>.

Naqib, F. (2003) 'Absorption of the Palestinian Refugee: Economic Aspects', Unpublished paper.

Ong, A. (1999) *Flexible Citizenship: The Cultural Logic of Transnationality*, Durham: Duke University Press.

Pedersen, J. *et al.* (eds) (2001) *Growing Fast: The Palestinian Population in the West Bank and Gaza Strip*, Oslo: Fafo.

Portes, A. (1985) *Latin Journey: Cuban and Mexican Immigrants in the US*, Berkeley: University of California Press.

—— (1998) 'Social Capital: Its Origins and Applications in Contemporary Sociology', *Annual Review of Sociology* 24: 1–24.

Reynolds, P.D., Hay, M. and Camp, S.M. (1999) *Global Entrepreneurship Monitor, 1999 Executive Report,* Babson College/Kauffman Center for Entrepreneurial Leadership/London Business School.

Roy, S. (1995) *The Gaza Strip: The Political Economy of De-development*, Washington, DC: Institute of Palestine Studies.

Saad al Din, I. and Fadil, M.A. (1983) *The Movement of Arab Labor*, Beirut: Center of Arab Unity Studies.

Salih, R. (2000) 'Transnational Practices and Normative Constraints Between Morocco and Italy: A Gendered Approach', paper presented at the First Mediterranean Social and Political Research Meeting, Mediterranean Programme of the Robert Schuman Centre, European University Institute, Florence, 22–26 March 2000.

Segev, T. (1986) *1949: The First Israelis*, New York: Free Press.

Sletten, P. and Pederson, J. (2003) *Coping with Conflict: Palestinian Communities Two Years into the Intifada*, Oslo: Fafo.

Uehara, E. (1990) 'Dual Exchange Theory, Social Networks, and Informal Social Support', *American Journal of Sociology* 96: 521–557.

Ugland, O.F. (ed.) (2003) *Difficult Past, Uncertain Future: Living Conditions Among Palestinian Refugees in Camps and Gatherings in Lebanon*. Fafo Report 409. Available online from <http://www.fafo.no>.

Van Heer, N. (1997) *New Diasporas: The Mass Exodus, Dispersal and Regrouping of Migrant Communities*, London: University College London Press.

—— (1996) 'Reintegration of the Palestinian Returnees', *Monograph No 6*, Ramallah: Shaml Publications.

CHAPTER 5

The return of Palestinian refugees and displaced persons: The evolution of a European Union policy on the Middle East Peace Process

Mick Dumper, Department of Politics, University of Exeter, United Kingdom

EXTERNAL INTERVENTION IN the return and repatriation of refugees is a common feature of most refugee situations. Examples can be drawn from recent United Nations (UN) and North Atlantic Treaty Organization (NATO) involvement in Afghanistan, Bosnia, Cambodia and East Timor. With regard to the Palestinian refugee issue, there is much evidence to suggest that the absence of a coordinated and coherent policy on the part of the international community is a major factor in the failure to achieve a resolution to the conflict. One of the major fault lines in the approach of the international community is the divergence between the European Union (EU) and the USA over approaches to the Middle East Peace Process (MEPP) and in particular over their respective policies on the Palestinian refugees.

The USA broadly concurs with an Israeli position that any return to the West Bank and Gaza Strip has to be subject to Israeli security needs and that any repatriation of refugees to Israel itself will be both nominal and in the context of family re-unification. On the other hand, the EU has sought to reconcile its stronger adherence to UN conventions on the rights of refugees and refugee repatriation with the constraints on those rights due to Israeli security and demographic concerns. At the same time, largely as a consequence of the marginalization of the EU in the MEPP by the US, the EU directed its energies towards economic development and co-operation in the region and the financing of the Palestinian (National) Authority (PA). Yet because any solution to the refugee issue would require large-scale investment and economic development, the EU has been able to engage more actively in the political aspects of the issue. It has been, therefore, obliged to face a conundrum: how to support a resolution of the refugee issue based upon international law yet find an accommodation with the Israeli veto on this issue, a veto which is broadly backed by the USA.

The wrestling with this conundrum and the evolution of a policy can be seen in the commissioning of two studies between 1999 and 2001 and in the consequent funding of a number of initiatives that sought to apply the findings of those studies. The first study focused on the absorption of Palestinian refugees into the West Bank and Gaza Strip while the second addressed the issue of the 1967 War Displaced Persons. This paper will examine the evolution of EU policy by discussing the second of the studies, including the factors that led to its commissioning and the impact it may have had on EU policy. The study in question was submitted in 2001 to the Refugee Task Force (RTF) advising the EU Special Envoy (EUSE) to the Middle East Peace Process. Entitled 'A Study of Policy and Financial Instruments for the Return and Integration of Palestinian Displaced Persons in the West Bank and Gaza Strip', the study was designed to assist in the formulation of EU policy on the Palestinian refugees. As coordinator of the research team that undertook the study and the final author of the report, I wrote this paper in part as a self-critique of the study and in part as a reflection on the context and processes contributing to the formulation of EU policy. As such the paper explores the dilemma confronting the EU in seeking to play an influential and relevant part in promoting a solution to the Palestinian refugee issue.

In addition, the paper draws attention to elements of the study which have been introduced into the discussions, and have helped frame the terms of references of the debate, around a fuller EU engagement in the Palestinian refugee repatriation process. Much of the economic and political data in the study preceded the second *intifada* and the Israeli re-occupation of the Palestinian territories, and therefore requires updating and will not be reviewed in this paper. Nevertheless, the study raised a number of important issues that are still relevant. These include the need for transparency over the legal principles in the construction of a repatriation programme;

the need for refugee participation in operationalizing priorities; the need to address the fragmentation of decision-making over the refugee issue in the Palestine Liberation Organization (PLO), the PA, the United Nations Relief and Works Agency (UNRWA) and the donor community; and the need to involve host countries in the planning and preparation of a repatriation programme and further examination of the role of UNRWA.

The paper is divided into five sections. The first part contextualizes the role of the EU in the refugee issue and discusses the background to the commissioning of the study. The second section outlines the Terms of References for the study and discusses the issues that led to their revision. The third section highlights the main issues raised by the study while the fourth discusses the policy implications of these issues and summarizes the key recommendations made. The final part attempts to assess the significance of the study and the subsequent activities of the Refugee Task Force.

CONTEXT OF STUDY

While Europe's long-standing and extensive links with the Middle East and North Africa (MENA) region are not the subject of this paper and have been discussed at length in many other publications it is important to refer to some of the main elements (Aliboni, Joffe, and Niblock 1996; Ludlow 1994; Weidenfeld 1995). Clearly historical links from the classical period, the Moorish invasion, the Crusades, the Renaissance, the Ottoman Empire and the colonial period have created a history of exchange and fusion which have been embedded in their respective cultures. More recently in the post-1945 period, economic interdependence between the two regions has increased with, on the one hand, European dependency on the region's hydrocarbons (80 per cent of its energy supplies come from the Middle East) and, on the other, the EU being the main trading partner of virtually every state in the region, including Israel (Ayubi 1995).

The result is that due to the MENA region's geographic proximity to Europe, any instability in that region, whether it be fluctuations in oil prices, the threat of uncontrolled migration or political radicalism, is perceived as threatening the security and interests of Europe. Thus European involvement in political and economic issues of the region can be seen as based on rational self-interest and not merely competition with the USA over access to markets, resources and political influence. In this context, the EU's lack of influence in the resolution of the Arab–Israeli conflict has been a strategic and critical policy failure in the defence of its future as a collective entity. Hence, there is likely to be constant pressure to undermine the attempt of the USA to monopolize the region.

The exclusion of the EU and its predecessor, the European Community (EC), from the MEPP is rooted in the imposition of Cold War dynamics in the region, particularly since the Suez crisis of 1956 (Dannreuther 2002: 3) The US–USSR rivalry over influence in the region during the 1950s and 1960s left little space for a 'European' policy. An additional factor in the lack of a European role has been the absence of institutions that could express a European policy. As a result European policy in the region was largely an aggregate of disparate bilateral relations. This is a pattern and dynamic that the USA sought to preserve. It resisted European involvement from the Venice Declaration of 1980, which called for the inclusion of the PLO in negotiations, down to the Madrid conference that launched the peace process in 1991, to the current reluctant acceptance of the existence of the Quartet (USA, Russia, the UN and the EU) as an actor in the MEPP. In the Madrid conference the co-sponsors were the USA and Soviet Union/Russia, with the EU being sidelined along with the United Nations. It was given no role in any of the bilateral negotiating tracks between Israel and its neighbours and was relegated to chairing the Regional Economic Development Working Group (REDWG) (Peters 1996).

However, two developments occurred in the 1990s that changed the pattern of external involvement in the region. First, the collapse of the Soviet Union and the emergence of a unipolar international system led to a growing US hegemonic control over the MENA region. Second, the Maastricht Treaty of 1994 that established institutions for a collective EU foreign policy (the Common Foreign and Security Policy, or CFSP) provided the basis for an EU challenge to its exclusion from the MEPP. Tensions surfaced with the USA over its refusal to intervene more strongly in the Washington round of negotiations that flowed from the Madrid conference. This had led to a paralysis not only in the Israeli–Palestinian track but also in the multilateral negotiations such as the REDWG. From the perspective of the Europeans, the impetus towards a negotiated solution following the Gulf War was being squandered. The Oslo Accords between the PLO and the Israeli government brokered by Norway was seen as a European initiative, despite Norway being a non-EC state. However, any advantage the EC sought was usurped by the USA as it recaptured the initiative by hosting the signing ceremony between the two parties in Washington. Likewise, while the EC sought to carve out a role for itself in the subsequent donor co-ordination meetings, the USA insisted on holding them in Washington and passing the chair on to the World Bank.

Nevertheless, EU pressure to be more closely involved has appeared to be unstoppable. While the Oslo Accords failed to revive the REDWG activities that were still chaired by the EU, Europe's expertise in economic development issues in the region came to the fore in the other multilateral forum established by the Madrid conference: the Refugee Working Group (RWG). In this working group, the EU was given responsibility for Social and Economic Infrastructure Development. This combination of involvement in one of the key Permanent Status issues in both the Madrid and Oslo frameworks for negotiations (the so-called 'deal-breaker') and in one which was bound to require a massive effort in economic terms, put the EU in a strong position to have a significant input into the outcome of the MEPP.

The EU had also played a significant behind-the-scenes role in the process set up by the Oslo Accords, particularly since the creation in 1991 of the post of European Union Special Envoy (EUSE) to the Middle East Peace Process, occupied during the period of the study by Ambassador Miguel Moratinos. Creating this post gave the EU a greater ability to respond to events and a greater visibility in the peace process. The EUSE undertook various small-scale initiatives aimed at building confidence between the parties, in a number of areas including refugees (Peters 2000: 159). The establishment of the Refugee Task Force, chaired by Karen Roxman, a Swedish diplomat seconded to the EUSE office, was an attempt to draw in the expertise of the member countries, and to coordinate their different agendas on the refugee issue. Its main brief, however, was to develop policy initiatives that would help the EU contribute to a solution to the refugee question. In addition, it was hoped that the work of the RTF would provide an alternative channel to the paralyzed RWG for fostering progress on the refugee issue (Peters 2000: 160).

Part of the impetus in the EU's efforts to strengthen movement towards the establishment of the Palestinian state was derived from the Euro-Mediterranean Partnership (EMP), launched at the Barcelona conference in November 1995. The EMP process (also known as the Barcelona process) included three programmes: the political and security partnership, the economic and financial partnership and the partnership in social, cultural and human affairs. The process was designed to create a Mediterranean Free Trade Area (MEFTA) and to enhance political security of the Mediterranean region. The process launched a series of Mediterranean regional conferences and meetings at the Foreign Minister level, with the EU providing the secretariat. Despite being seen as a separate framework, the EMP process nevertheless required progress on the Arab–Israeli conflict and the Palestinian refugee issue in order to attain its objectives. In this way, the EU became structurally involved in the progress of the MEPP (Xenakis and Chryssochoou 2001). In addition, the EMP process, in which the EU was the pre-eminent party, provided an alternative entry point to the MEPP outside of the US-dominated Madrid framework and the US-sponsored MENA economic summits that took place in Casablanca and Amman. For example, at the Third Euro–Mediterranean Ministerial Conference in Stuttgart in April 1999, the EU reiterated its commitment to a 'just comprehensive and lasting peace in the Middle East based on faithful implementation of the UN Security Council Resolutions 242 and 338 and the terms of reference of the Madrid Peace conference and the Oslo Accords' (Xenakis and Chryssochoou 2001: 89).

Thus, when the study was carried out in 2000–2001, the EU position on the peace process and on Palestinian refugees in particular was built on three pillars: the political framework established by the Madrid conference and the Oslo Accords; the EMP process; and also on legal principles based upon UN Security Council Resolutions

242 and 338 and other articles of international law regarding military occupation (namely, the Geneva Conventions). Continuing its role as 'outrider' of the USA, begun with the Venice Declaration, the EU followed this up with the Berlin Declaration of 1999, which announced its support for the creation of a Palestinian state as a prerequisite for a solution to the refugee issue. The EU provided substantial aid, to the tune of six billion dollars, in addition to an equivalent amount in loans from the European Investment Bank, with the purpose of laying the infrastructure for such an entity. In addition, the EU signed an interim trade agreement with the Palestinian Authority that focused on liberalizing trade and contributing to the economic development of the West Bank and Gaza as part of the EMP process.

Despite the extent of EU activity in supporting a future Palestinian state and its reiterations on a number of occasions of its belief in the importance of making progress on the refugee issue, it has, nonetheless, avoided formulating a clear position on the refugee issue as a Permanent Status question. A good example of this is a document which became known as the Bristol Report, submitted to the RWG by the EU. Despite being an attempt to break the impasse on the RWG, the report made no explicit declaration in support of refugee rights as understood by the United Nations High Commissioner for Refugees (UNHCR) in regards to refugee conventions (European Commission 1994: Point 12). In addition, while the Berlin Declaration had stated that no actions should be taken by either side that would prejudice the final status issues, there was no explicit support by the EU for the Palestinian refugees' right of return or compensation as laid down in UN General Assembly Resolution 194. Rather, during the 1990s the EU saw its main contribution to the refugee issue as being based on a humanitarian perspective – providing aid to Palestinian refugees via the European Commission Humanitarian Office (ECHO) and UNWRA (Tamari 1996: 19). One can note also that the EU sponsored a conference entitled 'Resolving the Palestinian Refugee Problem: What Role for the International Community?' held in Warwick in March 1998, comprised mainly of workshops on donor cooperation, economic needs and constraints and the issue of compensation (Warwick University 1998). In this context, the commissioning of two studies by the RTF can be seen as an attempt to make further progress on specific humanitarian and material steps.

The first study commissioned by the RTF was designed to ascertain, in the event of a negotiated settlement, the number of refugees that could be settled in the West Bank and Gaza Strip. This would assist the international community in drawing budgetary contingencies to support an eventual repatriation programme. It would also possibly reassure the Israeli government that such a repatriation programme was feasible and could be managed in a way which did not threaten Israel. Entitled 'Prospects for Absorption of Returning Refugees in the West Bank and the Gaza Strip' (Tsardanidis and Huliaras 1999), the study focused on the economic capacity of the West Bank and Gaza Strip to absorb returning refugees. Following an analysis of existing literature and studies on the economic performance of the West Bank and Gaza Strip, the authors presented three scenarios permitting a range of numbers of refugees that could return, with a top ceiling of 250,000. The capping of refugee return at such a low figure notwithstanding, the study was criticized in the RTF and by Palestinian bodies. EU member states argued that the conclusions did not tally with the evidence presented and insufficient care had been taken in establishing the political assumptions that underpinned the scenarios. A critique prepared by the PLO Department of Refugee Affairs called into question its 'gratuitous and pre-emptive political assumptions' regarding both the numbers and location of repatriation as well as the weak evidence for its quantitative conclusions (PLO Department of Refugee Affairs 2000). Despite being revised and re-submitted, the study was shelved and the EU turned to the World Bank for further research in this field. There was considerable embarrassment that the RTF's sally into this politically contentious field had been poorly executed (informal conversations with RTF members, October 2000).

PALESTINIAN DISPLACED PERSONS

The second study was commissioned in July 2000 with even a narrower remit. To some extent this was a victory of the 'pragmatists' over the 'idealists' in the RTF in that the focus was to be on a component of the Oslo Accords which was both humanitarian and agreed upon by all parties, including Israel. The aim of the study was to identify under different scenarios 'the policy and financial instruments essential for the successful return of Palestinian Displaced Persons (DPs) to the West Bank and Gaza Strip and their integration there' (Exeter University, 2001: Appendix, 117). A team based at Exeter University in the United Kingdom was asked to conduct a 'short and quick' study. Budgetary constraints limited the amount of fieldwork that could be conducted, so the study did not attempt to carry out new surveys. Instead it brought together existing material and the experience of other agencies in the field in order to offer policy recommendations concerning Palestinian DPs. In addition, the study was not a feasibility study. While some of the recommendations were quite detailed, they were not costed. Finally, the Terms of Reference did not include consideration of the compensation issue.

Almost immediately, however, the researchers encountered a series of political, conceptual and methodological problems that led to revisions in the Terms of Reference. Palestinians DPs are a sub-group within the generic category of Palestinian refugees who were displaced as a result of the 1967 War. They are specifically referred to in the 1993 Oslo Accords (Declaration of Principles, Article XII). The 1994 Peace Treaty between Jordan and Israel (Article 8, paragraph 2a) also provided the legal basis for the setting up of a Quadripartite Commission, comprising Israel, Jordan, Egypt and the Palestinians, to solve the issue of the DPs. The Quadripartite Commission failed to reconcile the different Palestinian and Israeli positions, but the agreement in principle provided enough of an opportunity for the PA and the donor community to begin the process of planning a return programme for the DPs.

However, due to the lack of agreement between the Palestinian and Israeli sides as to whom the term DPs actually covers, such plans remained at their early stages. The Palestinian position is that DPs should include Palestinians temporarily outside the West Bank and Gaza Strip in 1967; those deported after 1967; those who left voluntarily but were refused permission to re-enter; and, finally, the descendants and relatives of the above. The Israeli definition is narrower holding that the term should be limited to those individuals actually displaced as a result of the fighting in 1967, excluding descendants. The Palestinian definition pointed to estimates between 800,000 and 1 million. The Israeli definition led to estimates between 50,000 and 300,000.

The Exeter study noted that the term DPs in the Palestinian context was problematic. In some senses DPs are simultaneously both refugees and not refugees. They are refugees in the sense that in addition to being displaced in 1967, an estimated 50–80 per cent of them are also refugees from pre-1948 Palestine. That is, they became refugees for a second time in 1967. But they are not refugees in the sense that they do not fall under the original UNRWA mandate although many of them receive UNRWA services both as a result of their 1948 status and because UNRWA extended emergency relief to all DPs after the 1967 War for humanitarian reasons.

However, the term DP had considerable utility on the political level provided that the Oslo framework remained in place. Even in the political circumstances during which the study was conducted (November 2000 to January 2001), the Oslo framework was coming under question. In addition, on a programme planning level the term brought with it some serious problems of both principle and operational effectiveness. First, for possibly up to 80 per cent of DPs, a return programme to the West Bank and Gaza Strip would not be a return or repatriation to their place of origin. Therefore, unless it was designed and presented as an interim measure or as a prototype for a second repatriation to their original homes, the principle of refugee choice was being circumvented. Second, a return programme designed specifically for DPs but which did not address the needs of other refugees, was most likely to cause resentment and hostility, creating additional difficulties in implementation and successful integration. Third, the acceptability of a repatriation programme would be essential for successful integration. Refugees and DPs would be wary of any scheme that might undermine their right of return or which might deal with them as constituent parts or in an ad hoc and piecemeal fashion. Fourth, while most DPs reside in Jordan, they are difficult to isolate in terms of identifying specific financial and policy instruments or programme design that will assist their return to the West Band and Gaza Strip. Their definition as a sub-category is a result of a political event (the 1967 War) not of a particular socio-economic, regional, cultural, or religious characteristic. Indeed, they come out of the refugee environment and share the experiences and aspirations of that wider group.

As a result of these considerations, the Exeter team decided to interpret the Terms of Reference more broadly and locate its study in the wider context of the whole refugee issue. The challenge was to reconcile these divergent considerations and to design policy and financial instruments that had relevance to DPs of the Oslo framework but at the same time relevance for the return of the refugee community as a whole. These considerations were presented to the RTF at the interim report stage in November 2000 and accepted. Their acceptance by the RTF reflected an ongoing debate within the RTF, and by extension in the EU, about the extent to which the EU should engage in Permanent Status issues and challenge US dominance in this area. It also mirrored the changing dynamics in the region following the outbreak of the second *intifada* in September 2000 and the ongoing attempts to reach an agreement between the Israeli and Palestinian delegations which culminated in the Taba talks in January 2001. The prospect of a last-minute breakthrough at Taba running parallel with the total collapse of the Oslo framework, which the electoral defeat of Prime Minister Barak of Israel presaged, meant that the focus had moved away from DPs.

As a result the study comprised a broader perspective than had been envisaged in the original Terms of Reference. By introducing issues linking the operational feasibility of a repatriation programme to UN conventions on refugee rights and good practice, the support for a more comprehensive approach was made more credible. Adherence to UN resolutions could be dismissed as merely an idealist aspiration, but when it was seen to be part of an effective package and producing value for money then it was worthy of greater consideration. In this way the study tried to knit together various strands of existing EU policy: a positive track record in humanitarian assistance and economic development operating within the framework of international law; and the growing need to overcome the impasse in the Euro–Mediterranean Partnership – an impasse brought about by the lack of progress on Arab–Israeli conflict. Accordingly, the study aimed to produce a series of policy recommendations that were both practical and incremental.

MAIN AREAS OF STUDY

While not carrying out any primary data collection, the study surveyed the existing literature on the demographic profile of the refugee population. The aim was to identify key characteristics that would need to be incorporated into the design of a repatriation programme. Among these were: the relative youth of potential returnees; the importance of the family as an economic asset; the centrality of kinship links; the role of women in maintaining the cohesion of households; the relatively high levels of human resource development (education and training); and the labour skills in particular sectors. The study also highlighted the lack of gender-specific surveys to inform the design of a programme.

A major part of the study focused on the internal and external parameters and constraints for a repatriation programme to the West Bank and Gaza Strip. While the economic and political circumstances have dramatically changed since the study was submitted, many of the observations and issues raised are still pertinent. Internally, the study argued that the West Bank and Gaza Strip were not in an optimum situation to accommodate a massive return programme of either DPs or the wider refugee community. In the first place, demographic growth and projected return figures pointed to rates of job creation, health and education provision and infrastructure development in excess of projected local real GDP growth rates and beyond the internally generated fiscal revenues of the PA. The productive and financial sectors of the Palestinian economy are under-developed and would require significant investment for many years to come to meet existing and projected demand. In addition, the existing political framework and conditions of conflict were highly problematic as a context for the implementation of a successful return programme. There was a crucial lack of clarity over the role that a DP-only return programme would play in a wider return programme for refugees. The study also argued that the likely collapse of the Oslo framework would require a re-evaluation of a DP-only return programme.

The external parameters provided a more mixed picture. The regional economic climate had been buoyed by a period of unusually high oil revenues in 1999–2000. However, the specificity of the

Palestinian situation – with its political instability and dependence on economic relations with Israel – meant that any regional economic upturn would not significantly alter the poor prospects of the Palestinian economy. Another external factor to be considered was the way in which the international legal framework on refugees was evolving towards a more human rights-based understanding and away from a state sovereignty formula. This offered considerable support for a more comprehensive return programme, and for a negotiating agenda based around it. In addition, the role of the EU had become increasingly proactive which, from a Palestinian viewpoint, provided a counterweight to the close US–Israeli coordination on the refugee issue. The wide experience of the EU in development assistance in the area, its extensive contacts in the region and the fact that many of its political positions are based upon UN resolutions, positioned the EU as a crucial partner with the Palestinians over a return programme.

A distinguishing feature of the study was its attempt to place any planned return programmes in a comparative context by briefly examining refugee return programmes in other post-conflict situations. The first case study selected was the Bosnian return programme, asserted by many to be an example of how *not* to organize a return programme. The second was the Guatemalan programme that emerged out of a principled approach to the issue of return and strove to ensure its implementation met standards of good practice. It provided some useful learning points on the kind of challenges that can be faced when aiming to achieve high standards. Third, the Vietnamese programme was chosen as noteworthy in being one of the largest international return programmes, operating in the context of continued political tensions and involving the involuntary return of thousands of reluctant returnees.

The case studies highlighted a number of critical factors that should be taken into account when designing a return programme for Palestinian DPs and refugees:

- *Planning and preparation.* Thorough planning and preparation before beginning a return programme is a crucial issue. It took two years of preparation before the Guatemalan programme finally started. Factoring in this time ensures that the systems to co-ordinate the contribution of all stakeholders can be identified and put in place. In addition, joint standards of good practice can be discussed and agreed, and a common understanding of aims, objectives and ways of working can be developed.

- *Assistance packages.* The success of assistance packages is dependent on a number of crucial factors, such as consistency, legislative support and a gendered approach. The extent to which there is consistency in the level of benefit for each returnee and the degree to which the support given to returnees is seen to benefit the community as a whole is important in order to counteract resentment from the existing community not receiving benefits. Other factors include the provision of advice, training and ongoing support to individuals in the schemes, and the introduction of appropriate legislation to support the creation of micro enterprise while at the same time avoiding the saturation of the market for small businesses. In addition, it is important to introduce enabling systems for women to ensure, among other things, that women professionals benefit from and are equally attracted to return.

- *Country of origin participation.* The level of co-operation from government agencies in the country of origin is important as it determines how effectively the programme can be implemented, particularly in terms of the legislation needed to facilitate return programmes and the issuing of documentation papers.

- *Refugee and DP participation.* It is important to establish information systems that ensure information and advice is available in host countries which matches the reality in the country of return. This will allow returnees to plan for the particular needs of single women, young single men, the elderly, the disabled and unaccompanied minors. In addition, the involvement of returnees themselves in the design and implementation of return programmes is vital for the success of a return programme which builds up a sense of ownership and trust in the process.

- *Gender awareness.* Programs need to demonstrate a clear commitment to ensuring both men and women benefit from the programme and include a coherent and systematic gender component.

- *Integrated approach.* An integrated or holistic approach that considers the long-term well-being of the community as a whole has been shown to be the most effective approach.

The final substantive part of the study examined the range of options being discussed among the PA, local non-governmental organizations (NGOs) and the donor community within the context of the likely trends and projections for the economy of the West Bank and Gaza Strip and of the fiscal position of the PA. While at the time of the study there were no published plans for a refugee return programme, the implications of such a programme could be discerned from the long-term development plans of the PA. Particular reference was made to two documents: the Palestine Development Plan and the Pathway towards a Palestinian Vision of 2005 and Beyond (Palestinian Authority 1999; Palestinian Authority 2001). At the same time, the study recognized that strategic planning in the PA is highly diversified and uncoordinated, it therefore also examined the priorities expressed by different Palestinian institutions such as the Department of Refugee Affairs (DORA), the Palestine Economic Council for Development and Reconstruction (PECDAR), and the Negotiations Support Unit of the Department of Negotiation Affairs. The potential role of external aid in a prospective return programme was also examined.

The study noted that Palestinian planning for a return programme encountered a number of issues and debates. First, the political uncertainties regarding the future of the Oslo framework and the nature of relations with Israel mean that projections about numbers or target groups of returnees were largely speculative. Second, the economic conditions, even before the second *intifada*, were not conducive to a large-scale return programme. PA revenues failed to cover recurrent spending, leaving a total dependency upon external funds for capital expenditure on current infra-structural development. The sustainability of the then current and projected PA expenditure was contingent upon a level of private sector growth that was unlikely to materialize in the short to medium term. Private sector growth, with its knock-on effects in terms of overall economic expansion, job creation and higher fiscal revenues, would only become a significant factor when there was sufficient political stability in addition to legal, monetary and institutional reforms. In this context, during the short and medium term (five to ten years) the role of the international donor community would be essential in providing the means for the implementation of a return programme. Thus, if the EU was to be committed to assisting in the resolution of the Palestinian refugee problem in the long-term, it would be required to finance an array of measures from providing short to medium term budgetary support for the PA to the transformation of UNRWA.

Third, the nature of the return programme and the 'package' of infra-structural measures to be implemented were the subject of many debates. For example, approaches to the provision of refugee housing differed. One group, led by the Palestinian Ministry of Planning and International Cooperation (MOPIC), PECDAR and others in the international development assistance community, expressed a preference for new city development. This can be termed the 'Big Bang' school. It takes the position that large-scale projects in 'empty areas' of the West Bank should be a primary PA response to the practicalities of a return programme. Others in the local NGO community and individuals in the PA belonged to a second group, which can be termed the 'incrementalist' school. Their argument is that the existing absorptive capacity in the West Bank is much higher than assumed. Within the village context, for example, up to 50 per cent expansion would be possible in many neighbourhoods. It is feasible, they suggest, to begin strengthening the infrastructure of these villages now in preparation for the eventual return, rather than wait for large-scale developments pending a peace agreement. Full creation on the Israeli development town model would not be necessary or desirable except perhaps in the Jordan Valley. Even in the Gaza Strip, there are possibilities for some such expansion. A key benefit of the incrementalist approach would be the re-integration of small refugee communities back into Palestinian society, which is not likely to occur under the development town model.

Finally, there was the issue of implementation and the role of UNRWA. Officially there were no concrete plans for UNRWA to play a role in a return programme and, indeed, plans for its dissolution are referred to in the 1995 Annual Report (UNRWA 1995). With the stalling of the peace negotiations, discussion over the Agency's future had been stymied because of the political sensitivity of the refugee issue. However, researchers working on the study encountered two schools of thought over the future of UNRWA. On one hand there was what can be termed the 'UNRWA plus' school, which recognizes the need for the gradual handing over of UNRWA functions to the PA, but contends it still has a major role to play in the organization of a return programme. Under UNRWA plus, the agency would take on the logistical functions that UNHCR, or the International Organization for Migration (IOM) and German Technical Cooperation Agency (GTZ) have taken on in other refugee return programmes. This school of thought argues that transforming UNRWA in this way would have the added advantage of using the services of an organization trusted by the refugee community with staff who have extensive experience in humanitarian assistance and micro-enterprise development projects. In addition, UNRWA provides a collective and institutional memory that would contribute to the sensitivity required in organizing a return programme. UNRWA also has international legitimacy and would be able to maintain fruitful relations with the international donor community and with host governments.

On the other hand, the second school of thought, which can be termed 'UNRWA minus', argues that any return programme, whether it be for DPs or the whole refugee community, should fall within the ambit of a Palestinian immigration policy. Instead of an independent agency there should be a PA Ministry of Immigration and Absorption which would co-ordinate the relocation and absorption of returnees with other ministries and contract out the logistics of return to the IOM or GTZ. The advantage of this approach would be to delineate with greater clarity which party is responsible for which aspect of the return programme. The study recognizes that whether the UNRWA plus or UNRWA minus option is finally adopted, both options would involve the transfer of functions to the PA, which would have major fiscal and developmental implications for the PA, and hence the donor community.

The study concluded that if the return of refugees was not accompanied by improved management of public resources, better service delivery, and efforts to increase limited physical resources such as water supply, then the PA would struggle to accommodate the return of a mere 100,000 refugees. On the other hand, under improved circumstances in terms of increased water supply, good macro-economic management, a robust regulatory environment that encourages private sector investment and economic growth, better use of existing banking sector deposits and additional resources from the diaspora, the PA and the Palestinian economy might effectively absorb much larger numbers in a phased manner.

POLICY IMPLICATIONS DERIVED FROM THE STUDY

The final section of the study comprised 21 recommendations for policy initiatives based upon the following assumptions:

- That an EU-supported return programme would take place either in the context of a negotiated Permanent Status agreement or a series of interim agreements. It would not take place in conditions of open conflict or outright hostilities liable to jeopardize the safety and dignity of DPs and refugees.
- That if a series of interim agreements evolved, there would be sufficient regional stability and commitment to allow the implementation of certain projects of a preliminary nature, prior to actual return.
- That a return programme supported by the EU would adhere to UNHCR principles and international conventions and be based on refugee choice, giving due respect to principles of justice and fairness. Such an approach has been demonstrated elsewhere to be the most effective and successful.
- That an EU-supported return programme would form part of a larger commitment to the general short- to medium-term development of the West Bank and Gaza Strip and would thus adopt an integrated and comprehensive approach. That is to say it would include processes intended to assist the existing Palestinian population of the West Bank and Gaza Strip to absorb returnees, while also maximizing returnees' ability to contribute to building and strengthening Palestinian society.

Many of the study's recommendations related to the general economic and institutional development of the West Bank and Gaza Strip in order to facilitate the absorption of refugees and DPs need not be dealt with in this summary. Those recommendations that are specifically related to the refugee issue include the need to establish transparency in the form of a commitment to United Nations General Assembly Resolution 194 and United Nations Security Council Resolution 237 as a basis for a return programme, and the adoption of UNHCR principles of good practice. The study also recommended the introduction of mechanisms for better co-ordination between DORA, MOPIC, NAD, UNRWA and other host countries, including preparation for the creation of a ministry for immigration and refugee absorption. In addition, the study recommended that, in order to assist in the planning of a return programme, a series of symposia should be organized to bring into the public domain the needs and concerns of the host countries. Another recommendation was that the EU should assist in the formulation of plans to transform parts of UNRWA into a return programme agency including the retraining of key personnel and the incorporation of best practice from other repatriation schemes. A final series of recommendations focused upon the constituent parts of a return programme: preparation, transportation, housing, employment and orientation and follow-up services, and suggested specific tasks that the EU could undertake. One that did not require waiting for a Permanent Status agreement was the initiation of public discussion of the nature of Palestinian relations with Israelis and with the state of Israel. This would involve a consideration of what steps towards restorative justice and reconciliation might be taken in order to heal the emotional and psychological damage of the conflict along the lines of the Truth and Reconciliation Commission set up in South Africa.

OBSERVATIONS ON THE EVOLUTION OF AN EU POLICY

It is difficult to assess the impact of the study in any measurable way for at least three reasons. First, the arcane and opaque processes of the EU bureaucracy prevent a tracking of specific decisions taken in respect to the study. Minutes were not made available and feedback was given informally and on an erratic basis. Second, the submission of the study in February 2001 coincided with the intensification of

the second *intifada*, and the formal discussion on its recommendations took place during the Israeli re-occupation of the West Bank.
This led to a re-ordering of priorities in the EUSE office and the RTF
to focus more on direct humanitarian assistance. Follow-up discussion of the study and execution of the study's recommendations was
therefore delayed. Third, there was a series of changes in personnel
in the EUSE's office during the summer of 2001 that broke some of
the continuity in discussion.

Nevertheless, some results can be discerned. The study was
favourably received by most of the main officers involved, in that it
indicated a clear set of tasks that the EU could undertake. It was seen
as particularly valuable in suggesting policies that not only would
assist the pursuit of a Permanent Status agreement, but also others
that could be implemented prior to any agreement (e-mail communication from Karen Roxman, 6 February 2001). In addition, the con-
textualizing of the needs of 1967 DPs within the whole refugee issue
was seen as a helpful framework for formulating a return programme
for DPs. The main controversy occurred over the study's contention
that a prerequisite to a successful return programme would be the
adherence to UN resolutions and UNHCR guidelines. Some saw this
as unrealistic given the political conditions pertaining to the region.
During the final presentation of the study to the RTF in April 2001
there was considerable debate over this issue in both the formal and
informal sessions. No decisions as such were taken during the pre-
sentational session apart from the establishment of a working party
to identify which recommendations would be pursued. The research
team was not privy to the outcome of these discussions.

However, one can conclude from informal exchanges that the
study remained a basis for discussion in the Refugee Task Force, and
there are indications that some initiatives that originated from the
office of the EUSE have been partly framed by the analysis and recommendations put forward in the study. For example, the recommendation concerning the involvement of host countries in
discussing the refugee issue, was taken up through a series of semi-
nars co-ordinated by the Royal Institute for International Affairs and
the Oxford-based Centre for Lebanese Studies, an initiative funded
by the EC and the International Development Research Centre. The
importance of greater co-ordination between Palestinian agencies

dealing with refugee affairs was also recognized and was introduced as a result of a Canadian initiative which was supported by the EUSE. The initiative supported the establishment of a secretariat to promote coordination among the main Palestinian institutions working on the refugee issue, the Negotiations Support Unit, DORA and MOPIC. The issue of taking heed of the principle of best practice in the construction of repatriation programmes appears to have made some headway. In part this was due to the preference of EC and EUSE officers to adhere to UN conventions, but also because the destructive impact the Israeli re-occupation of the West Bank had on EU investments in infrastructure and institution building led to a re-evaluation of funding strategies. Although the office of the EUSE was reluctant to be more proactive than the Palestinian leadership itself is in adhering to international laws and conventions, there was a growing awareness that if the EU was to invest huge sums of money into a repatriation process it needed to be one that was going to be acceptable not just to the Israelis but also to the main stakeholders – the Palestinian refugees. Without their co-operation EU expenditure in this area may turn out to be a waste of money.

My own critique of the study has identified two weaknesses. First, the study suffered by trying to pitch itself at both the specialist and non-specialist members of the RTF, with the result that there was some duplication of previous work. The RTF is comprised of officials from the EUSE office but also representatives of member states, some of whom were more knowledgeable than others, and some of whom had a clearer agenda than others. Second, and more importantly, the study could have been improved by a greater knowledge of the decision-making processes within the EU. There are many different centres of power and financial channels in the EU ranging from the European Commission's control over the development assistance budget to the growing influence of the office of Javier Solana, the EU's High Representative for Foreign and Security Policy. In addition, it is clear that on the Middle East issue certain member states exert considerably more influence than others and scrutinize the refugee file in particular. Furthermore, the changing composition of the RTF, as member states sent different representatives to each meeting, led to a situation where a consistent dialogue, continuity and an institutional memory between the Exeter research team and the RTF was difficult to achieve. Thus, without an insider's grasp of the different levels of decision-making and budgetary authorization, it was difficult to identify specific activating levers which would drive a set of initiatives or policies through the different parts of the EU administration concerned with the Middle East.

In sum, during the period under review, EU policy towards a key element in the MEPP, the Palestinian refugees, appears to have undergone a subtle change. Greater institutional co-ordination among member states over foreign policy that flowed from the Maastricht Treaty; structural involvement in the region through the EMP process; active participation in Madrid-based frameworks such as the REDWG and RWG; budgetary support for the PA and UNRWA; and the creation of the EUSE, have all combined to place the EU in the forefront of external intervention in the Palestinian refugee issue. This was reflected in the way that an EUSE-funded study, originally intended to focus on Palestinian Displaced Persons, in the end included analysis and recommendations on the broader refugee issue. The initial narrower remit seems to have been superseded by a greater willingness to intervene in the formulation of a broader political agreement on the repatriation of Palestinian refugees.

BIBLIOGRAPHY

Aliboni, R., Joffe, G. and Niblock, T. (eds) (1996) *Security Challenges in the Mediterranean Region*, London: Frank Cass.

Ayubi, N. (ed.) (1995) *Distant Neighbors: The Political Economy of Relations between Europe and the Middle East/North Africa*, Reading: Ithaca Press.

Behrendt, S. and Hanelt, C. (eds) (2000) *Bound to Cooperate: Europe and the Middle East*, Gütersloh: Bertelsmann Foundation Publishers.

Dannreuther, R. (2002) 'Europe and the Middle East: Towards a Substantive Role in the Peace Process?', *Geneva Centre for Security Policy Occasional Paper Series* 39.

European Commission Shepherd of the Social and Economic Infrastructure Development Theme (1994) *Report to the Refugee Working Group of the Middle East Peace Process* ('Bristol Report'), Oxford: Office for International Policy Services and Refugee Studies Centre.

Exeter Refugee Study Team (2001) 'A Study of Policy and Financial Instruments for the Return and Integration of Palestinian Displaced

Persons in the West Bank and Gaza Strip: a Report Submitted to the Refugee Task Force of the European Union's Office of the Special Envoy for the Middle East Peace Process', January, Exeter University.

Ludlow, P. (ed.) (1994) *Europe and the Mediterranean*, London: Brasseys.

Palestinian Authority (1999) *Palestinian Development Plan 1999–2003*, Ramallah: Palestinian Authority.

—— (2001) *Pathway toward a Palestinian Vision for 2005 and Beyond*, Palestinian National Authority website, <http://www.pna.org>. Accessed January 2001.

Peters, J. (1996) *Pathways to Peace: The Multilateral Arab–Israeli Peace Talks*, London: Pinter Press.

—— (2000) 'Europe and the Arab–Israeli Peace Process: The Declaration of the European Council and Beyond' in Behrendt, S., and Hanelt, C. (eds) *Bound to Cooperate: Europe and the Middle East*, Gütersloh: Bertelsmann Foundation Publishers.

Palestine Liberation Organization Department of Refugee Affairs (2000) *Comments on the Report 'Prospects for Absorption of Returning Refugees in the West Bank and the Gaza Strip'*, Ramallah: Palestine Liberation Organization Department of Refugee Affairs.

Tamari, S. (1996) *Return, Resettlement, Repatriation: The Future of Palestinian Refugees in the Peace Negotiations*, Washington, DC: Institute for Palestine Studies.

Tsardanidis, C. and Huliaras, A. (1999) *Prospects for Absorption of Returning Refugees in the West Bank and the Gaza Strip*, Athens: Institute of International Economic Relations (unpublished).

United Nations Relief and Works Agency (UNRWA) (1995) *UNRWA Annual Report 1995*, Gaza: UNRWA.

Warwick University (1998) 'Proceedings', from Conference on *Resolving the Palestinian Refugee Problem: What Role for the International Community?*, Warwick: University of Warwick, 23–24 March 1998.

Weidenfeld, W. (ed.) (1995) *Europe and the Middle East*, Gütersloh: Bertelsmann Foundation.

Xenakis, D. and Chryssochoou, D. (2001) *The Emerging Euro–Mediterranean System*, Manchester: Manchester University Press.

CHAPTER 6

Refugees, repatriation, and development: Some lessons from recent work

Rex Brynen, McGill University, Montreal, Canada

THIS CHAPTER WILL examine the development challenges that will face Palestinian planners and decision-makers as a consequence of any voluntary repatriation of Palestinian refugees and displaced persons to a future Palestinian state. It will do so by highlighting 12 key lessons and policy implications drawn from analytical work undertaken by the World Bank and others in recent years. Many of these lessons are also relevant to donors, non-governmental organizations (NGOs), and analysts that may be involved in future Palestinian development efforts.

Before undertaking such a task, however, a few caveats are in order. First, this paper makes no assumptions about the relative mix of *return* (to 1948 areas), *repatriation* (to a Palestinian state, including any swapped territories formerly part of Israel), continued *residency* (in current host countries), and *resettlement* (in third countries) that might be part of a permanent status deal, other than to assume that all of these options will, in one way or another, form part of an agreement. If an agreement includes full recognition of the right of return to areas that are now part of Israel, many refugees may nevertheless opt to either move to, or remain in, a Palestinian state in the West Bank and Gaza (WBG). If refugee return is very limited (or even barred) under a peace agreement, the demand for repatriation will be much greater. In any case, there is a moral and practical obligation to address the demographic and developmental consequences of repatriation for Palestinian statehood. This is especially the case since, prior to 2000, little serious work had been done on the topic. By contrast, Salman Abu Sitta had undertaken substantial work on the practicalities of return to 1948 areas.[1]

Second, this paper presumes that the situations of 1948 refugees and 1967 displaced persons (many of whom are also 1948 refugees) will be dealt with at the same time. By contrast, the 1993 Oslo Agreement called for the situation of the displaced to be resolved during the interim period, while resolution of the broader refugee issue was postponed to final status negotiations.

A third caveat is that while this analysis is based in large part on World Bank data and draws upon a number of unpublished World Bank studies,[2] it is independent of the Bank. Thus, the author remains solely responsible for all views offered herein.

LESSON ONE: REPATRIATION FLOWS DEPEND ON MANY FACTORS, BUT REPATRIATION DECISIONS SHOULD BE VOLUNTARY

The developmental challenges of absorbing returnees in the WBG will be fundamentally shaped by three sets of factors: the nature of any final status agreement, the policies of host countries, and economic conditions in both host countries and the WBG. These elements will shape the total magnitude of population movement, the rate of flow, the voluntary or involuntary nature of population movement, and the social profile of those permitted or choosing to return.

The developmental challenges of absorption are most easily dealt with if population movements are voluntary and unbureaucratized, rather than somehow planned or 'managed'. In many or most cases, relocation decisions would be made by individuals and households based, in large part, on the relative degree of economic opportunity in the WBG, compared with conditions in their present host countries. Market Mechanisms, notably price levels and unemployment rates, will act as a natural regulator of population movement, with increases in these signaling scarcity in housing and employment, and hence causing the rate of repatriation to slow until a new equilibrium is reached.

Conversely, if refugees face substantial 'push' factors, and are even forced to migrate, their movement may be disconnected from local economic conditions. In such a case, returnees might find them-selves forced to repatriate to the WBG despite high local prices and high unemployment. Furthermore, the sudden involuntary arrival of a substantial number of persons would, in the absence of a buoyant economy, cause (at least in the short run) undesirable downward pressure on wages, upward pressure on prices, and increased unem-ployment resulting in a reduction in overall welfare.

What might be the major sources of 'push' migration? Lebanon, which hosts around 200,000 refugees,[3] has made it amply clear that it opposes any settlement (*tawtin*) of Palestinians in its territory. Lebanese authorities might, in the context of a refugee agreement, place additional pressures on refugees to leave. This population group would pose a particular absorption challenge to a Palestinian state, since Palestinians in Lebanon tend to be unskilled or semi-skilled workers, with lower levels of formal education, and little in the way of savings, legally held property, or other capital resources.

By contrast, it is unlikely that Palestinians in Jordan or Syria would face similar political pressures to repatriate: Syria has treated its refugees well, and most Palestinians in Jordan are Jordanian citizens. Jordan might, however, wish to see the eventual repatriation of non-citizen displaced persons. The most vulnerable population in this regard are Gazans, numbering approximately 50,000–100,000. To this group could be added a further 100,000–200,000 West Bankers holding temporary travel documents rather than Jordanian citizen-ship. Political realities in Jordan make it unlikely, however, that any draconian measures would be applied against either group to force an abrupt repatriation to a Palestinian state.

LESSON TWO: REPATRIATION AND DEVELOPMENT POLICIES SHOULD EMPOWER REFUGEE CHOICE, AND AVOID BUREAUCRATIC DISTORTIONS AND PERVERSE INCENTIVES

Fundamentally, a development strategy aimed at facilitating the social and economic absorption of repatriating refugees into the West Bank and Gaza should be designed so as to build on, rather than distort, the individual choices of returnees. Returnees should be empowered to select *when* to repatriate, as well as *where* they will reside. In doing so, they will likely be motivated by both economic factors (housing prices, employment and investment opportunities) and social links (family members and other social support networks). Perverse incentives, by contrast, would be those that might attract individuals to the WBG despite otherwise unattractive local conditions; for example, large grants or other entitlements that encourage rent-seeking migration.

To maximize flexibility and responsiveness, market and private sector mechanisms that respond to refugee choices (in the construction of new residential housing, for example) ought to be facilitated. State action and development initiatives may be needed in some cases, however, either to build private sector capacities, or to provide a suitable regulatory and enabling environment for private sector activity. Moreover, the state, in conjunction with the international development community, will need to play a key role in assuring the provision of critical infrastructure, and addressing the needs of especially vulnerable groups (such as low income families, especially those 'pushed' by host countries into repatriation).

Such a strategy would aim to maximize refugee satisfaction, while at the same time assuring that the natural link between migration decisions and underlying economic conditions is not distorted by bureaucratic procedures or perverse economic incentives. In this respect, such an approach would contain policy elements from – but go well beyond – the refugee integration policies adopted in most Western jurisdictions. It would more closely parallel the immigrant absorption policies successfully adopted by Israel since the 1980s.

What is *not* required is some centralized system of repatriation management, in which refugees 'apply' to return, and some sort of influx controls are applied to population movement. It is not clear whether such a process of management was envisaged by participants in the January 2001 Taba negotiations, where a 'return, repatriation, and relocation' committee was proposed as part of the architecture of implementing a refugee agreement (Government of Israel and Palestinian Authority 2001).

LESSON THREE: THERE IS NO SUCH THING AS 'ABSORPTIVE CAPACITY'

Overall, work by the World Bank and others has highlighted that there is no meaningful concept of 'absorptive capacity' that can be usefully applied to the West Bank and Gaza, especially under conditions in which population movement is relatively free and hence self-regulating. Given appropriate political and economic conditions – an end to current Israeli restrictions on the movement of Palestinian goods and people, and sound macroeconomic policies; appropriate frameworks to encourage private sector investment; efforts to improve the existing resource base (especially for water); and efficient delivery of public services – it is possible to envisage the absorption of a million or more returnees to the WBG. Conversely, given weak policies and poor economic conditions, the territories would struggle to deal with the arrival of a tenth as many persons.

Public income and employment-generation programmes should *not* be seen as a major component of absorption strategy. Governments are generally quite poor at 'creating' sustainable employment, and micro-finance programmes tend not to create new jobs. Instead, both have a limited role as social safety nets for specific, targeted groups. In the case of refugees, job creation would likely only play a modest and transitional welfare role for otherwise unemployed, involuntary returnees (for example, unskilled workers repatriating from Lebanon). Vocational training will also be important for this group.

It is particularly important to recognize that, in general, returnees will be a long-term economic asset, not a burden: returnees are workers, investors, taxpayers, and a source of valuable human and social capital. Although in the short term their repatriation requires capital investments in infrastructure and transitional costs for health, education, and social services, in the longer-term their economic activity (and the wealth and government revenues that it generates) is likely to cover the marginal cost of their consumption of public goods.

The one area in which there are constraints (although not limits) is the area of natural resources, and specifically water. This issue needs to be seen as part of an overall regional water problem, due not only to absolute scarcity and rapidly growing population, but also to inefficient pricing, usage and distribution. The repatriation of refugees from nearby countries to a Palestinian state would not increase the total demand on regional water supplies, moreover, but merely rearrange it.

LESSON FOUR: REFUGEE ABSORPTION OUGHT TO BE PART OF A BROADER STRATEGY OF PLANNING FOR DEMOGRAPHIC CHANGE

It should be noted that many of the policy issues and potential development initiatives associated with the possible repatriation of refugees to a Palestinian state are also highly relevant to general demographic growth in the WBG. Hence, policy planning on these issues should be seen as part of a larger effort to build Palestinian capacities to cope with demographic change.

Any return to the WBG would occur against a historic backdrop of high levels of demographic growth. Natural growth in the territories currently stands at around 3.5 per cent annually. This represents an increase of over 110,000 persons, or more than 17,000 households, per year. During peak periods in the years following the 1993 Oslo Agreement, population inflows pushed the net population growth rate as high as 6 per cent in some years, and year-to-year school enrolment increases peaked at 10 per cent in 1996–1997 (World Bank 2000: 2.75). During 1996–2000, an estimated 15,600 housing units were constructed per year in the WBG (World Bank 2002b: 2.13).

The effect of the current violence and Palestinian economic crisis on demographic growth and housing is not fully known. It would seem reasonable to assume that extremely depressed levels of economic activity and employment would severely restrict the ability of Palestinian families to acquire or upgrade housing, and increased overcrowding seems likely to result. This may create pent-up housing demand, which would be expressed in the future in more secure and economically buoyant times.

It is important to note that, in less abnormal years, the Palestinian private construction and housing sectors have proved capable of meeting quite high levels of demand, as have public institutions.

During this period, and despite the growth in the client population, the Palestinian Authority (PA) was, through substantial donor-financed investment, also able modestly to improve both education and health services. As the World Bank's June 2000 study of *Aid Effectiveness in the West Bank and Gaza* showed, this was evidenced by both objective indicators (such as student/classroom ratios, hospital beds per 1000 population) and by an opinion survey conducted among ordinary Palestinians.

At the same time, there are also salient differences between demographic expansion generated by natural growth, by the return of displaced persons, and by the repatriation of refugees. Of the three sources of demographic change, natural growth involves few or no problems of social integration. Integrating returning 1967 displaced persons poses more of a challenge. On the one hand, this population is physically proximate to the West Bank, often has substantial familiarity with the area, and has strong social links to the WBG. On the other hand, there could be problems of social friction if returnees were seen to get substantial benefits not provided to members of the existing population. Repatriated 1948 refugees pose an even larger challenge of integration, since relatively few have strong family links to the WBG, and many have had little or no personal familiarity with the territories.

LESSON FIVE: THE PALESTINIAN STATE OUGHT *NOT* TO CONSTRUCT HOUSING FOR RETURNEES

The construction of public housing for returnees was initially envisaged by a few Palestinian planners, some of whom seemed to imagine new towns and cities being constructed strategically along Palestine's borders on the model of Israeli development towns and settlements. This is a bad – and untenable – idea, for several reasons.

First, the experience with Palestinian public housing is limited and generally has been poor. Such a system is likely to be highly prone to abuse, mismanagement, cost over-runs, inflexibility and corruption. Indeed, the experience of Israeli immigrant settlement in the 1950s – with its emphasis on development town construction, and its continuing legacies of high unemployment, inadequate housing and infrastructure, political backlash, and social bitterness – represents a powerful argument why this is *not* the best approach.

Second, the provision of public housing to returnees, if coupled with rent or purchase subsidies, would create enormous perverse migration incentives, attracting returnees in numbers wholly discon-nected from economic opportunities in the WBG. It would also create significant equity problems, and considerable tension between returnees eligible for such housing and current WBG residents (including existing refugees).

Third, such a programme would be far too costly. In its 2002 study of the *Absorption of New Residents in the West Bank and Gaza*, the World Bank found that the total cost of accommodating returnees in new newly built housing on public land in the WBG varied from $8,924 to $13,275 per person, depending on location (including construction costs, and excluding the imputed cost of the land itself). If such housing were to be provided for returning refugees and displaced persons, the costs would be astronomical: between $4.4 and $6.6 bil-lion for 500,000 returnees, assuming the provision of free public land. Clearly, such outlays are well beyond any amounts of assistance that donors are likely to provide.

The only case where some public sector housing construction might be appropriate is in regard to emergency low-income housing for involuntary returnees who have been 'pushed' from host countries. However, even in this case it still may be preferable to stimulate private sector construction and provide other sorts of welfare support.

LESSON SIX: 'DECAMPING' OF REFUGEE CAMPS IS NOT FEASIBLE

Whatever political arrangements may be made in a permanent status agreement, it is inevitable that some refugees in the WBG would remain in their current locations. Initially, some Palestinian officials appeared to envisage a massive transformation of refugee camps, with the bulk of the population rehoused in new residential areas. This too would be prohibitively expensive, as World Bank data quickly demonstrates. Full redevelopment of all existing refugee camps in the WBG (that is, for approximately 650,000 persons comprising less than 20 per cent of the WBG population), involving the relocation of around 40 per cent of all refugees to new residential areas ('Type 3' upgrading, in the World Bank schema) would cost approximately $4.4 billion – well beyond Palestinian and donor capacities. Rehousing all camp refugees in new towns would cost even more, at approximately $7.3 billion.[4] In practice, the costs might be even higher than these estimates, due to the cost inflation associated with a massive reconstruction programme.

Instead, donor financing is only likely to be able to support much more modest improvements in existing camps. This would consist of modest infrastructure and access improvements, with only very limited relocation/de-densification in the worst cases.

It is similarly not feasible to 'decamp' Palestinian refugee camps in Jordan or Syria, where refugees, given a choice, may choose to maintain residence even after a peace agreement. In many cases, the camps act as low-income housing reserves, with refugees moving in and out depending on their economic circumstances. Instead, the focus would need to be on improving and regularizing these areas (with some de-densification), thus (further) transforming camps into urban neighbourhoods.

In addition to the overwhelming economic argument for not relocating existing refugee camp residents to new towns, there is a social one too: refugee camps have become poor but vibrant urban areas, with dense networks of social links, commerce, service, voluntary and community activities. Any redevelopment efforts should be careful to preserve, even build upon, these.

It is important also to recognize the enormous legal and other complexities that would surround land tenure within refugee camps. WBG camps are generally constructed on public land, but in Jordan, Syria, and Lebanon camps occupy a more confusing mix of public, charitable, and private lands. Despite a lack of formal legal title, refugees 'buy' and 'sell' camp properties. If camp residences and property were transferred to residents, the stark differences in potential land prices (between, for example, sea-front properties in Beach Camp versus the interior of Deir al-Balah or Rafah) could create substantial inequities. Some mechanism would need to be developed that provides refugees with clear legal title to their homes, but also mitigates the effect of variations in local property values.

LESSON SEVEN: EVACUATED SETTLEMENTS ARE ILL-SUITED FOR REFUGEE ABSORPTION

Many commentators have assumed that evacuated Israeli settlements in the WBG could provide suitable housing stock for returnees. While this may be true in some cases, simply allocating settlement homes to returnees could be problematic in many respects. First, there may be an inadequate number of homes. Second, settlements may not be conveniently located for Palestinian employment purposes. Third, there may be serious equity issues involved, especially given that most settler housing is relatively luxurious by local Palestinian standards. Why should some returnees acquire ex-settler homes with lawns, air conditioners and even swimming pools, while others acquire nothing at all, and local (and perhaps much poorer) WBG residents remain in their current inferior residences? Finally, there is substantial opportunity for abuse in any programme of using settlements as public housing for returnees, and even a well-run and transparent programme could be subject to politically costly accusations of favoritism in housing allocation.

Given this, it is preferable for the absorption of settler housing stock to be seen in the broader context of a Palestinian national housing strategy, rather than as a refugee specific asset. Most settler homes could be capitalized by selling them at appropriate prices to any interested Palestinian buyer, refugee or non-refugee. The resources thus received by the state could then be used to finance public infrastructure investments, housing finance incentives/subsidies, and other programmes for both returnees and the general population. Equity and transparency would be essential in the design of such a programme.

LESSON EIGHT: RETURNEES SHOULD BE ASSISTED IN VOLUNTARY RELOCATION IN A WAY THAT REDUCES THE TRANSACTION COSTS OF RELOCATION

The first basket of an overall policy package for returnees should involve relocation assistance. This would provide direct support, during the duration of the return programme, for the transportation and relocation costs of eligible refugees and displaced persons returning to the WBG to take up residency there. Such a programme might be generalized, or could be means-tested so as to direct benefits to low and middle-income families. It should, ideally, offset the economic cost of relocation without creating any particular financial incentive to relocate. Such a programme might take the form of per capita cash payments; vouchers, usable towards transportation costs for persons or possessions; organized and/or subsidized transportation; or some combination of these.

It is also possible to provide reintegration grants, to facilitate the initial transition to residence in new areas. Israel, for example, has provided rental assistance payments (usable, in essence, for any purpose) for newly arrived immigrant families since the 1990s. This policy has proved very useful in cushioning the costs and strains of first arrival, and supporting families while they arrange long-term housing solutions. It is doubtful, however, whether any such programme could easily be applied to the Palestinian case, for several reasons. First, the PA lacks the fiscal resources for such a programme, and donors may be reluctant to finance a programme that involves simple cash payments to individuals. Second, the weaker institutionalization of the PA might make a programme more vulnerable to abuse. Third, unlike immigration to Israel, returnees to the WBG are traveling relatively short distances, have opportunities to find housing solutions prior to arrival (especially if there were to be a relatively open border with Jordan), speak the local language, and thus face fewer problems of social integration.

Some form of housing assistance vouchers might be necessary, however, to address the urgent needs of low-income, involuntary returnees who have been 'pushed' from their current countries of residency. Ideally, such vouchers would form part of a broader low-income housing/welfare programme for which all Palestinians were eligible. However, in the absence of a national strategy, it might prove more practical to establish a limited-time, tailored programme focused on the needs of a particular group of involuntary returnees. Such vouchers could be used towards rent, housing purchase, or perhaps mortgage rate subsidies.

The relocation assistance basket would also include support for information and outreach programmes. Drop-in centres for returnees could be established in major urban areas, to provide a one-stop location for gathering information on housing, retraining programmes, and other relevant public and NGO services available to returnees. Similar information centres could also be established in the diaspora, to inform potential returnees, and to facilitate their efforts to secure travel and other needed documentation. Were relocation to be involuntary, there would also be an emergency need to assist individuals and families in securing documentation and making other necessary arrangements.

LESSON NINE: REFUGEE HOUSING POLICIES SHOULD FORM PART OF A BROADER NATIONAL STRATEGY TO STIMULATE HOUSING SUPPLY

The second basket of policies for the absorption of returnees would involve stimulating the housing sector to assure that adequate housing stock entered the market in a timely fashion and at a reasonable cost. In general, these policies would be aimed at increasing the general housing stock, rather than creating returnee-specific housing solutions. In doing so, such an approach reduces or eliminates the risk of both perverse incentives (attracting returnees through targeted housing) and social tensions between residents and returnees over differential access to housing solutions.

What is being suggested here is that resources be directed toward a programme that would see public land being made available for housing purposes at below market rates, whether to contractors for eventual sale or rent, or to qualified individuals undertaking their own construction. Such land would be made available to all, returnees or residents, although income criteria could be developed to limit the largest implicit subsidies to those projects intended for low-income housing or undertaken by low-income families. Affordability targets might also be set, requiring that contractor developments have a certain maximum sale price, or that a certain proportion of low-income housing be built. Increasing the pool of land available for housing in this way should have the added advantage of dampening increases in private land prices during the repatriation period, thus reducing or avoiding the sorts of sharp housing price increases that followed the Oslo Agreement and the establishment of the Palestinian Authority.

There is clearly enough public land to accommodate returning displaced persons in this way, quite apart from private land that would also be built upon. The World Bank's examination of a sample of just five representative urban areas in the West Bank[5] found sufficient land for 106,000–211,000 new residents in these locations, depending on assumptions about housing density. Although more costly, satellite towns could also be developed in new areas, each accommodating 20,000–70,000 residents (World Bank 2002a).

Sites would be made available as serviced lots, with roads, water, and sewage access and facilities provided. The funding for this, as well investments in the required social infrastructure (schools, health facilities, community centres), would be provided by donors. At present, poor infrastructure and the frequent requirement that developers provide feeder infrastructure represents a significant constraint on housing development, pushing prices up (World Bank 2002b).

It is envisaged that the implementation of such a programme would be highly decentralized, and focused at the municipal level. Local government units would be provided with incentive grants, proportional to the amount of construction undertaken on public land and the number of returnees attracted. Such grants would be sufficient to cover the cost of providing public infrastructure for new residents and housing, together with a bonus incentive amount intended to make it desirable for local governments to attract new residents.

Without such a programme, there is a danger that local governments will attempt to deter new residents, fearing that local infrastructure and services will be overwhelmed. With such a programme, local governments effectively will compete with one another to offer innovative programmes to attract newcomers, and hence the incentive grants linked to returnees. Such a programme would be devised so as to allow a variety of approaches to be adopted at the local level, reflecting different geographical circumstances, public and NGO capacities, demand, and other factors. It also focuses efforts at the municipal level, where Palestinian implementation capacity is often quite strong.

In addition to such locally directed incentives, there is a need to promote suitable reform and institution-building in the local planning, zoning, and taxation systems so as to provide a supportive environment for the housing sector. At present, only 25–30 per cent of WBG properties are properly registered, thus limiting collateral-based lending, slowing transactions, and rendering some purchases potentially insecure (World Bank 2002b: 2.17). In many cases, municipal zoning regulations are highly formalized and tend to restrict the supply of land for housing in urban areas (World Bank 2002b: 2.16). Reform in these areas is likely to occur faster if local officials see positive benefits accruing from attracting newcomers to their areas.

Reform is also important in the rental sector, so as to encourage growth of this housing stock. At present, only a very small proportion of Palestinian households reside in rental accommodation (12 per cent in the West Bank, 5.2 per cent in Gaza) (World Bank 2002b: Table 4). Rent controls, conversion restrictions, and existing tax laws do not encourage an expansion of the supply of potential rented accommodation.

In absorbing its immigrant flows since the 1990s, Israel provided landlords with exemption from existing income tax on rental income. There may also be scope in the Palestinian case for changes in tax rates, the provision of tax credits, or an expansion of investment amounts eligible for tax deductibility, so as to encourage the renting of existing vacant units, conversions, or investment in construction for rental purposes. However, such initiatives would also require suitable reforms of existing rent control laws inherited from Jordan and Egypt.

An enlarged rental market would provide a larger array of initial housing choices for returnees, and might lessen or spread out some of the initial demand for housing purchase. However, a strong social bias in favour of privately owned accommodation is likely to continue.

LESSON TEN: HOUSING FINANCE INITIATIVES ARE A CRITICAL ELEMENT OF ANY REFUGEE ABSORPTION STRATEGY

The third basket of required initiatives relates to the housing finance sector. At present, there is essentially no mortgage lending system in the WBG. Instead, purchasers typically use existing savings, family borrowing, remittances, land-swaps, and lease-to-own arrangements with developers. Developers have access to some commercial financing, but this is typically short term. As a result, it is common for developers to await initial sales or leases before completing or extending construction projects. Moreover, the absence of larger and longer-term commercial finance means that most developers operate on a relatively small scale.

Further development of the mortgage system being put in place in conjunction with the Palestine Mortgage and Housing Corporation (PMHC) would represent a substantial step towards the establishment of housing finance mechanisms that would facilitate housing solutions for returnees. While the current PMHC programme envisages most loans at levels of $30,000 or more, the programme has also conceptualized a lending window for smaller loans. A micro-finance component could further be added to support owner investments in housing expansion or upgrade, a particularly important consideration given the frequency with which extended families are accommodated within expanded housing, or additional units are built on to existing family plots.

Such a programme would be self-financing, and would include little or no subsidy component. However, it could be combined with a voucher scheme for low-income Palestinian and/or involuntary returnees that allows a buy-down in mortgage rates. Such a scheme of subsidized mortgages – a key element in Israel's immigrant absorption strategy – clearly would require the prior establishment of an effective mortgage system, as well as the establishment of the administrative structures required to determine eligibility, issue vouchers, and monitor the programme.

LESSON ELEVEN: COSTS ARE HIGH AND DONOR RESOURCES ARE LIMITED

It is important to note that the costs of even a relatively modest programme for supporting refugee absorption are high, and indeed well beyond the likely levels of donor support.

Table 6.1: *Costs of sample refugee absorption programme*

Programme	Cost
Modest support for moving and travel costs for returnees ($150/person)	$75.0 million
Repatriation information/drop in centres (32 in diaspora refugee camps, 13 in Palestinian cities, operating for three years)	$27.0 million
Infrastructure costs associated with the provision of modestly priced serviced sites for residential construction on public land, complete with road access, water and sewage connections, and local health and education infrastructure. (Excludes public income from sale of plots.)	$985.5 million
Incentive grants to municipalities designed to upgrade general community infrastructure and encourage the absorption of returnees, equivalent to an additional 50% of infrastructure costs above	$492.75 million
Housing finance support for 33% of returnees (and a similar number of low-income existing residents), equivalent to 20% of residential construction costs	$504.04 million
Transitional budget support for increased recurrent health and education costs associated with returnees, phased out over five years	$270 million
Modest improvements in social and public infrastructure refugee camps (utilities, roads and paths, improved access, health and education facilities)	$257.53 million
Modest housing improvements in refugee camps (relocation and housing of 20% of inhabitants). (Excludes income from sale or rental of upgraded housing.)	$3,039.4 million
Transitional budget support for former UNRWA programmes transferred to the Palestinian state, phased out over five years	$475.6 million
Annual cost	$612.68 million
Total cost (for ten-year programme)	$6,126.82 million

Table 6.1 offers rough estimates of the costs that might be associated with a ten-year programme to address the needs of 500,000

returnees to a Palestinian state, together with the needs of 650,000 camp residents in the WBG. These elements alone total $613 million per year, or $6.1 billion over the ten years of the initiative – an amount at the upper end of (and probably significantly beyond) the likely generosity of international donors. Moreover, these costs do not include support for refugee-related development efforts in Jordan or Syria, nor transitional support to Jordan or Syria for the costs of assuming former United Nations Relief and Works Agency (UNRWA) services, nor any costs associated with refugee return to Israel or refugee resettlement in third countries. They do not include income foregone by the Palestinian state due to tax incentives or the sale of public land at below-market rates. They also do not factor in an average population growth rate among refugees of 2.5 per cent per year, which could inflate costs further if peace is delayed.

LESSON TWELVE: REFUGEE COMPENSATION IS A KEY PART OF THE ABSORPTION PROCESS

Given the limited financial resources of a future Palestinian state and the finite availability of donor resources, refugee compensation payments may well represent the single largest source of investment in the living conditions and opportunities of refugee households. Much depends, of course, on how much compensation would be paid. At the time of the Taba negotiations, Israeli officials seem to envisage an Israeli contribution in the low single-digit billions, while Palestinian claims could easily top the one hundred billion dollar mark. If one assumes compensation in the $5–20 billion range, this still exceeds annual donor contributions to refugee absorption (over ten years) by around 10 to 40-fold.

Much also depends on the modalities of compensation. The rapid payment of significant individual compensation (whether in whole or in part) would provide refugees with resources that they will then be able to use according to their own family priorities, whether to relocate, improve existing housing and living conditions, save, or invest. At a state level, the availability of significant amounts of collective refugee compensation would help address the costs of public infrastructure investment, and cushion the burden associated with any eventual assumption of former UNRWA services by Palestine and host governments.

One method of assuring that refugees receive compensation payments in a timely enough manner to use them to support repatriation is to pay the bulk of these amounts through a fast-tracked system of per capita payments, in which refugee status entitles refugees to payments regardless of specific personal or family losses in 1948. Individuals with large losses over a certain level could then file claims for additional compensation, which would require evidence, adjudication, and identification of eligible heirs. Such a system would see most refugees receive their compensation much more quickly than would be the case if all refugees had to file specific claims for specific losses. Assuming that finite resources are available, such a system could also be designed to be progressive in its allocation of compensation, so that small-property owners receive proportionally more and large landowners proportionally less than would be the case under a losses- and claims-based system. Finally, a status-based per capita system does not suffer the gender inequities that are likely to result from a claim-based system in which payments would be made disproportionately to male heirs. At Taba in January 2001, the parties seemed to be moving towards acceptance of such a status-based fast-tracked per capita system (Eldar 2002).

It is important also to note that most or all compensation ought to be paid in cash, rather than through more complex systems of vouchers, entitlements, and/or community benefits. Compared to other more directive (and likely, more bureaucratic) processes, cash payments contribute to refugee choice and empowerment by maximizing flexibility, allowing individual refugees and families to decide how their welfare might best be improved. Households are likely to use the funds well – whether for immediate consumption, human capital, or longer-term housing and durable capital improvements – and such payments do not necessarily carry the danger of unproductive use. However, it is important that attention also be directed by both donors and the Palestinian state to enable refugees to use compensation funds most effectively, through increasing the capacity of the financial services sector, supporting infrastructure developments for housing, assuring adequate opportunities for human capital investments through higher education, creating a positive environment for investment, and similar developmental measures.

CONCLUSION

Much remains to be done in thinking about, and planning for, refugee repatriation in the West Bank and Gaza. However, among much of the work that has been done there has been substantial agreement that repatriation programmes should not create perverse migration incentives, that key decisions should remain in the hands of individual refugee households, that there are limits to what can be done given limited resources, and that any refugee compensation scheme will have profound repercussions for absorption, migration, and development. It is also clear that Palestinian absorption policies cannot be treated in isolation, but must be well integrated into the broader development strategies of the future state.

There is also much additional analytical work that still needs to be done. At the time of writing, the prospects for the peace process, and eventual final status negotiations, are uncertain. But despite that, there remains considerable value in continuing to explore *now* how best to meet the *future* challenges of a Palestinian state.

BIBLIOGRAPHY

Eldar, A. (2002) 'Moratinos Document: The peace that nearly was at Taba', *Ha'aretz*, 14 February.

Government of Israel and Palestinian Authority (2001) *Taba Negotiations: Refugee Mechanism (Draft II)*, Taba: Government of Israel and Palestinian Authority.

United Nations Relief and Works Agency (UNRWA) (2003) *UNRWA in Figures*, Gaza: UNRWA.

World Bank (2000) *Aid Effectiveness in the West Bank and Gaza*, Washington, DC: World Bank.

—— (2002a) *Absorption of New Residents in the West Bank and Gaza: Potential for Housing Accommodation on Public Land in Selected Areas in the West Bank and Gaza*, Washington, DC: World Bank.

—— (2002b) *Housing Finance for Returnees: Issues and Policy Options*, Washington, DC: World Bank.

—— (2003) *Housing and Infrastructure Scenarios for Refugees and Displaced Persons*, Washington, DC: World Bank.

CHAPTER 7

Planning in support of negotiations: The refugee issue

Khalil Nijem, Ministry of Planning, Palestinian National Authority

INTRODUCTION

Since its establishment in 1994, the Ministry of Planning (MOP) of the Palestinian National Authority (PNA) has been engaged in the formulation of various plans that have been used to guide the PNA, the private sector and civil society in meeting the challenges of Palestinian development. Forecasting future population levels in the West Bank and Gaza (WBG) is an integral part of planning. The increasing population, resulting from a combination of high natural growth and the anticipated influx of returnees, poses a challenge to development on all levels and across all sectors. In this respect, the refugee issue is one of the major challenging uncertainties facing Palestinian politicians and planners alike and shall continue to be so until it is resolved during final status negotiations between the Palestinian Liberation Organization (PLO) and the Israeli Government.

The PNA is anticipating that negotiations will include a discussion of Israeli responsibility for the creation of the refugee issue; recognition of the principle of the refugees' right of return; and mutual agreement on how the refugee issue will be resolved. During the last round of final status negotiations in Taba in January 2001, five options for refugee return and repatriation were discussed: (1) return to Israel; (2) settlement in a Palestinian state; (3) settlement in a host (Arab) country in which the refugees currently reside; (4) resettlement to a third country; and (5) settlement in 'swapped' lands that were formerly part of Israel. Compensation is also expected to be an integral part of the package offered to Palestinian refugees for lost land, homes, and livelihoods, as well as to account for the suffering they have experienced over the years. This compensation could be designed at an individual or group/state level, or a combination of both.

Based on these options, the planning tasks facing Palestinian planners as related to the refugee issue are three-fold: planning for absorption within a future Palestinian state, planning the future of the refugee camps and addressing the future of the United Nations Relief and Works Agency (UNRWA) after a peace agreement (the latter being a dimension not dealt with in this chapter). These issues, as well as the question of refugee compensation, highlight the need to integrate development planning and state building in a variety of ways, including land use, the development of infrastructure, housing, social services and job creation, poverty alleviation and economic recovery and development.

In addition to its linkages with future development planning and compensation, absorption is linked to other final status issues such as water, borders and Israeli colonies. It is necessary to address key questions such as: What amounts of land and water resources might be needed or available for use by returnees? What will happen to evacuated colonies and to what extent can these areas and infrastructure be used to accommodate future needs and can they be utilized in or facilitate the absorption process?

Likewise, the refugee issue is also linked to future regional relations (especially regional economic cooperation and the issue of citizenship) and, less directly, to the question of Jerusalem (notably physical land use planning and urban infrastructure development around the future Palestinian capital).

REGIONAL PLANS IN PALESTINE 1998–2010/2015: BASES FOR ABSORPTION PLANNING

In 1996–1997, a major task of MOP was to prepare 'first generation' spatial plans for the Gaza and West Bank Governorates, namely, the Gaza Regional Plan and the West Bank Regional Plan, which provided a basis for further planning within sectors as well as planning on regional/governorate and local levels. These plans were based on population growth predictions and distribution models and scenarios that took into consideration the inherent uncertainty in forecasting the future population of the West Bank and Gaza Strip. In both plans, the working assumption was that the Palestinians would return in great numbers immediately after the Palestinian State is established. Some assumptions about the number and the demographic structure of returning Palestinians were made. For planning purposes, it was assumed that by the year 2010 about 450,000 Palestinian immigrants would settle in the West Bank and about 260,000 would settle in the Gaza Strip. Their migration, it was assumed, would begin in 2005, at a rate of about 100,000 per year. As a result, immigrants/returnees would represent approximately one third of the total population increase by the year 2015.

These assumptions were deemed necessary in order to establish strategies for future spatial planning and development such as urban and rural development strategies, and sectoral development strategies including transportation, water and wastewater, solid waste, industry, agriculture, public services, housing and tourism. According to these plans, future population growth (including a large influx of returnees), their impact on land, and their potential to enhance the West Bank and Gaza settlement systems, economic growth, and the distribution of services have been incorporated in the delineation of developing areas and land use priorities, and in defining future spatial development patterns.

However, these assumptions could be challenged since it may take time for the new state to develop the needed capacity in order to accommodate the returnees. Furthermore, the living conditions in the newly established State may not compare favourably with places where many refugees now live. The challenge facing Palestinian planners is how to attract Palestinians in the diaspora to immigrate to the West Bank and Gaza, and to assess the possible impact of these immigrants on Palestinian society. While the main premise of the above mentioned plans remains valid in the overall sense, there is a need for more detailed and clearly defined development targets which, once implemented, will eventually lead to the realization of the goals and objectives of these plans. Stated differently, the dynamic and changing situation on the ground requires a clearly defined vision for the Palestinian future. Should there be movement from an 'interim arrangement' toward 'final' status, it is imperative that the PNA, together with the private sector and Palestinian civil society, strive toward a more articulated vision and strategy that take into account such a situation.

Moreover, an influx of more than 100,000 people per year to the West Bank and Gaza, as indicated in the Regional Plans, would represent both an opportunity and a challenge to Palestinian society. In order to avoid problems and to make the absorption and integration as smooth as possible, there is a need for further analyses related to the number of Palestinians that would be living in the West Bank and Gaza in 10–15 years; where they would settle; when they would move; how they would relocate; and how much money their move and resettlement would cost.

Similarly, more detailed analyses are needed to address the future status of the existing refugee camps and to investigate options for their integration within the Palestinian spatial system, once an agreement concerning the refugees is concluded.

In consequence, MOP has identified further planning tasks based on the Regional Plans, namely, the Physical Planning Initiatives (PPIs), that aim at developing national policies, strategies and programmes around two areas (among others): first, the receiving and absorption of Palestinian immigrants/returnees in the new Palestinian state and second, the urban regeneration of refugee camps and their integration in the Palestinian urban fabric.

PLANNING FOR THE ABSORPTION OF PALESTINIAN IMMIGRANTS/RETURNEES INTO THE PALESTINIAN STATE

Immigration is one of the most complex and least predictable components that will determine demographic change in the West Bank and Gaza. In the Palestinian context, immigration is considered to be part of the 'state-building' process. It is also one of the key factors in stabilizing and consolidating a durable peace in the Middle East. The proposed PPI concerning potential Palestinian immigrants/returnees aims at developing national policies, strategies and programmes for absorbing potential Palestinian immigrants/returnees in a way that considers the well-being of the individual as well as the benefit to Palestinian society. In general, it is anticipated that the analyses and plans would serve two purposes: first, they would provide input into future planning activities on the national and sectoral levels; second, they would provide additional information and support to the bilateral negotiations and in the formulation of Palestinian negotiating positions. Hence, the work of this PPI is dependent on and linked to the negotiation process and relies on ongoing political input and feedback from negotiating bodies.

There are several issues that absorption planning must address. First and foremost, it must determine the 'push and pull' forces that would influence the migration of diaspora Palestinians to the Palestinian state. These forces could be political (the nature of a final status agreement and the policies of the host countries), social, economic, or cultural, or they could be related to individual preferences and kinship ties. The major push or pull force, however, is likely to be economic.

It is therefore essential to try to estimate the number and profile of possible immigrants based on a comparison of socio-economic levels between the West Bank and Gaza and the refugees' respective countries of residence. Many families will compare the relative degree of economic opportunity in the Palestinian State with their current country of residence in deciding where to reside. To a significant extent, market mechanisms such as unemployment rates and prices levels in the West Bank and Gaza may act as a natural regulator of the population movement. The analyses and plans should be based on the assumption that the immigration should be voluntary and based on the free choice of refugees/returnees. The number of immigrants and the pace of voluntary immigration will depend largely on the capacity of the newly established Palestinian State to accommodate them.

Hence, an absorption plan must assess the associated needs for services, housing, and employment opportunities in the West Bank and Gaza. The State will need to be involved in providing infrastructure and opportunities, particularly for the vulnerable, low-income, and low-skilled Palestinians who may have been pushed from their country of refuge. At the same time, however, plans for the absorption of new arrivals must be developed as part of broader development plans for residents and immigrants alike, so as to smooth out inequities and minimize any social friction that might otherwise occur if one group is seen as receiving special benefits. Palestinians moving to the West Bank and Gaza should be seen as an asset, rather than as a burden. They can offer a valuable source of human capital.

The absorption plan for the new Palestinian State should be based on a determination of the absorption constraints of the West Bank and Gaza as well as the potential and availability of (public and private) land, accessibility of natural and economic resources, and institutional requirements (such as schools, medical facilities, and other infrastructures, as well as appropriate legal and regulatory frameworks and fiscal policies). In drawing up its absorption plans, the PNA will rely on various potential scenarios regarding the size of yearly immigration, and will develop estimates of required infrastructure, housing units, public services and potential for employment. The absorption plan will identify financial needs for the new immigrants as well as possibilities for financing, whether from outside sources, domestically, or by returnees themselves. The amount of compensation payments received by refugees will also have substantial effect on the level of resources available.

It would be useful to undertake comparative analysis of past Palestinian absorption experiences, and to draw lessons from these experiences that might be applicable to a future absorption process by the Palestinian State. They could include the return of a large number of Palestinians after the 1991 Gulf War, and the experience of returnees after the establishment of the PNA in 1994. In addition to examining past experience in Palestinian absorption for possible lessons and models, it would also be useful to investigate the experiences of other countries in immigrant absorption.

Absorption of Palestinian immigrants/returnees in WBG entails developing intervention measures that offer attractive and secure 'living conditions' for the people, economically, socially, politically, physically, and environmentally. Accordingly, a comprehensive assessment of the absorption capacity of WBG would involve the analyses of a set of complex and interrelated developmental, economic, social, legal, institutional, political, and diplomatic/negotiation factors. A series of interrelated studies and analyses are required.

A first step in this process has been to assess the capacity to provide adequate 'residential space' and, accordingly, identify and investigate strategic policy options for resettling the immigrants/returnees. A set of pilot studies was done in order to:

(1) Investigate different options for housing the immigrants/returnees.
(2) Develop and test analytical tools that could be used to assess the absorptive capacity of various types of locations. These could be new towns, satellite communities, as well as in-filling of existing urban areas.
(3) Investigate different land utilization options such as vertical expansion (apartment buildings), horizontal expansion, and mixed growth, as well as to analyse different density options.
(4) Identify the magnitudes and relative weights of land prices, housing construction costs, and related necessary public infrastructure – all essential pieces of information required for successful resettlement.

This work has been done in co-operation with the World Bank and as part of a broader package of research on housing and infrastructure needs for refugees and displaced persons in the West Bank and Gaza. The intention of the research was not to make concrete policy recommendations but rather to gain a better understanding of the technical issues that would need to be addressed at the time of the implementation of a negotiated political agreement. It should be noted that such planning work in no way undermines the legitimate rights of the refugees. On the contrary, the achievement of refugee rights has been and will remain a core Palestinian position in all final status negotiations with Israel.

Various options for creating new living spaces for the immigrants/returnees were investigated. The analyses were focused on determining the absorptive capacity of public and *waqf*[1] land in a number of selected sites. The results, however, should be taken in an 'illustrative' manner. Despite the generality of the assumptions and the simplification of the models used, the study still provides a reasonable assessment of the absorption capacity of the selected sites, as well as an indicative estimate of related land-utilization costs.

DEVELOPING NEW TOWNS

One option that was investigated is to develop new towns. Pilot planning studies were done for three selected locations: in the Eastern Slopes north-east of the West Bank, in Latrun area, and in an area south-east of Gaza Strip near the Airport. The selection of these three sites for possible development of new towns was based principally on their strategic importance within the overall urban development strategies for West Bank and Gaza Governorates, the land use plan proposed in the Regional Plans of 1998 for West Bank and Gaza Governorates, and on the Emergency Natural Resources Protection Plans of 1996 for West Bank and Gaza Governorates. The final location of the sites and the delimitation of the area are based on the availability of public lands and on land suitability analysis.

As an example, Latrun area, which is about 20 kilometres west of Jerusalem, has an area of 50 km^2 close to the Green Line and was the site of three Palestinian villages destroyed in 1967, namely, Imwas, Yalu, and Beit Nuba. The populations of these three villages took refuge in the West Bank and Jordan. It is expected that their numbers now have more than doubled since 1967. Their refugee status, however, is not recognized. After the villages were demolished in June 1967, the lands were confiscated by Israel and declared a 'closed area'. The confiscated areas were later declared as 'public' land, on which, in 1969, were established a recreation park (Canada Park) with an area of 1,257 dunums[2] and Mevo Horon colony with an area of 1,139 dunums and an estimated population of 500 persons[3]. The selected site for the new town in this area is limited to the area of the three villages inside the West Bank, namely, 13,307 dunums, excluding those areas that are in 'No Man's Land' and within the Green Line. It is assumed that the existing colony will eventually be evacuated within the framework of a 'Final Status Agreement' and could be utilized for absorption of immigrants and returnees. The analyses show that the new town can accommodate about 67,000 people. Its land retains high agricultural value. It also possesses many Christian and Islamic historical sites. In fact, up until their demolition by the Israeli army in June 1967, the three villages, whose history goes back to biblical times, were prosperous. Reconstructing these villages and creating a new town out of them would have great historic and cultural value. The selected area is located close to the Border Industrial Estate proposed in the West Bank Regional Plan of 1998. Its agricultural, touristic, and economic potential would render it highly attractive for Palestinian immigrants/returnees. Also, the reconstruction of these villages would encourage the return of its original population in addition to accommodating other immigrants/returnees.

USING VACANT LAND AROUND URBAN AREAS

A second option that was investigated is to resettle Palestinian immigrants/returnees on vacant public and *waqf* lands in and around existing urban areas. Pilot studies were conducted in several selected types of locations (large and small cities and satellite communities) to study their absorption capacity. The pilot studies also investigated whether expansion should take place 'vertically' (high-density housing) or 'horizontally' (low-density housing) and whether this expansion should happen within urban areas, on the outskirts, or a combination of both. In assessing the absorptive capacity of the available lands within each of the study areas, the following factors were taken into consideration: the provisions and guidelines of the Regional Plans for West Bank and Gaza Governorates; existing plan and zoning requirements in each location; and the experiences of the Ministry of Housing (MOH) and the Palestinian Housing Council (PHC) in the implementation of affordable housing projects.

Nine regional or local centres/cities were selected for investigation. The selection of these areas conforms to the developmental strategy proposed in the Regional Plans. Taking Jenin as an example and according to the Regional Plan for 2010, the population would surround the city of Jenin including Jenin camp in all directions using public land that is currently vacant. According to the study, such an expansion of residential space could accommodate some 29,000 persons in and around the city.

URBAN UPGRADING/REGENERATION OF REFUGEE CAMPS

The planning including refugee camps, on the other hand, is concerned with upgrading and integrating the existing refugee camps into the urban and rural structure of West Bank and Gaza after an agreement is reached between the Palestinians and Israel. The PPI aims at drafting a proposal for an urban regeneration plan of refugee camps in WBG including the assessment and formulation of policy/strategic options for this process. MOP's ongoing work in this area includes in-depth analysis of existing refugee camps, including the typology of camps, types of land, quality of housing, variations in socio-economic status as well as analysing various scenarios for the upgrading and integration of camps in order to develop policies and programmes for their rehabilitation and integration.

FURTHER STEPS

There are a number of further studies that the PNA could undertake to better understand and deal with residential issues. First, it could identify possible implementation modalities and conduct an assessment of institutional and managerial capacities of the various public and private institutions. It could also look at existing market mechanisms related to the housing sector, and the sources of any inefficiencies and market distortions that might cause bottlenecks in housing construction.

Another study should develop potential financing mechanisms and fiscal incentives (for example, offering low cost loans and mortgages). The PNA must develop a range of appropriate policy instruments and regulations to facilitate both house construction and housing purchase. It should also assess the capacity and involvement of local authorities in the planning and implementation of absorption and refugee camp upgrading programmes and should consider public-private partnerships. An assessment of the absorptive capacity of the existing education, health and social services systems is an essential ingredient to plan for a new immigrant population. Future work should also include a social and political assessment of absorption. Finally the role of civil society organizations in the absorption and refugee camps upgrading processes should be examined.

CONCLUSION

In conclusion, the interests of the PNA in the process of absorption and refugee camp urban upgrading are to develop implementation mechanisms (reception, resettlement, integration, and community acceptance) on national, regional and local levels, including physical, social, economic and cultural aspects; to determine the required policies and policy tools, and their formulation and implementation; to identify the institutional and administrative structures necessary to facilitate absorption and urban upgrading; to decide on the information and capabilities required to prepare and implement these plans; and to determine the roles and involvement of different stakeholders.

CHAPTER 8

Infrastructure scenarios for refugees and displaced persons

Nick Krafft and Ann Elwan, World Bank, Washington DC, USA

INTRODUCTION

In the event of a political settlement to the Palestinian–Israeli conflict, some refugees and displaced Palestinians may choose to move between the different countries as well as between particular locales; and the development or rehabilitation of infrastructure and housing to accommodate them could occur in a variety of forms. Some refugee camps may eventually be abandoned; but it is likely that some households in camps – particularly camps with more permanent structures that are well-placed for employment and other purposes – will, for a variety of reasons, choose to stay where they are. These camps may be converted to proper municipal urban areas. New extensions to villages, towns and cities, where there is already extensive infrastructure and capacity in place may emerge; existing towns and villages may intensify within their current boundaries; and the possibility of building new towns has been raised.

This chapter summarizes findings from several studies on refugees, carried out in two phases by the World Bank. The findings summarized here are those related to infrastructure and housing.[1] The Bank's purpose, in carrying out this analysis, was not to make recommendations, but to gain a better understanding of the technical issues that would need to be addressed as agreed solutions to the refugees issue are implemented; and to examine the likely costs of different proposals to inform the discussion on what is feasible and over what time frame.

The analysis recognizes that population movements and the upgrading or development of housing and infrastructure related to a political settlement are unlikely to take place as one large centrally planned exercise. It also recognizes that the developmental challenges of absorption are most easily dealt with if population movements are voluntary and not bureaucratized. In the absence of 'push' factors, relocation decisions will be based, in large part, on economic opportunities in, for example, the West Bank and Gaza as compared to present host countries. Many of the measures necessary to accommodate refugee or displaced households are also needed to improve living conditions for existing populations and better accommodate future growth. In the West Bank and Gaza, for example, there are deficiencies in infrastructure and constraints in the housing market that need to be addressed. In seeking to answer questions about how the accommodation can take place and how much it will cost, the Bank has drawn on its experience in upgrading camps and informal housing areas and developing new residential areas – experience which is very much in line with the measures that might be needed to accommodate some refugee/displaced households.

This paper summarizes findings from three internal reports in particular:

(A) The Phase I report *Infrastructure and Housing Costs: Technical Note*, June 2000;

(B) The Phase II report *The Absorption of Refugees in the West Bank and Gaza: Potential for Housing Accommodation on Public Land in Selected Study Areas*, September 2002; and

(C) The Phase II report *Housing Finance for Returnees: Issues and Policy Options*, March 2002.

For ease of reference, these are referred to as Reports (A), (B), and (C) in the rest of this paper. In the first phase of the studies, analysis was carried out on the need for, and costs of, upgrading typical public infrastructure (roads, water, sanitation, and electricity networks, etc.); social infrastructure (schools, health centres, and community centres), and private infrastructure (housing and on-plot infrastructure) in refugee camps and other areas with refugee concentrations (including de-densification where existing camps were heavily overcrowded), and for constructing new housing accommodation, both in extensions to built-up areas as well as new urban areas. Report (A) describes the framework for gauging the infrastructure requirements for a range of 'options', and estimating their costs, expressed in average per capita terms. The cost estimates were for on-site infrastructure only, and were not area-specific, allowing elements to be selected from the various options and to be applied in different locations/countries.

The second phase, *inter alia*, looked at the potential for accommodating significant movement of refugees between countries, building on the Phase I work by looking at some potential typical sites in West Bank/Gaza, and providing more detailed cost estimates. The 'absorption study' involved analyses by consultants, co-ordinated by the Ministry of Planning and International Cooperation (MOPIC) on the potential for, and costs of, rapid residential development on public land in several specific, but illustrative, study locations in the West Bank and Gaza. Three consultants' studies provided the analysis:

> Nijem, Khalil, *Absorption Capacity in the West Bank and Gaza Governorates: Public and Waqf[2] Land,* September 2001;
> Asa'd, Abdel Karim, and Anan Jayyousi, *Water and Wastewater Sector Investment for Refugees,* June 2001; and
> Zeidan, Khaled, *Estimating the Roadway Costs Associated with Absorbing Palestinian Returnees to the West Bank and Gaza,* September 2001.

Report (B) is a synthesis of the findings of these three studies on availability of public land, and the estimated needs and costs of critical off-site infrastructure (water, wastewater and transportation, that is the more binding constraints) for accommodating returnees on public land in the West Bank and Gaza. It complements the Phase I work, which was limited to estimating on-site costs and was not site specific. Again, the logic applied could be extended to other geographical areas.

In recognition of the extremely high costs of constructing or rehabilitating housing, and with no presumption that all costs could or should be borne by donors or any other particular source, the housing finance study carried out in Phase II looked at financing options, taking existing housing market conditions and ongoing or planned policy reforms into account. Report (C) summarizes the study, which was based on consultant and World Bank staff experience in the West Bank and Gaza and existing literature. The focus was on housing finance and housing market conditions in the West Bank and Gaza, although many of the findings are largely applicable in other host countries.

ON-SITE INFRASTRUCTURE AND HOUSING COSTS

Background

Palestinian refugees and displaced people are spread across Jordan, the West Bank and Gaza, Lebanon, Syria, and elsewhere. Nearly one third of the registered refugees – about 1.3 million people – live in 59 recognized UNRWA refugee camps in Jordan, Lebanon, Syria, the West Bank and Gaza; and a significant number live in informal settlements near camps.[3] Camps range from those where there is only an old rudimentary water reticulation system, no piped sewerage, unpaved roads and footpaths, and no surface drainage system, to those with water, sewerage and drainage systems, and paved and drained roads and footpaths.

Table 8.1: *Distribution of registered refugee population*

Location	Registered refugee population	Percentage of registered refugee population by location	Registered refugee population in camps, by location		Registered population not in camps, by location	
			No.	%	No.	%
Jordan	1,679,623	42.2	293,215 (18)	23.2	1,386,408	51.1
Lebanon	387,043	9.7	217,211 (56)	17.2	169,832	6.3
Syria	401,185	10.1	115,863 (29)	9.2	285,322	10.5
West Bank	626,532	15.8	168,507 (27)	13.3	458,025	16.9
Gaza Strip	878,977	22.1	468,071 (53)	37.1	410,906	15.2
Total	**3,973,360**	**100**	**1,262,867 (32)**	**100**	**2,710,493**	**100**

Source: UNRWA figures for June 2002.

Development options

The Phase I work looked at the requirements for (a) upgrading 'typical' refugee camps, including converting them to proper municipal standards, on the basis that some refugees will probably choose to stay where they are, particularly if the areas are upgraded, and (b) new extensions to existing villages and urban areas, where there is already extensive infrastructure and capacity in place, as well as (c) building new urban areas. It presented a framework for analysing various forms of upgrading or new development and estimating their costs. The forms analysed are referred to as 'options', although it should be understood that any or all of them could occur. Costs have been estimated for a number of upgrading options, ranging from minimal upgrading to full upgrading and/or redevelopment, as well as the development of completely new communities. The options analysed in Phase I are summarized below and in Table 7.2.[4]

Option 1: camp upgrading

Many camps are characterized by over-crowding, inadequate services and inadequate access to plots. A minimum level of upgrading within the existing camp form and layout has been carried out in some camps, and this level is included as Type 1 – the minimum type of upgrading in this study – involving the installation or rehabilitation of water, sewerage and drainage systems; properly paved roads and footpaths; street lighting; and telephone networks – but leaving road and footpath locations and widths and plot layouts unchanged. Camps upgraded to this minimum level generally do not meet municipal standards for road widths and access, plot setbacks and so on, and many plots remain overcrowded. In the six additional Types – 2 to 7 (see Table 7.2) – the objective was to retain existing infrastructure and superstructure to the extent possible, in order to minimize both public and private costs, and to maintain the social cohesion of the site; but also to improve access, allow additional services and facilities, and decrease density in some extremely crowded camps. Types 2 and 3 maintain the general plot layout and involve some plot amalgamation and de-densification. Where plot layouts cannot be maintained, Types 4 to 7 define a 're-development' approach, with parts or all of the camp structures being demolished and re-created to municipality standards. Types 2 to 6 all involve some demolition, and the costs of permanent resettlement of the affected households in an 'urban expansion' area (Option 3) are included in the upgrading cost estimates.

Option 2: upgrading in informal areas outside camps

This type of upgrading of informal areas is based on the recent experience of the Community Infrastructure Program (CIP) in Jordan. It involves little change in population density.

Option 3: urban expansion areas for resettlement/returnees

This option looks at resettling households around existing towns and cities where there is already infrastructure and capacity. Two modules were designed, one focusing on individual plots, and the other on apartments, although in practice, a combination of the two may evolve. These will allow a variety of urban structures, plot sizes and configurations, and varying building forms for housing and small-scale commercial use.

Option 4: new communities

Under this option, resettlement is assumed to take place away from existing habitations, that is, in new towns, requiring more extensive infrastructure, including municipal capacity, municipal buildings, and connector roads to other towns, etc. Costs for new free-standing communities were based on accommodating people in a number of modules, similar to those in Option 3–50,000 and 250,000 people for a new town and a new city, respectively, and on typical land use and infrastructure costs. The analysis is limited to outlining the infrastructure, housing and land requirements and costs of a hypothetical new town; it does not review the issues and significant risks associated with the economic and social viability of a new community.

Table 8.2: *Options for upgrading or new development of housing and infrastructure for refugees and displaced people*

Option	Summary description
I Camp upgrading	
Type 1	Utilities and road and footpath paving. No changes in plot boundaries or structures, except to accommodate the utilities.
Type 2	Utilities and road and footpath paving. Improved access. Relocation of around 20% of inhabitants.
Type 3	Utilities, road and footpath paving. Improved access, re-blocking and relocation of around 50% of inhabitants.
Type 4	Partial redevelopment (utilities, roads and plots to municipal standard). High density.
Type 5	Full redevelopment to municipal standards. High density.
Type 6	Partial redevelopment (utilities, roads and plots to municipal standard). Low density.
Type 7	Full redevelopment to municipal standards. Low density.
II Informal area upgrading	
	Utilities, road and footpath paving. Improved access. Minor relocation.
III Urban expansion	
Module A	A 30-hectare development scheme, focusing on individual plots with playgrounds, social facilities, community facilities, and commercial plots, designed to be adjacent to an existing village or small rural town. The module accommodates about 12,500 people with a density of about 400 p/ha initially, but with intensification over time, close to 19,000 people can be accommodated at a density of about 630 p/ha.
Module B	A 30-hectare development scheme, focusing on apartment buildings, with amenities as in Module A above, designed to be adjacent to an existing larger town or city. The module accommodates about 20,000 people, at a density of about 670 p/ha.
IV New communities	
New town	Scheme designed for 50,000 people, land requirement of 240 hectares.
New city	Scheme designed for 250,000 people; includes amenities such as tertiary education, potential for research or other industry-focus; land requirement of at least 1200 hectares.

Relocation because of demolition

All the types of upgrading and redevelopment under Option 1 (except Type 1) involve some demolition. In some cases demolition is only required in order to upgrade infrastructure to higher standards (i.e., more or wider roads) or to combine plots to more acceptable standards and to decrease density; in others demolition is required for redevelopment. Where these types involve demolition, they also involve relocating families. Some of this relocation is temporary, in order to accommodate the work on site; however, where the upgrading or redevelopment results in a lower population density on site, then the relocation is permanent. The issues of land tenure and compensation for demolition and their effect on beneficiaries are major considerations.[5] In this analysis, for the purposes of estimating the full costs of the options, it is assumed that families to be permanently relocated would be resettled elsewhere, as per the 'urban expansion' modules described below.[6] The costs of permanent relocation (for housing, land, public and social infrastructure at the resettlement site) are included in the total costs of the upgrading.

Cost estimates

Public and social infrastructure

Any of the options are likely to involve the basic elements of public infrastructure, social infrastructure (schools, health centres and community facilities), housing, and land. The costs of public and social infrastructure for these options are based on conditions in existing camps and sites, and on recent construction and upgrading contracts, but are not area specific. They are expressed in US dollars per 1,000 refugees and are indicative of costs on an average basis. Before finalizing any future plan, detailed site-specific appraisals would be required.

Public infrastructure

The estimated infrastructure costs in this phase of the analysis are for on-site construction of the infrastructure (roads and footpaths, water and sewerage, drainage, power, and telephone lines) needed to upgrade existing camps and informal settlements. Estimates are based largely on observed construction costs in Jordan. Construction costs vary significantly, depending, *inter alia*, on topography and soil type, and contracting market conditions. For upgrading works, they also vary according to road widths and housing density. Cost estimates in Table 7.3 are capital costs of utility infrastructure only; they do not include off-site works.[7]

Social infrastructure (schools, community centres and health centres)

The working assumption is that the existing built social infrastructure in camps will remain unchanged because the resulting lower population densities will reduce current overcrowding in the various facilities. The costs of social infrastructure for the appropriate number of 'relocatees' (that is those relocated from camps) are estimated according to the assumptions for the new urban expansion areas, which in turn are based on public planning criteria.

Several simplifying assumptions have been made regarding factors such as household size, residential densities and infrastructure requirements. As and when more specific information becomes available, more detailed costs can be estimated. Several issues have not been addressed, for example costs of public transport and other amenities, nor have any operation and maintenance costs been included. It is important to note that the estimated costs outlined in Tables 7.3 and 7.4 do not include any contingency allowance, and that they pertain to a period prior to the recent period of political and economic deterioration.

The seven types of upgrading/redevelopment were defined on the basis of observed layouts and existing plot sizes, housing structures, infrastructure networks, and land availability, and based on conditions in camps in the West Bank, Gaza, and Jordan. However, only a few camp layouts and structures have been reviewed in detail; more in-depth study would be needed to determine whether there are other 'typologies' that would produce significantly different results. Although the types are based on observations of specific camps, they are 'generic', and their relevance depends on current or 'starting levels', not particular locations. The cost estimates in Table 7.3 are based largely on costs observed in Jordan. Construction costs (for infrastructure and building) are higher in the West Bank and Gaza; indices are estimated at 1.5 for the West Bank, and 1.35 for Gaza. These estimates can be used as building blocks to estimate the costs of various scenarios. Similarly, indices could be developed for other geographic areas to estimate costs elsewhere.

Housing and land

Housing

In recognition of the inadequacy of much of the housing currently occupied by refugees and displaced persons, the costs of building new units or upgrading existing housing were estimated. However, the inclusion of housing and land in the cost analysis should not be taken as an endorsement of full-scale public construction of housing, which would not be feasible for several reasons – including equity considerations, as well as the extremely high costs.[8] Nor does this paper assume that donors or others would be willing or able to pay for housing construction.

For the purposes of this analysis, cost estimates for new housing (i.e., for Options 3 and 4, and for redeveloped areas within camps) were based on 120 square metres of built accommodation per household. A modest house of this size, typical of housing in the region, was estimated to cost (without finishings) in the order of $41,400 in the West Bank, $37,260 in Gaza, and $27,600 in Jordan.[9] In the camps, much of the existing housing is sub-standard, and needs to be expanded, modified, or re-built in some way to comply with safety and other regulations. The cost is roughly estimated at about 65 per cent of that for new housing cost, resulting in a range of $18,000 to $27,000 per house, depending on the location.

Land

Much of the land on which refugee camps are built is owned privately and land tenure arrangements need to be clarified in order for residents to be assured of retaining the value of substantial improvements. This is a major issue that will need to be addressed. Land values vary greatly in the study region; at one end of the range are urban sites with commercial value and sites near the Mediterranean in Gaza; at the other end are remote rural sites. In the absence of comprehensive information on land ownership and prices by area, land costs estimates in this paper are only indicative. Indicative camp land costs for upgrading range from as low as $200,000 per 1,000 people (using a low land cost, minimum level of upgrading, and no change

Table 8.3: *Estimated costs (US$ per 1,000 people) for on-site public and social infrastructure**

Option	Public infrastructure			Social infrastructure	Total		
	Remainees	Relocatees	Total		Remainees	Relocatees	Total
1 Camp upgrading							
Type 1	156,847		156,847		156,847		156,847
Type 2	195,342	35,169	230,511	52,416	195,342	87,585	282,927
Type 3	144,869	93,787	238,656	139,778	144,869	233,565	378,434
Type 4	130,118	63,307	193,425	94,350	130,118	157,657	287,775
Type 5	86,735	84,409	171,144	125,800	86,735	210,209	296,944
Type 6	309,805		309,805		309,805		309,805
Type 7	172,094		172,094		172,094		172,094
2 Informal area upgrading	175,050		175,050	103,916	278,966		278,966
3 Urban expansion							
Module A			168,817	251,600		420,417	420,417
Module B			77,213	239,683		316,896	316,896
4 New communities							
New town			205,026	313,624			518,650
New city			205,026	376,349			581,375

Notes: * 'Social infrastructure' here refers to schools, health facilities and community centres.
Construction costs are higher in the West Bank and Gaza. Indices for these locations are estimated at 1.5 and 1.35; the index for both Syria and Lebanon is estimated at about 0.85. Figures in Table 7.3 do not include any contingencies. The figures for all the upgrading forms, except Type 1, include the costs of relocation. Relocation costs per thousand 'relocatees' are based on the costs per person of urban expansion, module A. Figures are as in Report (A) Table 6.1, except that no costs of bulk water for new communities are included here.

in camp densities) to as high as $1.2 million per 1,000 people. Prices for urban development sites also vary greatly, and there is little history of large-scale land transactions for urban development. The land costs per thousand people would be in the order of $720,000 for Option 3 Module A, and $450,000 for Module B (which accommodates more people in the same area). Option 4 assumes a large remote site, where land values may be in the order of $2 to $5 per square metre. Taking the upper end of this range gives land costs in the order of $240,000 per thousand. Cost estimates for the various options can be refined further as specific sites are considered.

Indicative costs for housing and land are given in Table 7.4. Housing construction costs are very large relative to on-site infrastructure costs. From Tables 7.3 and 7.4, it can be seen that the ratio is generally higher than ten to one for both upgrading and urban expansion.

Report (A) provides a framework for discussions of options and broad 'order of magnitude' costs. The framework is capable of additional calibration as and when more detailed information becomes available, and can be used for further development as opportunities emerge. The figures and assumptions need to be used with discretion, bearing in mind their fairly severe limitations.

Aggregate costs

The costs in Tables 7.3 and 7.4 are additive – the total cost of, for example, upgrading a camp, or developing a new urban expansion module, would include the costs of the public infrastructure, the social infrastructure, and the land and housing costs, as appropriate. Using Tables 7.3 and 7.4, cost estimates for various scenarios can be broadened to allow 'order of magnitude' housing and land costs to be added to the public and social infrastructure costs.

LAND AVAILABILITY AND OFF-SITE INFRASTRUCTURE COSTS IN THE WEST BANK AND GAZA

Background

The Phase II analysis looked at the potential for, and costs of, accommodating some returnees on public land in the West Bank and Gaza

Table 8.4: *Indicative costs (US$ million, per thousand population), for housing and land*

Option	Housing (a)			Land			Total
	Remainees	Relocatees	Total	Base case estimate(b)	Low range(c)	High range	Housing + base land cost
1 Camp upgrading (d)							
Type 1	2.52		2.52	0.40	0.20	0.80	2.92
Type 2	2.00	0.80	2.80	0.54	0.35	0.94	3.34
Type 3	1.12	2.15	3.27	0.79	0.59	1.19	4.46
Type 4	1.99	1.45	3.44	0.52	0.39	0.77	3.96
Type 5	1.93	1.93	3.86	0.54	0.45	0.75	4.40
Type 6	3.11		3.11	0.60	0.30	1.19	3.71
Type 7	3.86		3.86	0.40	0.20	0.79	4.26
2 Informal area upgrading							
3 Urban expansion							
Module A			3.86	0.72			4.58
Module B			3.86	0.45			4.31
4 New communities							
New Town			3.86	0.24			4.10
New City			3.86	0.24			4.10

Note: Figures in Table 7.4 do not include any contingencies.

(a) Estimated costs are based on those observed in Jordan. Construction costs are higher in the West Bank and Gaza. Indices for these locations are estimated at 1.5 and 1.35; the index for both Syria and Lebanon is estimated at about 0.85.
(b) The 'base case' land costs for camps is $20 per square metre.
(c) The low and high land cost figures for camps are $10 and $40 per square metre, respectively.
(d) The figures for all the upgrading forms, except Type 1, include the costs of relocation. Relocation costs per thousand 'relocatees' are based on the costs per person of urban expansion, Module A.

following a political settlement. Consultants, co-ordinated by the Ministry of Planning and International Cooperation (MOPIC), studied public land availability and the off-site water, wastewater and transportation requirements (that is, the more binding constraints to accommodating new residents) in several types of selected study locations in the West Bank and Gaza. The study locations were representative and geographically diverse – initially including nine (existing) urban centres with possible expansion areas; two potential 'satellites' (existing villages or towns within commuting distance from larger urban areas); and three 'new town' sites.

The study did not attempt to estimate the overall absorption potential of the West Bank and Gaza. Rather, it estimated the cost of absorbing 100,000 to 200,000 new residents on public lands located in and around existing study towns and in a limited number of new town areas. Among the main limitations on the study's scope were: (a) only selected sites were included – the study did not address all public land in the West Bank and Gaza; (b) private land was not considered[10]; (c) no other aspects of accommodating new residents were addressed beyond land, housing, and some related infrastructure; and (d) only capital costs were considered.[11]

The existing situation

This section briefly describes existing conditions in the West Bank and Gaza, giving context to the analysis of off-site infrastructure needs. However, the information is illustrative. The methodology used for the study can be applied in other locations.

Water and wastewater service levels

Water demand in the West Bank and Gaza is suppressed as a result of both limited natural supply and artificial constraints, that is, restrictions on the development of new sources and infrastructure. Present water supplies are far below those needed. Consumption in the inland region, for example, for the 86 per cent of the population connected to a piped system, averages about 50 litres per person per day, about half the recommended World Health Organization (WHO) minimum for house connections in small communities. In areas without piped networks, consumption rates are considerably lower. The gap between water supply and water demand is increasing, due to population growth and increasing irrigation and industrial use, as well as increasing usage per capita. Wastewater treatment facilities at four operational plants serve nearly 15 per cent of the population; and most Palestinian localities, including some large towns, do not have sewerage systems. In the 19 localities with sewerage systems, many are partial. In the West Bank, about 60 per cent of houses in large municipal communities are connected to sewerage systems. The situation in the refugee camps is worse; in many camps, wastewater is channelled into open drains until it flows into either a sewerage network in a nearby city or is simply transported outside the camp boundaries. There are now three operating wastewater treatment plants in the West Bank (at Jenin, Tulkarm and Al-Bireh), and two non-operational plants at Hebron and Ramallah.

Transportation

The transportation system in the West Bank and Gaza is primarily the roadway network.[12] The total paved roadway length is about 5,900 kilometres, of which about 5,200 kilometres are in the West Bank, and 700 kilometres in Gaza.[13] Just over half of the roadway length is paved, and over 50 per cent of the roadways in the West Bank and Gaza are in poor condition. The cost of expanding and improving the system has been estimated at about $1 billion. The connection between the West Bank and Gaza is through 40 kilometres of Israeli land.[14] All in all, the roadway system is inadequate: poor roadway conditions and poor design and capacity limit accessibility between smaller population centres, and between larger population centres and smaller ones.

Public land availability in the West Bank and Gaza

Analysis was limited to public and *waqf* lands in the study areas.[15] The study areas were geographically diverse, and consistent with the regional plans for West Bank and Gaza. They should be viewed as illustrative, and should not be construed as representing any relocation decisions by either households or government agencies. The study areas were:

- Nine urban centres with possible expansion areas: Jenin, Nablus, Tulkarem, and Tubas in the North; Al-Jiftlik and Jericho in the East; Al-Bireh and Bethlehem in the middle region; and Hebron in the South. Seven of the nine urban areas are regional/district centres; Tubas and Al-Jiftlik are local centres.

* Two satellite villages/towns: Beitunya, west of Ramallah; and Tarqumia, west of Hebron.
* Three potential 'new town' sites: one in the northern part of the Jordan Valley; one west of Jerusalem/Ramallah in the Latrun area; and one in the southeastern part of Gaza, near Rafah airport.

Basic information on land ownership had to be compiled for the study, because much of the Palestinian land, especially in the West Bank, is not fully registered. The 11 (existing) study towns and satellite villages in the West Bank are estimated to be capable of absorbing around 300,000 immigrants by the year 2010, under the assumptions that all topographically suitable land that is not contraindicated (for environmental or other reasons) is considered, and land ownership is not taken into account. However, based on information gathered from the Surveying Department at the Ministry of Housing, *public land* within or adjacent to urban or village centres is quite limited. Only five out of the eleven study towns – four of the towns and one of the potential satellites – have 'vacant' public lands

Table 8.5: *Vacant expansion areas and public land in study locations*

Study towns	Built-up area (km²)	Total vacant area for expansion [a] (km²)	Total available public lic land (dunums) [b]	Percentage of total available public land to vacant area	Within municipal boundaries	Outside municipal boundaries
Jenin	4.4	20.6	907	4.4	205	702
Jericho	8.9	14.5	1,095	7.5	30	1,065
Nablus	11.6	37.0	1,629	4.4	1,550	79
Tarqumiya	1.9	7.4	274	3.7	140	134
Tubas	1.8	6.7	282	4.2	282	0
Total	28.6	86.2	4,187	4.9	2,207	1,980

Notes:

(a) Master plan area and urban expansion area according to regional plan.

(b) A dunum is 1,000 square metres.

sufficient to absorb a significant number of new residents.[16] The remaining six study towns had marginal or no available public land. Table 7.5 lists the areas in the five towns with sufficient available public land. *Waqf* land was found to be largely either already utilized or of small size, and was therefore not pursued further.

For the three potential new town areas, the final site locations for the study are based on availability of public land and site suitability. Table 7.6 shows the areas of public lands available in the three selected areas.

Table 8.6: *Available public land in the new town sites*

Study area	Available public land (km²)	Elevation range (metres above sea level) High	Low	Slope
Northern West Bank: Al Malih	7.2	200	−75	5% to 15%
Latrun	13.307	425	150	6% to 9%
East of Rafah	16.13	90	70	Negligible

Accommodation potential: West Bank and Gaza

Individual pieces of public land in the five remaining study towns and three new town areas were plotted, and locations were reviewed for land use restrictions and suitability of topography.[17] The suitable land areas were then analysed for their ability to accommodate new residents, taking into account guidelines related to population growth, land utilization density and urban expansion areas, and the zoning and building requirements in each location.

Three scenarios were constructed for the five existing towns and villages using different assumptions for land utilization (horizontal expansion) and type and height of buildings (vertical expansion):

- Scenario 1: Available public land is used to its maximum; i.e. depending on zoning requirements, maximum allowable construction percentages and number of floors is assumed, resulting in the highest possible number of new residents accommodated.

- Scenario 2: Only 50 per cent of available public land is used; however maximum zoning requirements for each plot is assumed.
- Scenario 3: All the available public land is used; but housing types are mixed – a combination of single houses and multi-storey buildings is assumed. Gross land utilization per person, for housing purposes, is assumed to be 24.4 square metres, double the overall average of 12.2 square metres for public housing projects.

Depending on the residential density assumed, and on whether sites inside and/or outside municipal boundaries were included, it was found that these five existing towns/villages could absorb from around 51,000 to around 211,000 new residents on publicly owned land. Table 7.7 shows results for two of the three density scenarios.

Table 8.7: *Potential for accommodating new residents on public land in or near existing towns*

Study area	Scenario	Within municipality boundaries	Outside municipality boundaries	Inside and outside municipal boundaries
		Potential numbers of new residents		
Jenin	1	13,225	45,287	58,512
	3	5,881	20,139	26,020
Jericho	1	6,028	55,351	61,379
	3	3,299	30,295	33,594
Nablus	1	54,895	3,416	58,311
	3	31,753	11,013	32,765
Tarqumiya	1	7,903	10,806	18,708
	3	4,016	3,844	7,861
Tubas	1	14,248	0	14,248
	3	5,924	0	5,924
Total	1	96,299	114,860	211,158
	3	50,873	65,291	106,164

The three new town sites were estimated to be able to accommodate some 130,000 to 165,000 people on public land. [18]

Table 8.8: *Potential for accommodating new residents on public land in new towns*

Selected areas/density		Potential numbers of new residents
North West Bank:		
Al-Malih	High density	36,364
	Low density	21,557
Latrun	High density	77,778
	Low density	57,082
East of Rafah (a)	Low or high density	50,000

Note:

(a) For the site east of Rafah, analysis revealed a large area of suitable land in this study area, sufficient to absorb large numbers of new residents, consequently a limiting number of 50,000 persons is assumed here.

Off-site infrastructure investment costs

Water and sewerage

In order to estimate the investment costs of providing water and wastewater facilities for the benefit of returnees to the West Bank and Gaza, several underlying assumptions were necessary, an important one being that service levels in the study towns, which are currently far below generally accepted norms, would increase gradually. This decision was based on equity as well as practical considerations; the study could not simply make the assumption that service levels for returnees would be substantially higher than for the existing populations in the same study towns. The underlying assumption is, therefore, that domestic consumption would increase from the current average of around 75 litres per capita per day (l/c/d) to an average of 126 l/c/d in 2010 (a level still substantially lower than the WHO average of 150 l/c/d). The analysis considered the investment needed to ensure this level of water (and related wastewater) service levels for existing populations as well as for returnees, taking natural growth of both into account.

For planning purposes, the important costs are therefore those of upgrading and expanding the whole system for a given town, to accommodate both the existing population and any returnees. The 'investment cost per returnee' for water and wastewater facilities, which ranged from around $1,150 to around $1,700 for the existing study towns, and around $1,800 for new towns, relates only to the additional cost of accommodating returnees, but should be used with reference to the costs for existing residents, as the underlying share of investment 'for the returnees' is not meaningful in isolation. For existing populations, the cost per person for water and waste-water ranged from about $800 to about $1500. Estimated water and wastewater costs are shown in Tables 7.9 and 7.10.

Roads

Limited information on traffic was available, and it was beyond the scope of the study to generate original data. Moreover, the current situation is very different from the traffic patterns that would prevail once conditions allow substantial numbers of Palestinians to return. Analysis was limited to the assumed access roadway linking the potential residential development areas in each study site to the existing roadway network and the associated intersections. The average road construction cost varied from a low of around $6 per person under a maximum density scenario in Jericho, to over $200 per person for a mixed housing use scenario in Tubas. For new town areas, the average per capita costs ranged from a low of about $160 per person in Gaza, to highs of $400 to $700 per person in the northern Jordan valley (Table 7.9).

COMBINING PHASE I AND PHASE II ANALYSES

Infrastructure (public and social)

The Phase II studies summarized above provide cost estimates for off-site water, wastewater and road infrastructure and housing for various densities and types of housing development for returnees on public land in the study sites. With additional assumptions, these can be combined with the costs of on-site public infrastructure (water

Table 8.9: *Summary of illustrative infrastructure cost estimates for new residents in study areas (US$/person)*[a]

Town	Off-site infrastructure		On-site public infrastructure[c]	Social (schools, clinics, etc.)[c]	Total cost (on- and off-site infrastructures, incl. social infrastructure)[d]
	Roads[b]	Water and wastewater			
Jenin	38	1,226	291	434	1,989
Jericho	11	1,417	291	434	2,153
Nablus	202	1,149	291	434	2,076
Tarqumia	34	1,658	291	434	2,417
Tubas	271	1,736	291	434	2,732
New town, N. Jordan Valley	556	1,520	354	541	2,971
New town, Latrun	244	1,501	354	541	2,640
New town, east of Rafah	159	1,475	318	487	2,439

(a) These estimates do *not* include the estimated cost of upgrading water and wastewater infrastructure for existing residents – and should be used only in conjunction with these costs (see Table 7.10).

(b) Average per capita road costs, using Scenario 3 for existing towns, and Scenario 2 for new town areas.

(c) Figures are based on cost estimates for urban expansion module A and for a new town, from Sections 2 and 3 of Report (B). Module A, with a planned capacity of some 400 persons per hectare, is more akin to the Phase II density assumptions than Module B; and the new town assumed population of 50,000 is closer to the potential/illustrative number of returnees in the Phase II analysis. The Phase I figures have been adjusted (i) for the West Bank and Gaza (50% and 35%, respectively); (ii) to include contingency (15%); and (iii) for the new town sites, to exclude the estimated bulk water costs from the Phase I analysis.

(d) does not include land, housing construction, off-site electricity infrastructure, or any recurrent costs.

and wastewater, roads, electricity, etc.) and social infrastructure (schools, health clinics and community buildings) estimated in the Phase I analysis of infrastructure costs and outlined above, to provide a more complete estimate of the total costs involved in accommodating new residents.[19] As noted, this methodology can be extended to other locations where returnees might settle.

The cost estimates can be combined in various ways, depending on the underlying assumptions. Table 7.9 shows an example; however, the estimates in Table 7.9, do *not* include the estimated cost of upgrading water and wastewater infrastructure for existing residents, and are shown only to illustrate how the more relevant figures in Table 7.10 were derived.

Table 7.10 applies the per person costs from the last column of Table 7.9 to an illustrative number of returnees – in this case, using density Scenario 2 (not shown in Table 7.7) which assumes use of 50 per cent of available public land for housing, and maximum zoning requirements for each plot) for the existing study towns. The medium density scenario is assumed for new towns. Column (4) shows the estimated cost of upgrading water supply and wastewater infrastructure for existing residents, to obtain the more relevant figure for total estimated cost. Column (5) then shows the total cost per 1,000 returnees. For planning purposes, a figure of $3–6 million per 1,000 returnees might be used, which includes the costs of upgrading water and wastewater services of those currently living in the towns. *It should be noted that the figures for existing towns in Column (5) include the costs of upgrading water and wastewater services for existing residents, and that the estimated costs for new towns do not take into account any considerations related to building viable new communities: the figures for existing towns are therefore not comparable to the estimates for new towns in the same column.* The costs for other density scenarios can be calculated similarly.

The cost estimates can be combined to yield illustrative estimates of the total costs per person; and ranges of possible costs can be estimated by using various assumptions about density or about using land inside or outside municipal boundaries, etc. Some of the important limitations in scope have been outlined above. It should be emphasized that the estimated infrastructure costs for new towns do not take into account the significant risks in planning a new town or city; for example, the risk that new industry will not be attracted, creating pockets of high unemployment (i.e., an urban slum) at some distance from other towns. An additional important caveat is that the figures used in this study have reference to a more stable period prior

Table 8.10: *Illustrative cost estimates of infrastructure for new residents in study areas, including costs of upgrading existing water/wastewater infrastructure for existing residents*

Town	(1) Cost of on-and off-site infrastructures, incl. social infrastructure (US$/person, from Table 7.9)[a]	(2) Illustrative no. of returnees[b]	(3) Total cost for returnees[c] (US$ m)	(4) Cost of upgrading WWS for existing residents[d] (US$ m)	(5) Total Cost (based on no. returnees in column 3) (US $m)	(6) Cost per 1,000 returnees[e] (5)/(2) (US$ m)
Jenin	1,989	29,256	58.19	44.68	102.87	3.52
Jericho	2,153	30,690	66.08	26.33	92.41	3.01
Nablus	2,076	41,000	85.12	160.09	245.21	5.98
Tarqumia	2,417	9,354	22.61	14.83	37.44	4.00
Tubas	2,732	7,124	19.46	22.42	41.88	5.88
New town, North Jordan Valley	2,971	26,966	80.11	n/a	80.11	2.97
New town, Latrun	2,640	67,172	177.33	n/a	177.3	2.64
New town, east of Rafah	2,439	50,000	121.95	n/a	121.95	2.44

Notes:

(a) Estimated costs do not include land, housing construction, off-site electricity infrastructure, or any recurrent costs.

(b) This illustrative table uses Scenario 2 (use of 50% of available public land, and maximum zoning) for the existing study towns, and the medium density scenario for new towns.

(c) The 'total cost for returnees' is calculated as the product of the numbers in the two preceding columns.

(d) From Table 16 in Report (B).

(e) For existing towns, includes the cost of upgrading water supply and sewerage for existing residents. Note that figures for existing towns are not directly comparable with those for new towns.

to the devastating impacts of the current political situation; and the cost estimates would need to be reviewed before further use.

Housing costs

Comparison of Phase I and Phase II estimates

Housing costs were estimated in both Phase I and Phase II, and the analyses were carried out independently of each other.[20] The Phase I analysis looked at the cost, in Jordan, of 120 square metres of built accommodation per household for new housing in urban expansion areas, towns and cities, and in redeveloped areas (upgrading, Types 4 and 6). The 120 square metre standard corresponds to modest housing, in line with 'typical' housing in the region.[21] It accommodates a living room, three bedrooms, and kitchen and bathroom for a six to seven person household, and is typical of the 'final' accommodation that a household with a median (or slightly lower) household income builds, incrementally, as resources allow.[22] Construction costs were estimated to be in the order of $200 per square metre in Jordan, that is a cost of about $27,600 per house.[23] This figure would be $41,400 in the West Bank (or around $6,000–$7,000 per person), and $37,260 in Gaza, using the assumed adjustment factors of 50 per cent and 35 per cent. Similarly, adjustment factors can be applied to other locations.

It was roughly estimated that the costs of expanding, rebuilding, or upgrading housing in the camps would be about 65 per cent of the new housing cost.[24] This results in a cost of about $18,000 ($27,000 in the West Bank, and $24,300 in Gaza) for upgrading each existing house. In order to estimate complete costs per 1,000 people, the costs of accommodating relocatees in new housing would also need to be considered.

In the Phase II analysis, which was carried out about a year later, housing construction costs were based on initial cost estimates from recent housing projects in the West Bank and Gaza, and ranged from around $6,800 to around $7,500 per person, depending on location and density (Nijem 2001: Appendix II). The housing cost estimates from the two Phases of the study are thus roughly consistent.

Given the consistency of the housing costs estimates, and since the Phase II estimates are both more recent and more detailed, they are used in Table 7.11 to illustrate the effects of adding the costs of housing to the various infrastructure costs to get a more comprehensive view of the overall costs. Table 7.11 demonstrates that the cost of housing is by far the largest element, often close to double the sum of infrastructure costs and costs of schools, etc., combined.

Table 8.11: *Illustrative cost estimates of infrastructure and housing for new residents in study areas*

Town	Estimated cost of infrastructure (US$m per 1,000 persons, col (6), Table 7.10)[a]	Housing construction cost[b] (US$m per 1,000 persons)	Infrastructure and housing construction cost[c] (US$m per 1,000 persons)
Jenin	3.52	6.84	10.36
Jericho	3.01	6.16	9.17
Nablus	5.98	8.21	14.19
Tarqumia	4.00	6.84	10.84
Tubas	5.88	6.84	12.72
New town, North Jordan Valley	2.97	8.23	11.20
New town, Latrun	2.64	10.64	13.28
New town, E. of Rafah	2.44	7.34	9.78

(a) Includes costs of upgrading existing water/wastewater infrastructure for existing residents, from Table 7.10.

(b) Housing cost estimates are from Appendix III in the Phase II consultant's report (Nijem 2001).

(c) Since the figures for existing towns include the costs of upgrading water and wastewater services for existing residents and the estimated costs for new towns do not take into account any considerations related to building viable new communities, the figures for existing towns are not comparable with the estimates for new towns in the same column.

HOUSING FINANCE OPTIONS

Given the magnitude of housing construction costs, it is clearly most unlikely that the full costs of housing construction and upgrading could be borne by any external source. Moreover, if a decision were made for the public provision of housing in a situation of insufficient funds, issues of locational incentives and equity would arise, as only a relatively small proportion of households could be accommodated. Another approach involves not funding housing construction directly, but providing lump sum payments and allowing individuals to build their own units. This would be more welfare-enhancing, but the provision of sufficient funds for a complete housing unit would require severe rationing, and would not remove the difficult equity question. A third, and perhaps most realistic approach, reflecting the reality of limited funds for housing construction and/or upgrading, would focus on funding infrastructure, and supporting public sector authorities in facilitating both an adequate supply of housing and households' access to housing finance.

Experience in many countries has shown that public housing construction often does not reach the intended beneficiaries, and that by far the most important part of the capital funding for new homes or for shelter improvements comes from households themselves, either up-front from accumulated savings, or through loan repayments.[25] However, public sector authorities have a crucial role to play in easing constraints in housing supply, in housing finance, and in administering any subsidies to needy households. Israeli experience in accommodating immigrants confirms the importance of addressing supply constraints, and shows that measures to treat housing supply at large have been more successful than those focusing on a particular group.

Housing market conditions in the West Bank and Gaza and housing policy priorities are briefly summarized below, followed by an outline of some options that could be considered by donors wishing to assist, whatever the locality.[26]

Housing in WBG

Housing demand in WBG is largely driven by a very high natural population growth rate. There may also be considerable pent-up demand, as evidenced by over-crowding in some levels of the market. The high natural growth rate predominates, even under the assumption of a large inflow of refugees. Housing finance is not well developed, and there is still little long-term financing available for homebuyers, despite the successful start-up of the Palestinian

Mortgage and Housing Corporation (PMHC). Commercial bank finance is limited to short-term loans for housing developers, whose operations remain limited in scale. Efforts to develop mortgage finance have begun, for example through PMHC, but are still at an early stage.

Construction is very important to the Palestinian economy, with construction investment accounting for about 75 per cent of private investment, and about 22 per cent of employed people working in construction. Lack of access to construction work in Israel has been a main cause of unemployment in the West Bank and Gaza.

The housing policy reform priorities are to remove the constraints which keep construction costs high, especially in land supply, infrastructure services, and planning and construction standards. On the demand side, there needs to be an increase in the availability of finance for consumers and developers. Efforts to increase the availability of housing supply and housing finance should focus on low-income households. However, to make a returnee housing programme viable, it is crucial to lower the costs of publicly supported housing solutions and to increase cost recovery, in order to gain sufficient programme reach. Measures to stimulate the supply of low cost units, both for rent and for sale, should be given priority, and constraints preventing the conversion of existing units to low-cost units should be addressed.

Programme options

Experience has shown that competing objectives should not be addressed in one comprehensive programme. Distinct sub-programmes are suggested, with the individual goals of:

- Mitigating property loss incurred during past conflict phases;
- Providing housing solutions based on need; and
- Stimulating additional housing production where returnees are likely to settle.

Given the size of the refugee population, the property loss mitigation goal is likely to create strong competition for resources with the housing policy goals. The housing finance paper, Report (C), proposes a vehicle for reaching compromise: its design principles

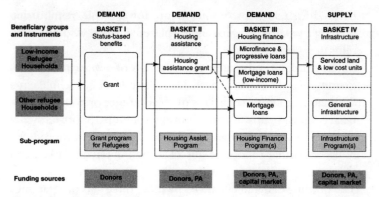

Figure 8.1 Returnee housing programme, design for the West Bank and Gaza

Note: dotted lines indicate potential instruments

include incentive neutrality for refugees with regard to the decision to move; consistency with local housing policy and the reform agenda; and efficiency of design and administration. It also allows donors to choose which sub-programmes to support.

The proposed programme, based on the design features above, includes 'baskets' or sub-programmes, as alternative funding options available to donors.

Within such a programme of 'baskets' for donors to select, the proposed eligibility requirements and benefits might include:

- In the first sub-programme, some refugees could receive a grant *benefit based on their legal status.*
- The second sub-programme proposes *housing assistance on a grant basis.* An important use of assistance on a grant basis could be for housing itself. However, it is proposed that only those fulfilling general pre-specified wealth and income limits could receive this assistance, and that domestic residents with housing needs who also satisfy the wealth and income limits would also be eligible. With this instrument, returnees and residents in need would be enabled to choose among a limited range of solutions in the housing market, including using the grant towards rent or housing purchase down payments. This type of assistance could also

be used for relocation/reintegration, for example, reimbursing moving costs for refugees and displaced persons who decide to relocate.[27]

- In the third sub-programme, a selection of *housing finance* programmes could be made available to enable *all* households in a destination country, regardless of their refugee or housing beneficiary status, to upscale their housing solutions. Short-term and micro-credit programmes would need to be introduced for households that cannot be absorbed by the rental market, and that have a low debt service capacity.
- The housing demand enhanced by these three sub-programmes could be supported by a fourth sub-programme to stimulate the supply of low-cost units. This could, for example, be specifically geared towards investment into land conversion and development, including funding for infrastructure, etc.

For equity reasons, the proposed instruments in the second and third 'baskets' would be available for low-income residents as well as returnees, but not to high-income households.

NEXT STEPS

The analyses summarized in this paper have necessarily been limited, both in the initial selection of study areas, and in investigating only public land sites. It has also been limited to a few geographical areas, but could be expanded to apply to other locations. The results, although helpful in identifying the likely orders of magnitude of the capital costs involved, fall far short of providing a blueprint for ensuring that sufficient infrastructure will be in place, and that appropriate and equitable housing solutions will be available, as the need arises.

There are several potential directions for further studies:

(a) *Widening the investigation to additional towns with absorption potential.* MOPIC now has the methodology to extend this work to other locations in the West Bank and Gaza not included in the original study; in particular to identify where there is additional public land.[28] In fact, the methodology can be applied to any location inside or outside the West Bank and Gaza.

(b) *Planning pilot projects in one or two of the study areas already identified as having available public land.* This would serve as a focus for identifying any policies, procedures, and specific actions required to provide infrastructure and ensure housing availability for accommodating new residents.

(c) *Investigating how private land could be brought into use for housing on a larger scale.* This may include a review of availability of private land within and near urban areas, the size of parcels, etc., and could also build on the initial review of the legal and institutional framework summarized in the consultant's paper (Nijem 2001).

Further discussion of some of the issues raised in connection with the analysis already carried out would help to move the work forward and avoid delays when the time comes for designing programmes to accommodate returnees. Issues to be discussed could include:

• Possible incentives for municipalities to provide the various infrastructure or other facilities needed to attract and accommodate refugee or displaced households, within an overall policy framework of improved housing market operations (particularly targeting low-income families) and infrastructure service provision, also benefiting existing residents;
• The role of the public and private sectors in construction of infrastructure and housing; and
• The types and extent of subsidies (explicit and implicit) in the various options for providing housing and infrastructure. The subsidies need to be sufficient to act as an incentive to ensure the full co-operation/participation of municipalities, but need to take into account the limited availability of financial resources.

BIBLIOGRAPHY

Asa'd, A.K. and Jayyousi, A. (2001) *Water and Wastewater Sector Investment for Refugees*, Washington, DC: World Bank.
Nijem, K. (2001) *Absorption Capacity in the West Bank and Gaza Governorates: Public and Waqf Land*, Washington, DC: World Bank.

World Bank (2000) *Infrastructure and Housing Costs: Technical Note*, Washington, DC: World Bank.

—— (2002) *The Absorption of Refugees in the West Bank and Gaza: Potential for Housing Accommodation on Public Land in Selected Study Areas*, Washington, DC: World Bank.

—— (2002) *Housing Finance for Returnees: Issues and Policy Options*, Washington, DC: World Bank.

Zeidan, K. (2001) *Estimating the Roadway Costs Associated with Absorbing Palestinian Returnees to the West Bank and Gaza*, Washington, DC: World Bank.

CHAPTER 9

Land and housing strategies for immigrant absorption: Lessons from the Israeli experience

Rachelle Alterman, Technion-Israel Institute of Technology, Haifa, Israel

INTRODUCTION

Israel offers one of the world's largest scale and most consistent experiences (relative to population size) of absorption of legal immigrants since the Second World War. Due to shared aspects of geography, history, demography, and national development trajectories, Israel's experience is particularly salient to its Palestinian neighbour. At the same time, there are also significant differences that call for care in the interpretation of the Israeli lessons and their transfer to the Palestinian context.

This paper details the lessons from the Israeli experience with the absorption of mass immigration in the last five decades. It will examine different immigrant absorption waves and analyse the range of absorption strategies. The conclusions point to the elements of Israel's evolving immigrant-absorption policies that have been more successful, and those to avoid.

This paper is based, in part, on a larger unpublished study prepared for the World Bank. It draws upon a variety of sources: an extensive literature review (in Hebrew and English) of the various aspects of Israel's immigration policy, including land-use, housing, economic, and social dimensions; official documents from the various periods; and official statistics. It also reflects the author's ongoing research and publications about Israel's land-use, housing, and urban policies and laws; as well as international comparative research on planning, land-use laws and policies (Alterman 1988; Alterman and

Cars 1991; Alterman 1997; Alterman 2001; Alterman 2002), housing, and neighbourhood policies (Alterman 1988; Alterman and Cars 1991; Alterman and Churchman 1991). The information about policy-making during the mass-immigration wave of the early 1990s and its outcomes draws on this author's in-depth analysis of policy-making during that crisis period (Alterman 2002).

A BRIEF INTRODUCTION TO ISRAEL'S IMMIGRATION POLICY

A cross-national comparative perspective

Israel is a small, densely inhabited country with a natural population growth rate higher than other advanced-economy countries. Palestine is even smaller and denser, and with a much higher natural population growth rate – one of the highest in the world. Yet both countries have parallel histories that have made them – and will continue to make them – nations that absorb immigrants at a much higher rate than most other countries.

The impact of mass immigration on a small country such as Israel – and in the future, on Palestine – is very high, compared with that of another advanced-economy country among the few which, in recent history, were ready to receive many immigrants, such as Germany. One should take into account the relative size of the population, the economy, average individual wealth and the available land resources. In 1990, when the most recent wave of mass immigration started, Israel had about one fifteenth of Germany's population, Israel's gross national product (GNP) per person was about half of Germany's, and among the lowest among advanced-economy countries. The size of Israel's economy was approximately 3 per cent of Germany's, and its population density, though not the highest among the group of countries, is expected to become the highest in the near future, mainly due to Israel's higher natural growth rates (Alterman 2002: 10–12). The argument, in sum, is that the impacts of mass immigration on Israel's economy, society, geography, and environment have been objectively greater than the impact of immigration on most other advanced-economy countries.

Immigration policy, endemic uncertainty and crisis-proneness

In many ways, Israel's immigration policy is not only different from, but opposite to that of most countries. The goal of the immigration policy of most countries is to turn the demand for immigration from an unknown and potentially unmanageable factor, into one where both the number and traits of the immigrants are controlled and predictable. Israel's policymakers knowingly place the country in an endemic state of uncertainty about the number of immigrants at any given time, their human-resource traits, and the potential impact of mass immigrations. Through this policy Israel has willingly made itself vulnerable to immigration-generated crises. This happened during Israel's formative years (1949–1955) and once again in the early 1990s.

Israel is unique among advanced-economy countries in its consistent open-doors policy toward (Jewish) immigrants, as expressed in law and policy (see below). In this respect, the future Palestinian state is likely to be similar to Israel.

As might be expected, Israel's immigration policy is controversial, being an integral part of the Middle East conflict. While Israeli immigration law and policy is extremely open towards Jews and their non-Jewish family members, it is very restrictive toward others (Rubinstein 1996: 124, 877–893). The rationale for this policy is to preserve the country's scarce land and water resources as a potential haven for Jewish refugees, should there be a resurgence of anti-Semitism anywhere in the world. A related goal is to maintain a Jewish population majority.

Within the ebb and flow of immigration to Israel since its establishment in 1948, one could in retrospect identify more-or-less distinguishable periods characterized by differing contexts and different policies for absorption. Table 9.1 presents a rough division into ten periods, showing the number of immigrants, their dominant countries of origin, the size of the initial population, and the key economic indicators. The division into periods roughly parallels the evolution of strategies for immigrant absorption.

The policy variables for designing absorption strategies

In retrospect, one is able to identify several policy variables that served as the basis for immigrant-absorption policies (in the realm of land use and housing). In the next pages I shall take a close look at

Table 9.1: *Major periods of immigration to Israel, by number of immigrants, existing population and GDP per capita*

Key periods and their characteristics	Typical annual number of immigrants	Israel's population in initial year	Total number of households	GDP per person	
				1996 prices (US$)	Average annual growth
I: 1948–1951 Mass immigration of refugees	170,000	872,700		3,410	6.2
II: 1952–1959 Moderate, mainly North Africa, Romania	44,000	1,629,500	474,900	4,490	5.3
III: 1960–1966 Moderate, mainly North Africa	50,000	2,150,400	549,000	9,494	6.3
IV: 1967–1970 Low, mainly western countries	22,000	2,776,300	653,900	9,346	4.9
V: 1971–1976 Moderate, mainly USSR	50,000	3,022,100	933,300	11,770	5.2
VI: 1977–1985 Low, South America and western countries	21,000	3,653,200	1,102,500	12,748	0.62
VII: 1986–1989 Stagnation: emigration balances immigration	12,000	4,331,300	1,162,000	14,301	2.4
VIII: 1990–1992 Mass immigration wave from USSR (Commonwealth of Independent States – CIS)	140,000	4,559,600	1,398,100	16,080	2.5
IX: 1993–2000 Moderate wave from CIS	70,000	5,327,600	1,647,000	19,150	1.9 (high till 1996 then dipping into recession)

X: 2001–2004
Moderate-low rate
from CIS and
elsewhere   30,000   6,508,800   1,815,000   18,000   –3.0

Source: Israel Central Bureau of Statistics, Statistical Abstract (annual reports for the relevant years) 1950–2005

each of these policy variables to see how they varied over time. Thus, Israel can serve as a 'laboratory', so to speak, of policy variables for immigrant absorption that are 'tested' under varying contextual conditions.

Whenever decision-makers design an immigration absorption strategy they are likely to consider all or most of the five major policy variables depicted in the following list. These are the building blocks out of which Israeli policymakers constructed the country's immigration policies, and altered their choices over time. I don't wish to imply that such decisions were made in a concerted, synchronized or comprehensive way; public decisions are rarely of that nature. The decisions may have been made in an incremental, disjointed manner, but *de facto* at any given time period they did add up to an identifiable set of policies.

The policy variables for designing immigration absorption policies are:

1 Planning law and regulation of development.
2 Land and property rights policy: the role of publicly owned land.
3 Regional development: direction to preferred geographic regions.
4 Housing production:

  • Production side: type and extent of public intervention in production.
  • Housing standards.
  • Consumption side: type of consumer subsidies and targeted populations.

5 Living support 'absorption basket' (for initial period after arrival).

Some of these policy variables have been more reactive to mass immigration and crisis situations, others less so. The most flexible policy variables used to adjust to crises have been housing and living support. Also reactive, but somewhat less flexibly, have been land policy, regional development and (surprisingly?) planning law. Least adjustable to crises through policy instruments have been economic development and employment policy.

In the sections to follow I shall analyse each of the policy variables (grouping some of them), showing how it evolved over time and how it interacted with each of the other policy variables.

PLANNING LAW AND THE REGULATION OF DEVELOPMENT

Most accounts of Israel's immigrant absorption policies – indeed, of any country's immigration absorption policies – neglect a major variable: the role of planning law. Would planning regulations enable the large-scale housing starts and other construction projects triggered by accelerated growth?

Until 1966, land-use planning and development control in Israel were carried out according to the Town Planning Ordinance that Israel inherited from the British Mandate over Palestine and integrated into the Israeli legal system. When the 1965 Planning and Building Law was enacted, the waves of mass immigration that typified Israel's first decade had already subsided. The 1965 law was suitable (or barely suitable) for the country's 'regular' pace of development. However, when mass immigration resumed in 1990, Israeli policymakers found that the planning law was unsuited to dealing with massive development pressures.

The legal status of state-initiated construction

Under the British Mandate over Palestine's Town Planning Ordinance (that stayed in force until 1965), projects constructed by government were exempt from the control of planning law. The British Mandate government was engaged in construction mainly of major infrastructure and military projects. Most housing and social-service construction was left to the initiative of the two major local populations – the Arabs and the Jews. Both communities had an active private construction and non-profit sector.

When the state of Israel stepped into the shoes of the British Mandate Government in 1948 and faced mass immigration, it undertook state-initiated construction at a larger scale. This included the construction of hundreds of large-scale housing projects, entire new neighbourhoods, over 30 new towns, and hundreds of new co-operative and communal villages (for an extensive description of this mammoth project, see Brutzkus 1964, 1969). In addition, the government also undertook many infrastructure construction projects of roads, water supply, regional drainage and sewerage, hundreds of schools, health facilities, and some social facilities (others were initiated by various quasi-public organizations not legally exempt from planning controls). Indeed, by 1965 when a new planning law was enacted, the majority of Israel's currently existing towns, cities and villages, were already on the map. Many of the horses had already run out of the stable.

This massive planning and development effort was not worse, and at times better, than public-sector development carried out during that period in many other countries, including western ones. But its huge scale in a short time (relative to the country's size) magnified the usual maladies that accompany government construction in most countries: Many of the new towns were look-alike copies and oblivious to each unique setting, the housing types were repetitive, and construction standards were not always adequate (Swirski and Bernstein 1980; Darin-Drabkin 1959; Carmon and Czamanski 1990; Carmon 1999; Tanne 1959). Some decision-makers felt that government too should be regulated to some extent.

The 1965 Planning and Building Law went to the other extreme. It did not exempt *any* state-initiated construction projects from going through the full planning and building-permitting process. The reasons for this about-turn have not been well researched, but I will surmise that they reflected three interconnected views: a feeling that since Israel had 'come of age', the need for massive government projects will no longer be as acute as during the country's first initial years; a critical view of the outcomes of the massive construction projects that had bypassed the planning bodies; and an optimistic belief – which turned out to be over-optimistic – that the planning system under the new Planning and Building Law would be able to handle not only private-sector initiatives but also state construction initiatives. However, the 1965 Planning and Building Law did not meet all of these expectations.

The Israel Planning and Building Law in a nutshell

After some 70 mostly minor amendments, the Israel Planning and Building Law still stands today as Israel's main planning law. It is a rather centralized law compared with the planning laws of most other advanced-economy countries (Alterman 2001a). Most planning decisions at the local level require the approval of the District Planning and Building Commission composed of representatives of central government ministries. The Minister of the Interior has extensive oversight powers. At least on paper, the system calls for a co-ordinated hierarchy of plans, from the national, through the district, down to the local levels. Lower level plans have to be strictly consistent with all higher level plans. Every action of development or demolition, big or small, requires a building permit; there are hardly any exemptions.

Before I mention the Planning and Building Law's shortcomings in handling the accelerated development brought about by mass immigration, I should say that it has also had some important achievements. It has enabled a large slate of national (mostly sectoral) plans for essential infrastructure projects, has protected parks, and has contributed to the preservation of farmland and coastlines. A less recognized achievement, but perhaps the most significant for the subject at hand, is the fact that after only a few years of adjustment, all state agencies did indeed learn that they must ask for planning approval for all their construction initiatives. This means that since 1966, all state-initiated housing, public services, or infrastructure projects have been subject to planning review, to (some) public exposure, to the growing slate of environmental controls, and (presumably) to better co-ordination with other public and private projects.

These achievements aside, the 1965 Planning and Building Law came under severe criticism soon after its enactment. The level of criticism increased with time, as land became scarcer and as the level of planning and environmental controls increased. The criticism centred on the multi-layered approval process and the rampant delays. Statutory planning was (and still is) regarded by many as chronically lethargic, and an unnecessary impediment to economic development. While the problem of perceived excessive delay in development approval is not unique to Israel, many Israeli decision-makers view it as *the* major problem in the planning system. Their sensitivity to this issue may be due to the fact that Israel's demographic, economic, and physical-development growth rates are high even during periods without mass immigration, and are higher than most other advanced-economy countries. Palestine's will be higher yet.

Special legislation to meet the needs of mass immigration in 1990

As long as the pace of development reflected relatively moderate immigration and growth rates, during the period from 1966 to 1989, the planning institutions managed to handle the country's needs, more or less. However, and not surprisingly, when the major immigration crisis broke out in late 1989 to early 1990, the single major target for legislative change was the Planning and Building Law and its institutional system (Alterman 2000; Alterman 2002).

The 1990 Planning and Building Interim Law achieved its goal by establishing six Housing Construction Commissions (HCCs), one for each district of Israel. These were to serve as 'single stop' planning institutions for approving any proposed development with at least 200 housing units (public or private) or extension of an existing industrial area. These new bodies were composed of six representatives of the key central government ministries: Interior (two), Housing, the Lands Administration, Transportation, and the Commission for the Preservation of Agricultural Land.

The new law entirely bypassed the local planning commissions that, under the regular law, were an important first station in the approval process. Under the Interim Law the local authorities only had partial representation on the HCCs. Although three local representatives (the mayor and his appointees) would be members of the Commission, their membership would be on a 'musical chairs' basis, for only as long as a plan within their jurisdiction was on the agenda. The elected officials from the opposition would have no voice at all. Ostensibly set up as combined local-district bodies, the six new Commissions functioned more like organs of the central government than as mid-way bodies.

In the name of cutting down approval time, the law also drastically cut citizen review and objection time (from two or three months to a period of only 20 days, including weekends and holidays). Furthermore, it severely limited the time allocated for scrutiny by the planning support staff and for deliberations by the HCCs.

The Interim Law also placed severe limits on the authority of the National Planning and Building Board. It thereby challenged the logic of the entire hierarchy of national, district, and local plans. The HCCs were authorized to approve development that did not accord with a district plan, without requiring the prior approval of the National Board. The new Commissions were even authorized to approve development that contradicted existing national plans as long as they allowed the National Board 20 days in order to halt the HCCs' decision. Otherwise, the HCCs' decision would prevail.

Another goal of the new law was to reduce the powers of the national agricultural land protection body. Under the regular law, all proposed development that impinges on declared agricultural land required the review and approval of the Commission for the Preservation of Agricultural Land (CPAL). The Interim Law brought the CPAL 'down' from its elevated position by making its representative a regular member of each Housing Construction Commission and by authorizing the new commissions to review all plans, even those that convert agricultural land. Although the CPAL representative had the power to call in particular plans for the CPAL's direct review, in the crisis-time atmosphere, that power was rarely used.

There is no doubt that during the height of the crisis, the Interim Law did succeed in enabling a highly accelerated rate of approval of housing and ancillary facilities. It did so in a reasonable time frame that, under the circumstances, balanced the need for fast decisions with a degree of planning scrutiny (Alterman 2002: 90–97; Borukhov 1998). However, compared with non-crisis decision-making, the decisions under the Interim Law often did compromise on environmental assessment, design control, open space preservation, and timely infrastructure completion (Alterman 2000; 2002: 129–169).

Even though the 1965 Planning and Building Law was not abolished and continued to operate side by side with the Interim Law, the latter was to dominate the Israeli land-use planning scene for the next four and a half years (it was extended three times). And even after the crisis was over and the Interim Law was allowed to sunset, in the eyes of pro-development government and private interests, the Interim Law continued to serve as a model of how to bypass the 'planning bureaucracy'. So far, the more draconian of such initiatives have been aborted, thanks to the actions of environmentally conscious groups and government agencies in charge of regulative planning and the environment, but in 2002 an amendment to the Planning and Building Law instituted a special national body and a streamlined procedure for approving plans for 'national infrastructure' projects.

LAND POLICY AND REGIONAL DEVELOPMENT

In this part I shall discuss the second variable in the list – land policy and property rights instruments as they pertain to immigrant absorption. In addition, I shall also refer to the third variable, Israel's regional development policies and their interaction with immigrant absorption policies.

Introduction to Israel's land system

Israel's immigrant-absorption policies have relied to a large extent on a factor unique to Israel – national ownership of the majority of the country's land area (approximately 93 per cent). The majority of private land is concentrated in pre-state towns (about half of which are in Arab–Israeli villages and towns). Within the major cities, national land holdings are not as large, and are mostly concentrated on the urban outskirts. Municipal land holdings in Israel have always been minimal, consisting at most of local roads and some other public facilities. Nationally owned land figures prominently in most day-to-day activities, such as housing and industry. From a cross-national perspective, the quantitative and qualitative characteristics of Israel's public land holdings place it in a category of its own. It has no equivalent today either in an advanced-economy country (Alterman 2003), or in the Palestinian Authority. Today, Israeli land policy presents an interesting (and counter-intuitive) mixture of public powers alongside a very high level of protection of private property rights – whether on private land or on long-term public leaseholds (Alterman 2006).

The national land holdings served as a major policy instrument for immigrant absorption in each and every one of the immigration waves noted in Table 9.1. Despite the series of decisions that have gradually brought the public leasehold system closer and closer to a freehold system (Alterman 1999, 2003; Benchetrit and Czamanski 2004), public land policy has played a major role in immigrant absorption even during the most recent mass immigration wave of the 1990s (Alterman 2002: 85–86, 97–103, Cohen *et al.* 1993).

In addition, the fact that the state controls most of the land reserves has enabled the linkage that Israel has made throughout its history, between immigrant absorption and nation building through regional development policies.

The evolution of land policy and regional development instruments

Table 9.2 summarizes the key land policy and regional-planning instruments applied in the various periods of immigrant absorption (combining several of the immigration periods in Table 9.1, as relevant to the discussion of land policy). In the Israeli context, these policies almost invariably were articulated by central government rather than by municipal governments. Central government decided, for the most part, where and when new development for new immigrants was to be located.[1] Municipal involvement (whether promoting or opposing these policies) was very low during most of the periods discussed. The slightly greater municipal involvement of recent years has not manifested itself directly in land policy, but rather indirectly, through local planning and development controls and through lobbying central government (Alterman 2001b).

Table 9.2 presents the evolution of the land component of immigrant absorption policies in terms of the initial allocation of public land; the determination of the price of land allocated; and the tenure status of the immigrant residents. The Table is therefore closely linked to the evolution of housing policies, to be discussed in the next section.

Table 9.2: *The evolution of public land policies as related to immigrant absorption*

Policy evolution periods (approx. dates)	Public land, property rights and regional policies related to immigrant absorption
1948 to early 1950s Mass immigration waves	• Allocation by central government of large tracts of national land for temporary housing sites and ancillary public services (at no cost to the residents and no official establishment of property rights), mostly on the outskirts of existing cities. • Allocation of built-up housing units vacated during the 1948 war (mostly belonging to Palestinians) as temporary housing. Some become the immigrants' secured-tenure permanent housing through pre-State tenant-protection laws, through public long-term leasehold, or though outright freehold purchase by the occupants.
Mid-1950s to mid-1960s High immigration rate	• Land allocation (at no cost or artificially low price) for public-sector construction of new permanent neighbourhoods on the outskirts of existing cities and towns. • Allocation of large tracts of national land for the construction of about two-dozen new towns, mostly in peripheral areas, to be inhabited by new immigrants. Land is allocated to state and quasi-public developers at artificially low price. • The property rights of the urban residents in the new housing is initially mostly rental. Gradually (during the 1970s and 1980s) most rental units become 'owner occupied' (more precisely, on long-term urban-sector leaseholds akin to freehold). • Allocation of large tracts of national land for the establishment of scores of new agricultural villages in peripheral areas,

Table 9.2 (*cont.*):

	most inhabited by new immigrants. Public land allocated for housing, agriculture, and ancillary industrial sites through rural leasehold contracts, usually at no initial cost to the residents and very low leasehold fee (but in retrospect, the property rights turned out to be insecure).
Mid-1960s to late 1970s Low to moderate immigration rates	• Public-land allocation recedes in importance as a direct instrument of immigrant absorption. • Exceptions: allocation of national land for several Immigrant Absorption Centres (hotel-like facilities for initial housing and language courses). • Establishment of new towns ceases; new urban neighbourhoods and new villages are built on public land but are not directly earmarked for new immigrants. Initial market mechanisms developed for valuation of public land before allocation. • More former immigrant renters of public housing upgrade their tenure to 'ownership' (in fact, long-term leasehold).
Late 1970s to 1989 Low immigration rate	• Public-land policy is *de facto* fully disengaged from immigrant absorption strategies. No more construction earmarked for new immigrant housing • Immigrant Absorption Centres continue until 1986, then are phased out in favour of the 'direct absorption' policy. • A major new city (Modiin), as well as scores of new small exurban non-agricultural communities are planned on national land, but are targeted mostly for long-term Israelis to be lured from the central region.

- Market mechanisms for allocation of national land for housing and industry become sophisticated and simulate market prices closely. Lower-than-market prices are used as a lever for population distribution (not earmarked for new immigrants). Prices are reduced in part (Galilee, Negev regions) or in full (along the borders).
- Project Renewal seeks to upgrade the housing of declining neighbourhoods – mostly those targeted for the immigrants of the 1950s and 1960s. The Project indirectly further stimulates transfer of more rental housing to the 'ownership' of the residents. Lower-than-market prices may be charged.

1990–1992
Mass immigration wave

- Available tracts of national land are once again allocated for mass construction of entire new government-initiated urban neighbourhoods and facilities.
- These are not exclusively earmarked for new immigrants but are triggered by the mass immigration from the former USSR.
- The market mechanism for pricing public land for government-initiated housing is put 'on hold' and developers are given land at no cost or (in high demand areas) at half-cost.
- A very small proportion of the housing units are designated for rental; the vast majority is for sale (long-term lease).
- Most development towns ('new towns') and some exurban neighbourhoods planned at the previous stage receive a population boost from the immigrants.

1993–2000
Moderate immigration rate

- Land policy is once again disengaged from immigrant absorption strategies.
- The market mechanisms for allocating national land are resumed. Lower-than

Table 9.2 (*cont.*):

	market prices are still used only for population distribution target areas. New immigrants are indirect beneficiaries but the policies are not earmarked for them. • Experimental land-subsidy programmes are developed for targeted socially deprived communities or social groups.
2000 to date Low immigration rate (*intifada*, terrorism and deep recession)	• New policies of lower-than-market-price allocations of public land in peripheral areas were introduced in 2001 to stimulate the recession-depressed housing market. New immigrants were indirect beneficiaries. But these incentives were almost fully withdrawn in 2003–2004. I predict that they will be reintroduced for border regions in the future.

Lessons to be learned from Israel's land and tenure policies

Several conclusions emerge from Table 9.2:

1 Avoid illegal squatting and ensure that temporary sites are phased out

Unlike most countries with a developing economy that face large waves of immigrants or migrants, Israel's immigrants rarely have found themselves as squatters without established property rights. Intentionally, the temporary sites (camp sites, transit sites) did not give any property rights to the residents, yet their stay there was legal. These sites were planned to be temporary (Jewish Agency 1959) and indeed, most (but not all) were vacated within a few years, usually not beyond the early 1960s (Namir 1972). The residents knew that they were likely to be offered permanent housing. But the precise timing, location, and type of housing were often not known in advance. When such housing did come through it was not always to the immigrants' liking (see lesson 3). The policy that immigrants should be offered permanent housing has become one of the hallmarks of Israel's housing policy.

The need for temporary housing for mass immigration recurred in

1990–1991. At that time, various policy means were used (such as a 'sunset clause' in planning permits, and agreements signed with local authorities) in order to assure that the sites would not become quasi-permanent and would be phased out within a maximum of five years (Feitelson *et al.* 1992). That did not always hold up, but most sites were indeed cleared within a considerably shorter period than during the 1950s (Borukhov 1998; Alterman 2002: 132–135).

2 View national land holdings as a possible instrument for immigrant absorption

The availability of large vacant tracts of nationally owned land became the major instrument of Israel's immigrant-absorption policy during the 1950s to the early1960s (Brutzkus 1964: 6) and once again, during the massive wave of 1991–1992 (Alterman 2002: 85–86, 97–103; Cohen *et al.* 1993). Central government was thereby able to control the size and timing of development by using large tracts of vacant land rather than relying on infill. Public ownership enabled government to avoid the need to assemble private land through expropriation or other means of onerous intervention in property rights.

3 Consider the pros and cons of linking regional development policy and immigrant absorption

National land ownership was a major instrument in the Israeli government's ability to link the need to house masses of immigrants with regional-planning goals such as population dispersal to the peripheral and border areas (Brutzkus 1964; Law Yone and Kalus 1995; Garon 1992). In the uncertain geopolitical situation of Israel's early years when the armistice-lines were not yet recognized as national borders, government adopted a planning policy of distributing towns and villages as widely as possible to the country's peripheries in order not to leave entire regions without a 'Jewish stronghold'. These national-development goals were buttressed by environmental and land-use policy goals that sought to deconcentrate the population away from the central region (Brutzkus 1969). These regional development goals were accomplished through the establishment of some 30 new towns and hundreds of new agricultural co-operative villages (Brutzkus 1964, 1969). Nationally owned land was the key instrument for the implementation of this policy.

But the policy of linking national land ownership and immigrant absorption, while being a potent tool for achieving regional-distribution goals, also had major negative outcomes. It has resulted in some of the worst social disparities within Israeli society. The lucky, better-connected or better-off households got access to housing in urban locations, but others were encouraged (often without being given other options) to go to peripheral locations such as new towns or co-operative villages. This period was responsible for much of Israel's social inequality to date. Those who went to the peripheral regions in order to gain permanent housing tended to be the less socially mobile groups among the immigrants (Kipnis 1990). The deprivations that characterize peripheral locations as such, compounded with initial social deprivation of many of the immigrants, created regions where the new immigrants of the 1950s and early 1960s joined the lower rungs of the socio-economic ladder (Swirski and Katzir 1978; Swirski and Bernstein 1980; Lifshitz 1990).

The policy of dispersing the new towns and villages as widely as possible created nodes with few employment opportunities and usually with an undiversified economy base (Soen and Kipnis 1971). Geographic isolation away from the country's major cities exacerbated social disparities between the new immigrants and the existing Jewish population. The design of the new towns to look 'urban' and be composed of apartment blocks without offering most of the benefits of urban concentrations did not enhance the value of the housing units (Lerman 1976). The more upwardly mobile households tended to leave for better employment in the country's central region, so with each wave of immigrants, the average socio-economic indicators of these new towns and villages tended to decline further.

During the 'comeback' of mass immigration in 1990, some Israeli politicians sought to re-link immigrant absorption, national land ownership, and population distribution. But other decision-makers regarded the availability of jobs to be an overriding condition for good immigrant absorption, and they opted to reduce incentives for immigrant location in the peripheral regions. The result was a compromise position that was guided by the *de facto* availability of land reserves (Alterman 2002: 86–87).

4 Encourage gradual disengagement of national land policy from immigrant absorption

Since the late 1970s, Israel's public land allocation and pricing policies gradually became disengaged from immigrant absorption (though not necessarily through an explicit decision). That is, public land was no longer allocated specifically for projects earmarked for new immigrants, nor were special pricing mechanisms used to subsidize land for immigrant housing. However, the public land instrument was by no means entirely dropped from public policy; rather, it became more targeted to general regional-development goals such as the 'population distribution' policy rather than directly to immigrant absorption.

The mass immigration wave from the Soviet Union in 1990 led the government once again to view the allocation of national land for immigrant housing as a major policy instrument in the immigrant absorption strategy. Government planners scanned all areas of the country for tracts of national land available for development. However, the 1990 land policies differed significantly from the policies of the 1950s and 1960s. While the trigger was the mass immigration wave, and the original notion may have been to renew the policies of the 1950s, the policy that was finally developed turned out to be much more sophisticated. Only a minority of the tracts were allocated for housing for immigrants, while the majority were allocated to new government-subsidized mixed housing available for purchase by any interested households. As soon as the mass immigration wave subsided, government resumed the full disengagement of national land policy from immigrant absorption strategy (Alterman 2002: 97–103).

5 Increase reliance on the market place in allocating public land

The pricing mechanism for the allocation of public land for immigrant and other publicly initiated projects changed over time. In the initial periods, a zero or close-to zero price was charged for land allocated to immigrant housing. Gradually and incrementally, a market-emulating pricing system was developed. During the 1960s and into the 1970s this mechanism was called 'chart prices', policy-driven decisions about the pricing of land according to categories of preference. This mechanism was widely criticized for its arbitrariness, inequities and potential misuse, especially where high-demand areas were concerned. The artificial pricing mechanism was therefore gradually phased out and replaced by a tender-based mechanism that applied to most allocations of national land for any purpose (Alterman 2003).

However, when mass immigration resumed in 1990, policymakers reinstituted subsidies of housing production through the pricing mechanism for national land. Such land was allocated at no cost anywhere outside the central region, and at half cost in the high-demand central region where land values were very high. The decision-makers soon discovered that in high-demand areas, the subsidy through the land component would rarely reach the consumers, but would be pocketed by the developers (Alterman 2002: 99). They therefore reduced the subsidies in land in the central region. In 1992, when the massive wave tapered down, these subsidies were phased out entirely. The market-emulating mechanism for the pricing of most national land allocations was reinstated. The only remaining exceptions were the regular subsidies that applied to peripheral and border regions (and since 2004 these too have been phased out).

6 Aim for a high rate of home ownership generally and among immigrants

Finally, Israel should be a target of envy for other countries because it has offered secure property rights in housing to most immigrants (in urban areas). This has occurred gradually and incrementally. Three sets of policies have contributed to this outcome: the consistent reduction in the amount of new public housing for rental (Israel Ministry for Immigration Absorption 1975; Alterman 2002: 47–58); restrictions on eligibility for such housing (only the very poor or old); increasing public expectation that households be able to purchase (or long-term lease) a housing unit; availability of (modest) mortgages for this purpose (to be discussed later); and a policy of encouraging gradual purchase of public-housing rental units by their occupants – most of whom are former immigrants or their offspring. Another possibly relevant factor (though likely never to have been thought-out as linked to the above policy) is that Israel has never had rent-protection laws for housing constructed after statehood.

The outcome is that today, the majority of the new immigrants who arrived at any time after the state's establishment own their apartment or house. No such statistic has ever been assembled, but my assumption is that the figure is approximately 65–70 per cent. There are, however, marked differences in the number of years it has taken the immigrants of the different waves to achieve home ownership. The latest wave of new immigrants from the former USSR achieved an over 70 per cent home ownership rate within a few years of their arrival (Alterman 2002: 113–114). But for the immigrants of the 1950s and 1960s it has taken many years, at times a generation, to reach that point. Among the latter, there were large disparities among ethnic groups – immigrants from Europe tended to reach home ownership faster than immigrants from North Africa and the Middle East (Law Yone and Kalus 1995).

Home ownership (usually condominium-apartment ownership) is the main capital asset of most Israeli households. It has proven to be a major determinant of social mobility, and therefore a major tool for immigrant absorption (Carmon 1999, 2001 for Israel; Alba and Logan 1992 for the USA). Compared with rental, home ownership has other important positive benefits regarding residents' motivation for upkeep and maintenance. It is therefore generally recognized as an important player in physical and environmental quality of life (Megbolugbe and Linneman 1993).

HOUSING PRODUCTION AND CONSUMPTION POLICIES

In forging housing policies, government institutions must decide on three main issues: *type and extent of public intervention in the market, desired housing standards, and targeted populations.* Among these three issues I shall use the first issue – the type and extent of public intervention – as the main prism for viewing the evolution of Israeli policies for housing immigrants. The other two issues will be incorporated in that discussion.

I don't mean to imply that Israeli government institutions have developed housing strategies for immigrant absorption in a comprehensive manner; that is rarely the way public institutions anywhere make decisions. However decided, these three issues were part of housing policy at any given time – whether as overt decisions, or by default. However, before focusing on these particular aspects, one should look at the position housing has occupied among the plethora of policy issues relevant to immigrant absorption.

Housing as lead issue

Unlike immigration absorption policies in many countries, including the USA and Canada, in Israel housing has been viewed as the lead issue with which government decision-makers must contend. In many countries, immigrants are expected to look for housing on their own. They often occupy substandard housing in inner cities or squat in makeshift housing on the urban outskirts. This has never been part of Israeli public policy regarding immigrant absorption. In setting public policy regarding priority areas in which government should invest, housing has always taken the lead. This preference held even during the 1990 mass immigration wave when Israel was already an advanced-economy country (Alterman 2002: 81–89). It had a well-developed private housing sector that conceivably may have been able to adjust itself to the increase in demand, but with a long time lag. During the interim, many immigrants would not have had adequate housing and the unmet demand would have driven up housing prices. So policymakers once again identified housing as the lead issue, and directed the largest portion of public investment into housing rather than into other areas such as economic development.

The reasons why housing has always been seen as the lead issue in immigrant absorption are probably deeply embedded in Israeli social values and political expectations. The sight of homeless families has been socially and politically unacceptable throughout Israel's history, irrespective of the country's economy at that time. Politicians have consistently viewed adequate housing as a mark of success in immigrant absorption, and homeless immigrants or their concentration in substandard housing, as a starkly visible mark of failure.

The policy spectrum: type and extent of public intervention

Beyond the long-term consensus about housing as a priority area in immigrant absorption, the particular strategy of housing provision varied over time, reflecting changes in the economy, society, and the role of government.

Figure 9.1 shows a schematic spectrum of housing policies on the *production* side. The spectrum runs from direct government

From direct government intervention to private-market production				
◄───►				
Direct government construction	**Direct subsidies**	**Indirect subsidies**	**Indirect public incentives**	**Private market**
and financing public land; centralized design	in land and public infrastructure; 'public programme' construction by quasi-public companies	and direct incentives to private developers	such as economic development	with planning regulation only

Figure 9.1 Housing production strategies: conceptual policy spectrum

intervention by means of state-initiated and financed construction on the left, to reliance on the private market for all or most of housing construction initiatives and financing on the right. In the intermediate parts of the spectrum one could place various mixes of public and private roles in housing production, according to the degree of government intervention in the marketplace. The three interim-range policies included in this spectrum refer to particular mixtures of policies applied in Israel at various periods, as will be described in the sections below. The policy on the extreme right has never been practised in Israel and is added here only for the theoretical completeness of the spectrum. A similar spectrum constructed for another country's context might show slightly different policy mixtures in the interim stations.

In 1990 the special policies developed for the absorption of a massive number of immigrants from the former Soviet Union, were a combination of policies from both the far and immediate past (Alterman 2002: 97–103). Because the progress along the spectrum of housing production policies has not been entirely linear, I have not indicated the periods along the spectrum.

A concomitant set of policies applies to the *consumption* side. These pertain to the manner in which households get access to public-sector

From government allocation to purchase on the open market			
(approximate dates)			
1949 to 1965	mid-1960s to late 1970s	1980 to 1989	1990 to date
Immigrants directed to temporary, later rental or low-cost housing; later purchase options with subsidized mortgages	Choice: uniform public housing or subsidized mortgages for varied but size-limited housing by quasi-public developers	Purchase on open private market or 'programme' housing; size limits upgraded and adjusted by household sizes; subsidized mortgages	Purchase on open market of private or 'public-programme' housing with help of subsidized mortgages; may combine families; no size limits

Figure 9.2 Housing consumption policies: *de facto* spectrum of subsidies and approximate periods

housing. Figure 9.2 presents the policy spectrum regarding consumer-based subsidies as they progressed through time. The policy movement along this spectrum has been entirely linear; therefore, I have added approximate dates.

The discussion below will follow the division into periods set out in Figure 9.2 and will deal both with the production side and the consumption side policy spectrums. I shall devote more space to the discussion of the two periods that I believe are most relevant to the Palestinian Authority because they deal with mass immigration: the first period where direct government production policy dominated and Israel – like Palestine – was in its most important nation-building stage; and the most recent period where highly innovative approaches were developed.

First period: direct government housing production from 1949 to 1965

During the early periods of mass immigration – 1949 to the early or mid-1960s – the dominant production-side policy favoured direct government construction. This was viewed as necessary to house the masses of new immigrants. Construction took place on national land and through government or quasi-government financing. This was true both for temporary housing sites and for permanent housing construction (the land policy component was discussed above).

Temporary housing sites

At first, the major concern was finding shelter for recently arrived immigrants, much of which had to be temporary. Between 1948 and 1950 about 400,000 immigrants arrived, almost all with no financial means. The Jewish Agency was the main body in charge of temporary accommodation. It was the pre-state governing body of the Jewish sector, which in Israel's early years was better organized than the embryonic government bureaux.

During those stressful years of war and incipient statehood, the authorities were able to offer the majority of immigrants only temporary housing. The types of housing 'solutions' delivered during 1948 to mid-1950 – the period of greatest urgency and poorest public resources – included immigrant camps, various dormitory facilities, rural temporary housing, and cohabiting with relatives. These categories total about 55 per cent of the accommodation types used by recently arrived immigrants (Jewish Agency 1959). In addition, about 124,000 (31 per cent) were to be housed in Arab houses and apartments vacated during the war (Carmon and Czamanski 1990: 514; Jewish Agency 1959). Some of these housing units turned into permanent housing, others remained temporary because they were sub-standard. I estimate that during 1948–1950, 65–70 per cent of the immigrants received temporary housing. This percentage increased still further in the following years since the formerly Arab housing stock had been exhausted during this early period, while permanent housing had not yet been completed in any significant amount. The role of the temporary camps and transit sites increased, and hundreds of thousands passed through them.

The temporary camps and transit sites deserve further description because they have become the symbol of the time in both collective and individual recollection. In 1949 the Jewish Agency established its 'Camps Division' whose first project was to prepare a site on the outskirts of the port city of Haifa where immigrants received initial shelter. This massive tent camp handled about 1,000 immigrants entering or leaving daily. In total, 127 camps had been built by 1951 and 250,000 people had lived in them (Bernstein 1980: 6). Each family received a tent of some 16 square metres, and the toilets and bathing facilities were collective (Darin-Drabkin 1955: 36). Conditions in the tent camps were often intolerable, especially during winter.

The fear of social unrest and the financial burden of supplying the immigrants' full needs (employment was hardly possible for these short-term residents) led the Agency in 1950–1951 to begin the construction of 'transit-housing sites' (*ma'abarot*) (Bernstein 1980). These were to supply interim housing until permanent housing was ready. In these sites a variety of temporary inexpensive structures were tried out: 'cloth housing', 'tin housing', 'asbestos housing', wooden shacks, and housing made of a mixture of temporary and some permanent construction materials (Darin-Drabkin 1955: 36–35). These units were tiny in size, with external toilet facilities, although some had running water. The number of immigrants who lived in these transit sites is estimated at 260,000 (Bernstein 1980: 6).

Of all the housing categories of the first period, it is the tent camps and transit sites that have remained as a collective symbol: a symbol of hardship for the hundreds of thousands of Israeli families who passed through them; a symbol of ethnic discrimination; a rallying flag for some politicians; and a symbol for decision-makers and planners of what to avoid in the future.

Permanent government-constructed housing

In 1952, the Jewish Agency and the government set out on one of the world's most ambitious housing agendas – to supply permanent adequate housing to the new immigrant households who were living in temporary housing and to those who were yet to arrive. By 1964, despite the country's low GDP, a hefty 500,000 units were constructed by the public sector (Carmon and Czamanski 1990: 519). This represented some 70–80 per cent of all housing starts in those years (ICBS 1997). It included both housing constructed directly by government, and housing constructed by a variety of quasi-public agencies. Among these were the Jewish Agency's housing corporations, the Labor Union's (*histadrut*) housing and construction corporations, and various other ideological or political party-based organizations. All these agencies received national land at no or very low cost.

The desire to construct as many housing units as possible in a short time often led the authorities to compromise on building design and construction quality. The government's chronic shortage of foreign currency for importing building materials and equipment also contributed to this negative outcome. The construction standards were basic, and inexpensive materials were used (Carmon 1997; Darin-Drabkin 1959). The need to save on costs of construction (or at least, the perceived short-term savings) led central-government planners and architects to opt for very small apartment sizes (Glikson 1958).

The massive construction project was conducted centrally, and was only marginally sensitive to differences in residents' needs and preferences. Yet, even in the early years, the physical standards for newly constructed housing usually required in-house toilet, running water, electricity, and sewerage connection (Darin-Drabkin 1959: 90). These standards represented a higher physical-facilities level than at that time prevalent in most Eastern European countries and even some western European ones.

The floor areas of the housing units constructed were extremely small. In the early 1950s, the urban housing constructed typically was only 24 square metres in size, often in low-rise double-attached or row housing. Located on the outskirts of urban areas, this housing had a quasi-rural design with relatively large lots that were planned to serve as home vegetable gardens to supplement the families' income (Glikson 1958). In many cases, however, the food-supplement assumption never worked out, whether due to economic reasons or the planners' faulty cultural assumptions. The extra land could not compensate for the sizes of the grossly inadequate housing units. The gardens lay barren in Israel's hot climate, whereas the cost of the dispersed infrastructure was very high.

In order to overcome these deficiencies, from the mid-1950s onwards, decision-makers changed the policies regarding housing design in favour of more urban densities (though by no means high). Walk-up apartment buildings with two to four stories were constructed, with ample spaces among them (once again reflecting the absence of a pricing mechanism for land and the modelling on European-type housing). Apartment sizes were gradually increased, at first to 28–32 square metres, then to an average of 44 square metres, and by the mid-1960s, to 60 square metres (ICBS 1997). The increases in size applied only to new units, so that the cumulative stock contained many very small apartments. But even the improved apartment sizes were still grossly inadequate for most families, especially for the many large families who arrived from North Africa and the Middle East.

The consumption side: group focus, rental public housing and purchase options

The focus during this period was on the immigrants as a *group* whose basic needs had to be met rather than on *individuals* and their choices. Since immigrants usually arrived in groups, often from the same country, the group focus also enabled the authorities to 'send' people to particular housing sites, temporary or permanent.

At this initial period, a large proportion of the publicly constructed permanent housing was allocated via rental. Rental charges were low, and heavily subsidized by government. Very early on during this state-building period, the central government and the Jewish Agency developed policies to encourage renters to purchase (usually, to long-term lease) their housing units (Jewish Agency 1959: 72). These included rent-to-buy programmes, subsidized mortgages with a low initial payment, and an artificially low appraisal of the value of these units.

The eligibility criteria for both temporary and permanent housing were simply that the family in question was a newly arrived immigrant family.[2] No income or property tests were used (nor were they relevant in most cases since the vast majority of immigrants during this period were penniless). For permanent housing, the eligibility criteria also included a determination that the household had no other permanent housing. In later years during this period, families who were housed in permanent but substandard structures became eligible to move to better housing, if such were available.

The outcomes of government-constructed housing

The goal of the mammoth public-housing project was to provide a permanent housing unit for each immigrant household. That goal was more-or-less achieved by the early to mid-1960s (Namir 1972). So, in quantitative terms of output (and in comparison with other countries of a similar per capita GDP) the national housing project was immensely successful. Furthermore, as we saw in the section on land and property rights, though much of the housing was initially in rental tenure format, gradually many of the residents or their off-spring managed to gain ownership of their original apartment or a future one (Jewish Agency 1959). Thus the public housing stock has served as a capital jumping-off point for many families, who were then able to gain mobility to better housing.

Today, the residents of public rental housing are not a large group in Israel. Many are elderly persons or descendants of the immigrants of the 1950s and 1960s; others are new immigrants from the former Soviet Union. The total public rental housing stock in 2004 is estimated at about 75,000. It is further declining through a variety of purchase-by-residents programmes. Only part of this housing stock dates back to the 1950s and 1960s (and has been upgraded since), while the rest was built later. The very fact that today there are only several tens of thousands of public-rental units indicates that the bulk of the housing stock constructed by the government in the 1950s and 1960s has been purchased by the residents. This attests to the success of Israel's housing policy even during Israel's initial years of very tough circumstances.

However, in other terms the public housing project was less successful. The sizes of apartments constructed by government and quasi-government bodies contrasted sharply with the sizes of apartments constructed by the private or associations sector[3] (ICBS 1997; Darin-Drabkin 1959). The private sector continued to operate after Israel's establishment and catered to those sectors of the population that could afford it. Statistics show that the disparity in sizes is maintained throughout this period. Thus whereas in 1950 the average size of housing built by the public sector was about 34 square metres, the equivalent in the private sector was about 63 (ICBS 1997). By 1965 the respective numbers were 60 compared with 90.

This disparity is compounded if one looks at household sizes and degrees of crowding. Those who could afford to purchase housing on the private market tended to be of European origin and had, on average, smaller families than the average for the new immigrants from North Africa and the Middle East. The outcome was that there was a stark disparity between the average levels of crowding among population groups, depending on their length of stay in Israel. In 1957 about 70 per cent of the immigrants who had arrived since 1948 lived in crowded conditions of over two persons per room (including the living room) and a hefty 19 per cent had an average of more than four persons per room (Darin-Drabkin 1959). By contrast, among those who had arrived pre-State, only 6 per cent had over four persons and only 39 per cent over two persons per room. Criteria of crowding were not applied in the allocation of housing until a decade or so later. Only then did public policy attempt to adapt housing-unit sizes to family sizes.

The mass construction of apartment blocks by a central body often also fell short in the qualitative aspects of design. The buildings were designed in a modern style of rectangle blocks modelled on European social housing of the time (Tanne 1959). This reflected the norms according to which most of the architects had been educated. The architecture was almost uniform, irrespective of difference in geography, climate, water availability for garden maintenance, or topography. The architects were oblivious to the differences in family, residential, and design cultures among the many ethnic groups of immigrants (Carmon and Czamanski 1990; Carmon 1999; Lerman 1976). There was little room for adjustment to different modes of living, and little room for individual stamping. The greatest disparity pertained to immigrants from the Middle East and North Africa, many of whom had been accustomed to living in a large common room or perhaps two, and a large courtyard (Swirski and Bernstein 1980: 32). The format of a small apartment divided into small rooms was alien to their lifestyle.

This type of disparity is likely to apply to many of the potential Palestinian returnees, especially those who have been living in refugee camps or villages.

Many of the buildings directly constructed by government deteriorated within a few years, not structurally, but functionally. In retrospect, the 'saving grace' of this housing was the spacious layout and the relatively small number of floors (three or four). This fact turned out to be the major unanticipated asset that in the 1980s enabled the national large-scale Project Renewal to target many of the early immigrant neighbourhoods and upgrade them. The most effective upgrading went beyond renovation, to upgrade the size of apartments. Before Project Renewal, this was done mostly by joining together two adjacent original-size apartments into a larger combined one. After the 1980s, a more audacious programme was applied, which enabled construction of entire new slabs attached to the original apartment building. These slabs added significant floor space to each apartment in the buildings, but only if the residents were interested in such intervention (Carmon and Hill 1993; Carmon 2002). Such additions were made physically possible thanks to the ample spaces between adjacent apartment buildings constructed in the 1950s, and would have not been possible had the layout been more dense or the buildings much taller.

Second period: from direct government production to direct subsidy policies –1965 to late 1970s

By the 1960s government planners and politicians realized that continued reliance on centrally designed and constructed housing would be a mistake. Herewith began a consistent trend of gradual reduction in the proportion of direct state-constructed housing and a concomitant rise in the role of the private sector in meeting national housing goals. National housing policy gradually moved along the spectrum of housing policies depicted in Figures 9.1 and 9.2, away from the public extreme, edging its way towards the second station on the way to the private-sector side.

The termination of the temporary and transit housing sites necessitated a new solution for those newly arrived immigrants who did not go directly to permanent housing of their choice. I shall first discuss the 'Absorption Centres' idea that emerged during this period, and will then move on to discuss the policies of this period concerning housing production and consumption.

A substitute for temporary housing: the absorption centres policy

From the late 1960s until 1987 Israel's immigrant-absorption policy featured the idea of 'absorption centres'. These centres combined several functions in one: temporary housing along with essential services such as restaurant, laundry, and storage; a language learning centre and lecture hall (since Hebrew was not, nor is it today, the mother tongue of most immigrants); childcare facilities such as daycare, kindergarten, and playground, a youth club and a synagogue.

The philosophy behind these centres was that new immigrants often encounter 'culture shock', and that these centres would provide the social and educational means and the mutual exchange of information to cushion this shock. Each immigrant had the right to spend several months in an absorption centre. It was assumed that since all their daily needs were taken care of, the immigrant family would be able to use their stay in the absorption centre and the guidance provided in order to search for permanent housing of their choice. But in fact, the centres tended to isolate the immigrants, often lengthening rather than shortening the immigrants' integration into Israeli society and the economy. Some immigrants developed a dependence on these centres, reducing their drive to find housing and work in the 'real world' (Leftman *et al.* 1986).

In 1986–1987 these shortcomings brought about the decision to phase out the absorption centres in favour of a new policy, the 'direct absorption' policy, the epitome of the individual-focused approach (Mikonovski and Caspi 1991). The absorption centres were subsequently used only to house immigrant groups with special needs, such as Ethiopian Jews who immigrated in groups in the 1980s and 1990s.

The consumption side: from group-based to individual-based

The group-based policy of immigrant absorption continued until the mid-1960s. In 1965 the policy was changed, to focus more on the individual household. This change of course followed the decline in numbers of immigrants. It also reflected the accumulated dissatisfaction with the outcomes of the earlier policies, especially those that directed new immigrants to 'development towns' and mass-constructed neighbourhoods (Soan and Kipnis 1971; Lichfield 1972; Swirski and Bernstein 1980; Kipnis 1990; Lifshitz 1990; Gonen 1990). Instead of a policy that offered the immigrants only limited choice about the desired housing type and location, the new policy encouraged private choice, though still within limits.

Beginning in 1965, Israeli social housing policy, which in the 1950s had been largely focused on immigrants, expanded to cover broader groups of the population. This became necessary as new families were formed, most of whom could not afford the type of housing size or location that the small private sector was constructing.

So, planners and decision-makers at the Ministry of Housing set up the rudimentary elements of Israel's 'housing eligibility' policy that has become a major attribute of Israel's housing strategy to date. The concept was that certain categories of households would be considered as 'eligible' for financial help in purchasing (or long-term leasing) a housing unit. As during all periods of Israeli housing policy, public rental housing remained restricted to the very poor and the elderly.

The main categories of eligible households were (and still are)[4]: new immigrants; young couples married within a specified number of years; and households living in substandard or crowded housing (the definition of crowding has changed over time with the rise in housing standards) (Fialkoff 1988: 11). New immigrants were, and still are, eligible for better levels of rent support, mortgage sizes, and mortgage interest rates than non-immigrant Israelis.[5] Unlike the immigrants, the levels of financial support for which non-immigrant households were eligible were based on socio-economic characteristics of the couple's parental families. The eligibility assessment method evolved gradually over the years, becoming more and more sophisticated in the use of socio-economic indicators.

Direct production subsidies: public-programme housing, 1965–1979

The gradual reduction in direct housing production by government agencies did not mean a retreat from the high position that housing held in Israeli public policy priorities. I'll even hazard to say, that the reduction in the onerous load of designing, financing, executing, delivering, and managing housing production allowed government agencies the 'space' to develop a broader and better housing policy. Rather than focusing mainly on new immigrants, the Ministry of Housing (and in the rural sector also the Jewish Agency) gradually extended its concern to broader sectors of the population and tried to tailor policies to fit a variety of household needs and capacities to pay. A variety of subsidy policies were developed, some instituted temporarily and experimentally, others applied on a long-term basis.

The quasi-public housing corporations

From the mid-1960s to the late 1970s, government policies stood at the second 'station' of Figure 9.1 and were based largely on direct subsidies to quasi-public producers. A small portion of the units was still to be constructed through direct government initiative and funding (Israel Ministry of Immigration Absorption 1975). However, the main part of the new housing policy relied on quasi-public development corporations as producers of social housing by means of production subsidies (Carmon and Czamanski 1990: 519–521). These corporations (most of which have since been privatized) were owned by the National Labor Union (*histadrut*), the Jewish Agency, various political organizations, and various other organizations recognized by the Ministry of Housing.

The housing corporations were obliged to build the subsidized housing in designated locations, according to the specific guidelines of the particular 'Program Specifications' defined by the Ministry of Housing for each site. The Ministry's planners were guided by an overall national target of annual production of units and their desired distribution among the various population groups and regions (in accordance with the national population distribution policy). The programme developed by the Ministry of Housing's architects and planners for each site became part of each developer's contract. It was rather detailed, specifying the number of units, their sizes, their target populations, and even their detailed design. The development companies had little leeway for making decisions. To ensure affordability, there were also restrictions on the maximum size of housing units. The result was that much of the public-sector housing units could easily be distinguished (in the negative sense) from private-sector ones.

During this period, the developers of public-programme housing received direct subsidies in land and infrastructure (see also the above discussion under 'Land policy'). In brief, public land was usually allocated to these corporations at a price much below market value. Some of these corporations received tracts of land that were much larger than needed to fulfill their foreseeable share of building public-programme housing. (In some cases, this accumulation of land turned out in subsequent decades to be a great source of enrichment of these later-privatized corporations). In addition, some or all of the infrastructure and public services were also subsidized by government budgets. The actual construction of these services was sometimes done by state Public Works Department, at other times by the quasi-public development corporations with government financing.

It is important to note that during the period 1965 to 1979 (approximately), those who had 'eligibility status' for subsidized mortgages could use them only towards the purchase of public-programme housing produced by the authorized corporations (Sasson 1992: 18–19). The eligible households were allowed to use their subsidized mortgages only toward the purchase of housing-corporation units (and not private-market housing). Thereby, the housing corporations were in fact ensured a consistent level of demand. Thus, the public-programme housing units were in effect subsidized both on the production side and on the consumption side.

The outcomes of the 1965–1979 housing policy

The outcomes of this period's housing policy were mixed. This policy was in part a reaction to the centralized uniformity of design and construction standards. In this respect it succeeded somewhat in softening the edge of public-sector housing. Nevertheless, the degree of control imposed on the developers through the detailed 'public programme' concept still produced less variety in housing types and sizes than the market demanded, and too much uniformity of design (Carmon 1997; Tanne 1959). This led to continued tagging of subsidized housing and in many cases, to their long-term deterioration (some became the targets of Project Renewal in the 1980s).

At the same time, this housing policy was socially more successful than the direct government-constructed housing of the 1950s. The fact that households with different backgrounds and different levels of need (expressed in a variety of eligibility levels) could purchase housing in the same neighbourhood or apartment block created a greater social mixture than before. New immigrants were no longer concentrated in housing earmarked for them. Furthermore, since the eligible households could shop around a variety of semi-public producers, this policy produced a quasi-market process. The developers built housing units with some variety in price levels that reflected location, and to some extent also differences in apartment size, density, and design. Socially uniform housing was partially avoided. Such outcomes were better for immigrant absorption than the policies of the previous period, but not yet good enough. The proof is that within a decade or two many of these units deteriorated in upkeep and price levels, trapping their residents in low-value housing units that would hamper the residents' capacity for social mobility.

Third period: indirect production incentives – Public-programme housing, 1979–1989

Starting in the later 1970s or early 1980s, Israel's housing policies moved into the third 'station' of the production-policy spectrum in Figure 9.1, mostly relying on *indirect* subsidies. Partly reflecting the all-times low in the rate of immigration and partly the privatization trends in the general economy, Israel's housing policy took several large steps towards the private-sector side of the spectrum.

Opening the private housing market to eligible households

The main change was to enable eligible households to use their subsidized mortgages on the open housing market, whether new or second-hand. Subsidized mortgages could be used towards the purchase of any housing type, in any urban area (Sasson 1992: 17). (The levels of support continued to vary by region, according to the population distribution policy.) That meant that decision-makers could relax the reliance on housing produced or directly subsidized by the government.

By 1988, the government's *direct* share in housing construction steeply declined, reaching only 5 per cent of housing starts (Alterman 2002: 53–56). Most of the quasi-government corporations were privatized (often along with the public land reserves they had accumulated during the previous period). The public programme share of housing starts also shrank greatly, from about 60 per cent in the 1970s to only 15 per cent in 1989 (CBS 1997).

The circle of developers who were eligible to participate in public-programme housing production was gradually enlarged. Private developers could present their candidacy to become authorized housing corporations and the Ministry would assess their size, capital, past performance, and reliability. These companies could then compete in tenders put out by the Ministry of Construction and Housing (or at times, by the Lands Administration).

Indirect incentives to private developers in the public-programme housing

The Ministry of Housing's goal was to ensure that housing remained affordable to eligible households. Therefore, the locations where the housing was to be built were not in high-price areas (Haber 1975). At the same time, the Ministry of Housing's policy was to serve all regions of the country, not only the peripheral regions. Affordability was to be enabled by placing caps on the sizes of apartments permissible for purchase with a subsidized mortgage by households of various sizes (Sasson 1992: 18).

The public programme specifications that the Ministry of Housing gave out to developers became more flexible and market-oriented than during the previous period. While the location of the housing project, the number of housing units, and approximate breakdown into types and sizes of apartments would be predetermined in the programme, the detailed architectural design was no longer done by the Ministry of Housing but by the developer's architect (Carmon and Czamanski 1992). To promote social mixture, the Ministry adopted a policy that required the developers to design a variety of housing types and apartment sizes within each housing complex.

The subsidies offered to the developers were smaller and less direct than during the previous period (Sasson 1992: 15–21). The system of large bonuses granted through artificial land prices was abolished in favour of a system of tender, but because the minimal price was set by the public land appraiser's office, in some cases there might be a small subsidy folded into the price of the land. However, in regions outside the high-demand areas, land prices were subsidized outright, the rate of subsidy changing from time to time and from region to region. In high-demand areas, local infrastructure costs were to be largely financed by the developer, with the Ministry or the Lands Administration participating to a lesser extent than in the past. Some land or development-based taxes were also relaxed. In addition, the degree of uncertainty about demand that developers faced was at times lower than on the open market because the Ministry had already performed an assessment of the market of households eligible to buy the public-programme housing.

The outcomes of the 1979–1989 housing policy

The quasi-privatization policies of the 1980s on both the production and the consumption sides had very positive outcomes. The sizes of apartments and their variety were greatly increased compared with the public-programme housing of the 1970s, but were still smaller and therefore more affordable than the private sector was building (CBS 1997). The architectural designs became highly varied, and the quality of construction was high. All in all, public-programme housing became almost physically undistinguishable in quality or design from private-sector housing, yet the prices were usually lower. Because the categories of 'eligible households' had been expanded, and thanks to the Ministry of Housing's policy of encouraging a mixture of apartment sizes in each apartment complex, the socioeconomic mix of residents became potentially more heterogeneous than in the past (Sasson 1992: 22–23).

However, in some locations the contrary occurred: the social mixture was more uniform than in the past. The fact that more and more eligible households chose to use their housing support to purchase housing on the open market meant that public-programme housing attracted households that had few other choices. The Hebrew term for 'housing for the eligible' increasingly became a euphemism for housing for the poor. The 1980s that saw accelerated social change in Israeli society, also brought about an increasing number of exclusionary decisions by local planning bodies along socio-economic lines.

The fourth period: the housing production strategy developed for the 1990s mass immigration wave

In 1990 when mass immigration resumed, the consistent movement towards the private-market side of the policy spectrum took a sudden partial turn-around. The government found itself having to move partly back towards the public intervention side of the spectrum – but with a difference. Public policymakers feared a repeat of the housing policies of the 1950s and tried to develop policies that would have 'antidotes' against 1950s-like policies.

The decision-making process that accompanied the most recent wave of mass immigration was unlike any that came before. By November 1989, when the gates of the USSR suddenly opened for Jewish emigrants, Israel had thoroughly changed compared to its earlier decades. The 1980s were the lowest immigration years since Israel's founding. The general public had almost forgotten the housing crises of the early years and the policies that accompanied them.

Israel had entered a decade of relative stability. The trends of privatization and deregulation in the economy had progressed far. Suddenly, between late 1989 and the beginning of 1990, came the mass-immigration crisis. The estimates were that within three to five years, between one and two million people would arrive. Government policymakers had to ensure enough housing so as to avoid two dangers: homeless immigrants on the one hand, and a hike in general housing prices due to over-demand on the other hand. So, urgently they sought for ways of increasing the housing stock as quickly as possible (Alterman 2002: 88–90).

The strategic dilemmas facing decision-makers

The 1990s housing production programme had clear, quantifiable goals: to maximize quantity and minimize production time, while yet ensuring a reasonable quality of housing. In the spring of 1990, when the official estimate of new immigrants was one to two million within three to five years, planners at the Ministry of Housing estimated that the public-programme housing sector would have to increase its production rate 14-fold, from the pre-crisis rate of some 5,000 units to 70,000 units annually. These would be added to the 15–20,000 units supplied by the private sector in a typical pre-crisis year. (Alterman 2002: 109–113).

In the initial stages of policymaking during this crisis, government decision-makers faced the following strategic dilemmas (Alterman 2002: 86–87).

- *Government or private-sector construction?* Should the government resort to direct construction of public housing, or should it harness the financial and production capacities of the private sector to the greatest extent possible? Recall from the previous section that, by the 1980s, direct public-budget housing constructed by the government had declined to a small fraction of the housing starts. Even public-programme housing, built on public land with private capital, and usually for market-rate sale, had declined to about a sixth of housing starts.
- *Build a stock of temporary housing for the short range or only permanent housing?* Should there be extensive reliance on temporary housing that can be built quickly with public funds, or should resources be

directed to permanent housing, even at the risk of having to use interim emergency shelter facilities?

- *Concentrate or disperse temporary housing sites?* If large-scale temporary housing were necessary, should it be concentrated in large sites, or should it be dispersed? Could temporary housing be planned and designed to minimize its long-term negative effects and enable the transition to permanent housing?

- *Target new construction for new immigrants or increase the general housing stock?* Should the government opt for new housing starts designed specifically for new immigrants, or should it prefer a social mixture of new immigrants and Israelis? The latter option would mean that the general stock of new housing should be increased. To be marketable, the standard of such housing would have to be higher than housing designated for new immigrants only, thus requiring a greater investment of both public and private funds.

- *Should new housing be located in regions of national priority, or where there are more job opportunities?* In the selection of locations for the new housing, should the opportunity of mass immigration be used to boost the long-standing policy of population dispersal to the peripheral regions, or should employment opportunities in the country's central region be the overruling consideration?

The crisis atmosphere enabled decision-makers to question entrenched 'sacred cow' policies. The Ministry of Finance's economists were the first to address the dilemma of population dispersal versus jobs. For the first time in Israel's history, a government body recommended a departure from the policy of population dispersal by halting any new incentives for development in the periphery. However, the Ministry of Finance's recommendation was not adopted at that time. Its document was also the first to suggest relaxation of the hitherto 'untouchable' policy of agricultural land conservation. That policy had for decades been a major stumbling block before both public and private developers who proposed the conversion of agricultural land for development on a large scale, especially in the country's central areas where demand was concentrated. The Ministry of Finance document was also the first to state the need for new land-use planning legislation to streamline the processes of plan approval (rezoning) and building permits.

The components of the 1990 housing production programme

After debating these dilemmas, planners and policymakers in the Ministry of Housing finally developed a programme that, they believed, would provide enough subsidies and incentives to stimulate the construction of the needed amount of housing. Their programme strategy was a compromise between two views: the first was that large-scale direct government-constructed housing was the right solution. The second view was that government should limit its role to regulation and the provision of approved sites on public land, but the private sector should carry out the actual construction with private capital, according to market demand, in a manner akin to the strategy developed during the 1980s – the third period discussed above (Alterman 2002: 53–56).

The compromise solution called for a relatively small number of several thousand 'emergency' units to be built as early as possible through direct government financing. However, most of the housing starts would be built with private capital but with government incentives and subsidies. This type of strategy was not new – it was similar to elements of the public-programme housing that prevailed in Israel's housing policy during the second and third periods discussed above. What was totally new was the highly fortified formula of subsidies developed for this crisis – a formula very different from anything that had existed before. In terms of the Figure 9.1 spectrum, the new strategy combined elements from the third and fourth 'stations' on the one hand, and the first station on the other.

Also very new was the overriding policy of 'direct absorption' (Mikonovski and Caspi 1991). That is, most immigrant groups would be expected to find housing on their own – whether rental housing (with rent allowance) for the initial period, or permanent housing with a subsidized mortgage. The Absorption Centres concept, phased out in 1987, was not reintroduced, except for a small number of very needy groups.

Government-supplied temporary housing

The direct government-constructed housing was of two types: temporary sites for mobile homes ('caravans') and permanent but (hopefully) rapidly constructed and modestly priced low-rise housing ('emergency housing').

The Minister of Housing wanted to import 60,000 mobile home units because he feared that permanent housing construction would take too long and thousands of families would lack any 'housing solution'. The Ministry of Finance, fearing a gross waste of national resources, wanted to minimize the number. The compromise was that 27,000 units were imported from several countries, after a worldwide tender. Planners from the Ministry of Housing and the Lands Administration located undeveloped sites, each of which could accommodate several hundreds or thousands of caravans (Feitelson *et al.* 1992; Borukhov 1998: 211).

Government-constructed permanent housing (tagged 'emergency housing')

The second component of government-constructed housing was 12,000 so-called 'emergency housing' units. This was a misnomer because these were permanent but small (45–60 square metres) low-rise units ('ground-attached' in Israeli planning jargon). These were designed so as to allow for expansion in the future either laterally or through a second floor. These units would be located on sites that could accommodate a few hundred, at a density of about 16–20 to the net acre (40–50 to the hectare). These were to be constructed only in development towns, especially in peripheral areas – the Galilee and southern area. The construction was to be inexpensive and with few frills.

The government-constructed units of the 1990s turned out to be sustainable both socially and environmentally, thanks to their low-rise format, and their wise design as 'expandable units' through a second floor.

The subsidy and incentives formula for the public programme private-capital housing production

At the beginning of the crisis, the Ministry of Housing's planners and the developers spent months bargaining over the incentive package. The developers held back action, and were tough negotiators. Only in late summer and autumn of 1990 did the Minister of Housing convince the Cabinet to override the Ministry of Finance's opposition to a more generous package of incentives to the developers (Alterman 2002: 97–100). The package of incentives and conditions was composed of several main elements:

- *Bonuses for speed and innovation in construction modes*: This incentive offered very generous bonuses to stimulate the speed of construction. These could reach $15,000 (per unit?) if a unit were completed within seven months or less. Bonuses for longer periods were also generous.

- *Allocation of public land*: The second type of incentive called for the allocation of public land to developers at no cost. This policy was applied equally in most parts of the country excepting the high-demand central region where subsidies were at 'only' half-price. Since land prices there were much higher than on the periphery, the value of this bonus was very significant. In late 1991, this policy was abolished for the central region, as evidence corroborated initial expert opinion that in a 'sellers' market' subsidies accrue to the developers and are not passed on to the immigrants or other consumers.

- *Infrastructure costs covered*: This incentive did not draw as much attention as the previous two. The Ministry of Housing offered to cover virtually all developers' infrastructure costs – roads, sewerage, and public services.

- *The buy-up commitment*: This subsidy was perhaps the most significant. The developers argued vehemently that a buy-up commitment was necessary, but government was very reluctant to grant it. The developers were concerned that they would need to commit huge resources in the face of great uncertainty. They argued that to increase production capacity dramatically, they would have had to invest large sums in new equipment; import manpower; train local labour, and absorb high financing costs. Yet, the immigrants might suddenly stop coming or might not have enough income to obtain financing for mortgages. After tough negotiations, government finally agreed to buy up any units that developers did not succeed in selling within a specified period of time, and to pay the developers 100 per cent of the agreed-upon value of each unit. In the high-demand central region, the government committed itself to buying up 'only' 50 per cent of the units. The buy-up commitment, however, had a price ceiling, as noted next.

- *A price ceiling*: A ceiling of approximately $80,000 was set for the buy-up commitment. Since most developers wanted to be eligible

for the exercise of the buy-up commitment, if that became necessary, it was assumed that they would keep to the price ceiling.
The ceiling was intended to serve two purposes: to ensure that the
new housing would be affordable, and to save on public funds
should the government have to activate its buy-up commitment.

- *No restrictions on the 'status' of the potential buyers:* This incentive was
  a notable departure from the traditional policy of public-
  programme housing in which the housing was specifically designated for new immigrants and other earmarked households such
  as young couples. Since the purpose of the crisis-time programme was to increase the *total* housing stock, it was decided
  that all the units could be sold on the open market, to anyone.
  This policy also served the planning goal of avoiding social seg-
  regation and neighbourhood deterioration, and the developers'
  goal of opening the market to anyone who could pay. This rule
  helped increase the potential demand for the public-programme
  housing, making it even more attractive to developers.

- *Uniform application:* The incentive programme was to apply coun-
  trywide, to all local authorities and all sites on public land that the
  government slated for public-programme housing (with a distinc-
  tion between the central and peripheral regions). But despite the
  ostensible uniformity, the price ceiling was not always maintained,
  as the Comptroller General noted in her 1992 Report (Alterman
  2002: 111). Furthermore, some astute local authorities were able
  to negotiate minor variations in the programme, such as better
  design control or use of external materials, as I have shown in previous research that compared how two 'matched' local authorities
  handled the ostensibly uniform centrally imposed guidelines in
  significantly different ways (Alterman 2002: 146–169).

The economically sophisticated formula for public programme
private-capital housing of the 1990s turned out to be very successful
in stimulating the private housing construction market to produce an
amount of housing ten-fold its usual production.

Tax exemption to encourage the private rental market

The only incentive provided during the crisis to the private housing
market was an exemption from the 10 per cent income tax that

applied to private rentals before the crisis. This initiative, proposed jointly by Housing and Finance, was enacted in 1990. In the virtual absence of housing constructed especially for rental (this has been so throughout Israel's history), the ad-hoc rental market by individuals who own more than one apartment or are abroad has provided the major rental stock in Israel. Many economists and planners credit the tax exemption with the great increase in the rental housing stock that suddenly appeared during the mass-immigration crisis. I have my doubts because much individual rental income was never reported either before the crisis or during it. The increased supply was due to a steep increase in demand and the resulting hike in prices that made it lucrative to rent out vacant, poorly maintained, or previously converted housing units.

Consumption-side policies in the 1990s: the evolution of subsidies to eligible households for rental and for purchase

The policies developed during the 1990s were the most sophisticated not only on the production side, but also in the consumption side. Before introducing these in detail, I shall summarize the evolution of these policies until the 1990s.

The evolution of consumer-side policies until the 1990s

A consistent element of Israel's housing financial support policy to immigrants has been to provide them with enough money to rent housing during their start-up years, but to encourage them to purchase housing as soon as possible. This meant that, unlike non-immigrant Israelis, immigrant households are eligible for initial rental support, but only for a limited number of years (except for the very needy or elderly). Alongside the opening-up of the private housing market to eligible households, the rental support system too was opened up and gradually deregulated. The particulars of the rental support policy have changed with time, but the details are beyond the scope of this report.

While Israel's policy of encouraging housing purchase has been a consistent leitmotif, the subsidies towards housing purchase have not always been in direct relationship to housing or immigrant absorption goals. Being a major government expenditure item, the levels of support have changed with Israel's macro-economic and social policies, or in response to interest-group political consider-ations. The size of the mortgages and the levels of subsidy of the interest rates were not always very generous, often lagging much behind the hikes in housing prices, especially during high-inflation periods. The levels of subsidy have consistently been part of the national population distribution policy (Alterman 2002: 50–56; Gal'on 1998). This has meant that the size of mortgages and the levels of subsidy would be higher for the same eligibility category in peripheral and border areas than in the central region.

During the early stages of the mass-immigration period of the early 1990s, the consumer-side strategy was very similar to what had been in effect in the 1980s. That is, under the 'direct absorption' policy, new immigrants were offered rental subsidies for a limited period of time so as to substitute for temporary housing. After that period, it was hoped that most new immigrants would be able to buy (or long-term lease) a housing unit, with the help of subsidized mort-gages available to immigrants at privileged terms compared with other eligible categories of Israeli households. The basic categories remained the same as in the 1980s (Israel Ministry of Housing 1989, 1990: Table 11). However, with time, as feedback accumulated from the Ministry of Absorption and the Ministry of Housing, several lessons were learnt.

There has been a gradual shift from rental support granted to the house owner (requiring immigrants to give the authorities copies of the rental leases) to a policy that made the rental support entirely liquid, to be used at the family's discretion. The length of time during which immigrants would be granted rental support and the levels of support varied from time to time in accordance with the monitoring data about the rates of housing purchases (Gal'on 1998).

Rental allowances and the living-support 'basket'

As a result of feedback, several important policy improvements were made in the rental allowances. The first change pertained to the target of the allowances. At first, the allowances were earmarked for housing only, and renters had to produce the leases to prove that the allowances were used legally. This not only caused difficulties for the immigrants, but also led to a hike in rental prices as renters realized that the immigrants had a particular assured sum earmarked for rental only. So, decision-makers changed the policy, later allowing immigrants to receive the rental allowance as part of the total absorption-support 'basket'.

The second change pertained to the permission to pool allowances. Initially, only one rental allowance could be used per household. With time, this was relaxed to allow more than one family to share an apartment with relatives or non-related persons. This turned out to be the 'great saviour' in that it allowed the rental housing stock – very limited at the outset of the crisis – to 'stretch' itself according to demand and prices.

The third policy improvement dealt with the time limit of the allowances. Initially, the rental allowances were limited to a short period of time and were tied to the production of an actual rental contract. This caused not only stress to many households, but also misinformation, and a tendency by some to delay housing purchase in order not to lose out on the free allowance. Decision-makers found that it was best to lengthen the period of time to allow more households to stabilize their job situation and to have a longer horizon before making the decision to take out a mortgage for housing purchase.

Subsidized mortgages

The key consumption-side policy remained as in the 1980s (the third 'station' of the spectrum in Figure 9.2). That is, households were each eligible to take out a mortgage according to the number of persons, and these could be used towards the purchase of any unit on the open market (Israel Ministry of Housing 1990: Table 11). With time, a very important relaxation was made that moved the strategy of the 1990s further along our spectrum of policies, into the fourth station. Whereas during the early periods each family had been eligible for only one mortgage, in the early 1990s policymakers reacted to the many requests to combine mortgages. They made the highly critical decision to allow more than one mortgage to be used towards the purchase of a single housing unit (Israel Ministry of Housing 2004: 5).

Many immigrant households have made extensive use of the new flexible policy. For instance, some families took in one or two grandparents, while some parents pooled their eligibility with that of an unmarried adult child. Because there was a housing shortage during the early 1990s, this new policy was not only helpful to the immigrants, it also helped to stretch the housing stock and to increase the rate of housing purchase. While the permission to combine mortgages has generally been a very successful policy, allowing households to set their own priorities and to gain tenure security faster, there have been cases of misuse within families. All in all, however, this policy has been an important factor in the success of the 1990s housing strategy.

The immigrant mortgage system that evolved after the mass-immigration wave of the early 1990s is the most successful in Israel's history (relative to the country's resources). The additional flexibility introduced regarding household choices has been important in enabling an exceedingly high rate of immigrants to gain housing security in a relatively short time – probably one of the highest rates of success in the world. The majority of immigrant families have been able to buy a housing unit within 5–7 years of their arrival.

The outcomes of the public-programme housing of the 1990s

By 1993, the results of the housing-production onslaught were visible everywhere. The policy formula developed led to the delivery of some 100,000 'affordable' housing units, mostly in the form of condominium apartments. These generally were built to a good standard, despite the speeding-up incentives. In some towns, especially the smaller ones, entire new neighbourhoods sprang up, thoroughly changing the physical and social landscape of these towns. The construction blitz added a much-needed stock of medium-sized and smaller apartments to Israel's housing market (Alterman 2002: 104–114).

The housing programme largely relied on the 'trickle down' process. The policymakers' goal was not just to increase the general housing stock so as to avoid homelessness; they hoped that the majority of immigrant households would be able to become homeowners (usually meaning apartment owners) just like the general population. Like the other eligible population groups since the 1980s, the new immigrants were allowed to use their government-subsidized mortgages towards the purchase of *any* housing unit of their choice, whether in the public or private sector (Alterman 105–113).

By September 1999, 73 per cent of the immigrant households that had arrived during the 1990s had already purchased their own housing unit, despite the hike in housing prices that occurred until 1996. Remarkably, this figure is about the same as the equivalent figure for home ownership by the total Israeli population! (Alterman 2002: 113–114). The picture becomes even more impressive if the immigrants are classified by year of arrival in Israel. The new immigrants may achieve an even higher home-ownership rate than the total Israeli population. Among the immigrant households who arrived in 1990, a hefty 91 per cent have already purchased their home, and of those who arrived in the massive wave of 1990 and 1991, 88 per cent and 81 per cent, respectively, have bought a housing unit (Alterman 2002: 114). Even among the immigrants who arrived in 1996, about half had managed to buy a housing unit within three years. These figures also provide an indirect indication of the reasonable success of employment and economic integration.

CONCLUSION

The Israeli experience with immigrant absorption, especially in the area of housing policy, has been very successful in international comparative terms. One of the keys to success has been the capacity of decision-makers to learn from their own mistakes and adjust their policies. This is not to say that the learning process has been adequate, or that mistakes were not repeated. However, in many countries, housing policy suffers from governmental failure more than some other areas of socio-economic intervention. Furthermore, government failure in immigrant absorption is also a common malady in many countries, often compounding the problems encountered in forging housing policies particularly for new immigrants (Carmon 1996).

In the above pages I have attempted to point out those elements of Israel's evolving immigrant-absorption policies that have been more successful, and those to avoid.

In conclusion, I present in Table 9.3 a comparison of the outputs and outcomes of the housing strategies applied in Israel over the various periods. The table shows the gross public investment (in constant IS). These figures should be seen, of course, in relation to the country's economy at each period. In the 1950s, the investment in housing constituted some 35 per cent of the government's total

Table 9.3: *The outputs and outcomes of the housing strategies in key policy periods*

Key periods and their characteristics	Gross annual public investment in housing (million NS)	Average no. public housing units built annually	Average size of private initiated housing unit in m²	Average size of public-initiated housing in m²	Percentage of population living in crowded housing *
1948–1951 Mass immigration	804		50	28	
1952–1959 Moderate, mainly North Africa	1,202	19,372	75	45	58
1960–1966 Moderate, North Africa, Romania	1,939	44,760	92	61	39
1967–1970 Low immigration	1,441	8,750	104	74	29
1971–1976 Wave from the USSR	3,805	21,130	110	73	23
1967–1985 Low level – South American and affluent countries	2,180	10,580	126	86	16.2
1986–1989 Stagnation: Immigration and emigration balance	886	3,520	144.4	98	12.5
1990–1992 Mass immigration from former USSR	5,569	34,660	148	85	11.5

1993–2004 Moderate wave from CIS tapering down after 2001	2,867	18,475	152	105	7.9

Source: ICBS 1997, 1998

Note: * More than two persons per room ('room' includes bedrooms and living rooms but not kitchen).

expenditures (Darin-Drabkin 1959). In later periods, this percentage declined.

The table also shows how despite the intake of mass immigration, housing standards in Israel have risen constantly.[6] The rise in housing standards has applied both to private and public sector housing. In fact, during the 1990s' mass immigration crisis, the government had to make a special effort to reduce the average size of apartments constructed (Alterman 2002: 111–113), which can also be seen in Table 9.3.

So, despite the fact that during Israel's initial years the economy was similar to Palestine's today, and in the 1950s the degree of crowding was 58 per cent, it has declined to 8 per cent today. If one adds an important indicator not shown in the table – the rate of home ownership among all Israelis and the even higher rate among the newest immigrants (well over 70 per cent), one can support the conclusion that Israel's housing policy offers important lessons for other countries.

I personally hope that this report will contribute to the transfer of knowledge among the closest next-door neighbours and that the lessons from the evolution of Israel's policies – both successes and mistakes – can soon be applied usefully to address the intake of Palestinian returnees and the upgrading of current refugee and other inadequate housing. Hopefully, a peaceful settlement between Israel and Palestine will arrive soon.

BIBLIOGRAPHY[7]

Alba, R.D and Logan, J.R. (1992) 'Assimilation and Stratification in the Homeownership Patterns of Racial and Ethnic Groups', *International Migration Review* 26 (4): 1314–1341.

Alterman, R. (1988) 'Opening up the "Black Box" in evaluating neighborhood programs: The implementation process in Israel's project renewal', *Policy Studies Journal* 16 (2): 347–361.

—— (1997) 'The Challenge of Farmland Preservation: Lessons from a Six-country Comparison', *Journal of the American Planning Association* 63 (2): 220–243.

—— (1999) *Between National Land Ownership and Privatization: A Future Land Policy for Israel*, Jerusalem: Floresheimer Institute for Policy Research (Hebrew).

—— (2000) 'Land-use Law in the Face of a Rapid-Growth Crisis: The Case of the Mass-immigration to Israel in the 1990s', *Washington University Journal of Law and Policy* 3: 773–840.

—— (ed.) (2001) *National-Level Planning in Democratic Countries: An International Comparison of City and Regional Policy-Making*, Liverpool: Liverpool University Press.

—— (2001a) 'National-level Planning in Democratic Countries: A Cross-national Perspective', in Alterman, R. (ed.) (2001) *National-Level Planning in Democratic Countries: An International Comparison of City and Regional Policy-Making*, Liverpool: Liverpool University Press.

—— (2001b) 'National-level Planning in Israel: Walking the Tightrope between Centralization and Privatization' in Alterman, R. (ed.) (2001) *National-Level Planning in Democratic Countries: An International Comparison of City and Regional Policy-Making*, Liverpool: Liverpool University Press.

—— (2002) *Planning in the Face of Crisis: Land Use, Housing, and Mass Immigration in Israel*, London: Routledge.

—— (2003) 'The Land of Leaseholds: Israel's Extensive Public Land-Ownership in an Era of Privatization' in Burassa and Yu Hung Hong (eds) *Leasing Public Land: Policy Debates and International Experiences*, Cambridge, MA: Lincoln Institute of Land Policy.

Alterman, R. and Cars, G. (eds) (1991) *Neighborhood Regeneration: An International Evaluation*, London: Mansell.

Alterman, R. and Churchman, A. (1991) *Israel's Neighborhood Renewal Program: The Great Experiment and its Lessons*, Technion: Samuel Neaman Institute Books.

Alterman, R. and Haddadin, M. (forthcoming) *Transfer and Adaptation of Planning Laws: How British-Based Planning Legislation Has Persevered in Israel and Jordan.*

Benchertrit, G. and Czamanski, D. (2004) 'The Gradual Abolition of the Public Leasehold System in Israel and Canberra: What Lessons can be Learned?' *Land Use Policy* 21 (1): 45–57 (January).

Bernstein, D. (1980) '*The Transit Camps in the 50s*', *Notebooks for Research and Criticism* 5: 5–47, Haifa (Hebrew).

Borukhov, E. (1998) 'Immigrant Absorption and Housing: Influences on the Construction Sector', in Leshem, E. and Sikron, M. (eds) *Profile of Aliya: Absorption Processes of the Former Soviet Union Immigrants 1990–1995*, Jerusalem: The Hebrew University in Jerusalem, pp. 207–231 (Hebrew).

Brutzkus, E. (1964) *Physical Planning in Israel: Problems and Achievements*, Jerusalem: Israel Ministry of the Interior.

—— (1969) *Regional Policy in Israel*, International Federation for Housing and Planning, Israeli Section.

Carmon, N. (1992) 'Israel's Project Renewal: Evaluation of Goals Achievement', in Elazar, D.J. and Marom, Z.R. (eds), *Urban Revitalization – Israel's Project Renewal and Other Experiences*, New York: University Press of America.

—— (1996) 'Immigration and Integration in Post-Industrial Societies: Qualitative and Quantitative Analysis', in: Carmon, N. (ed.) *Immigration and Integration in Post-Industrial Societies: Theoretical Analysis and Policy Implications*, London: Macmillan, pp. 21–35.

—— (1999) 'Housing in Israel: The First Fifty Years', in Nachmias, D. and Menahem, G. (eds) *Public Policy in Israel*, Jerusalem: The Israel Democracy Institute, pp. 381–436 (Hebrew).

—— (2001) 'Housing Policy in Israel: Review, Evaluation and Lessons', *Journal of Israel Affairs* 7 (4): 181–208.

—— (2002) 'User-Controlled Construction and Renovation: Desirability and Feasibility' *European Planning Studies* 10 (3): 285–303.

Carmon, N. and Czamanski, D. (1990) *Housing in Israel: From Planned Economy to Semi-free Market Management*, Haifa: Center for Urban and Regional Studies, Faculty of Architecture and Town Planning, Technion-Israel Institute of Technology.

Cohen, Z., Yehezkel, F. and Israel, K. (1993) *Land Policy in a Time of National Immigrant Absorption 1990–1991: Examination of Economic and Physical Aspects*, Jerusalem: Center for Information and Economic Analysis, Israel Ministry of Housing (Hebrew).

Darin-Drabkin, H. (1955) *Housing and Absorption in Israel 1948–1955*, Tel-Aviv, Gadish (Hebrew).

—— (1959) *Public Housing in Israel: Surveys and Evaluations of Activities in Israel's First Decade (1948–1958)*, Tel-Aviv: Gadish.

Feitelson, E., Margalit, Y., and Pilzer, D. (1992) 'The national Outline Scheme for Emergency Housing', in Golani, Y., Eldor, S., and Garon, M. (eds) *Planning and Housing in Israel, in the Wake of Rapid Change*, Tel-Aviv: Israel Ministry of Interior.

Fialkoff, C. (1988) 'Building Policy for Urban Dwellings: A General View', in Harlap, A. (ed.) *Israel Builds*, Jerusalem: Israel Ministry of Housing (Hebrew).

Gal-On, Z. (1998) *The Integration of the Former Soviet Union Immigrants at the Housing Market in Israel* (MA Thesis), Tel-Aviv: Tel-Aviv University (Hebrew).

Garon, M. (1992) 'The National Outline Schemes for the Geographical Distribution of the Population', in Golani, Y., Eldor, S., and Garon, M. (eds) *Planning and Housing in Israel, in the Wake of Rapid Change*, Tel-Aviv: Israel Ministry of Interior.

Glikson, A. (1958) *Problems of National and Town Planning in Israel*, Japheth Printing Press.

Gonen, A. (1990) 'Population Distribution and Immigrants Absorption as Collision Assignments', in Gonen, A. (ed.) *Geography of Immigrant Absorption: Lessons from the Past and a Glance Toward the Future*, Jerusalem: Department of Geography, The Hebrew University in Jerusalem (Hebrew).

Haber, A. (1975) *The Population and the Construction in Israel: 1948–1973*, Jerusalem: Israel Ministry of Housing (Hebrew).

Israel Central Bureau of Statistics (1950–2005) *Statistical Yearbook*, Annual Reports, Jerusalem: Central Bureau of Statistics.

—— (1997) Special publications series – *Housing in Israel*, Jerusalem: Central Bureau of Statistics (Hebrew).

—— (1998) Special publications series – *Immigrant Absorption*, Jerusalem: Central Bureau of Statistics (Hebrew).

—— (1999) Fiftieth anniversary publications series – *National Accounts*, Jerusalem: Central Bureau of Statistics (Hebrew).

Israel Ministry of Housing (1989) *Assistance for New Immigrants*, Jerusalem: Ministry of Housing (Hebrew).

—— (1990) *Assistance for New Immigrants*, Jerusalem: Ministry of Housing (Hebrew).

—— (2004) *Assistance for New Immigrants*, Jerusalem: Ministry of Housing (Hebrew).

Israel Ministry of Immigrant Absorption (1975) *Immigration and Its Absorption 1970–1975*, Jerusalem: Ministry of Immigrant Absorption (Hebrew).

Jewish Agency (1959) *11 Years of Absorption: Facts, Problems and Numbers for the Period 15 of May 1948 to 15 of May 1959*, Tel-Aviv: Jewish Agency (Hebrew).

Kipnis, B. (1990) 'Did We Unwind the Population Distribution Policy?', in Gonen A. (ed.) *Geography of Immigrant Absorption: Lessons from the Past and a*

Glance toward the Future, Jerusalem: Department of Geography, The Hebrew University in Jerusalem (Hebrew).

Knesset Information Center (2001) *Report by Yifat Shai on 'Requests to Move by Residents of Public Housing'* Available at: <http://www.knesset.gov.il/ mmm/doc.asp?doc=m00111&type=pdf> (Hebrew).

Law Yone, H. and Kalus, R. (1995) *Housing in Israel: Policy and Inequality*, Tel-Aviv: ADVA Center.

Leftman, A., Tzarfaty, D. and Asmara, D. (1986) *The Absorption Center Direction: From Absorption Center to Aliya Center*, Jerusalem: Jewish Agency (Hebrew).

Lerman, R. (1976) *A Critical Overview of Israel Housing Policy*, Jerusalem: Brookdale Institute.

Lichfield, N. (1972) 'Development Policy of New Towns in Israel', *Environmental Planning* 19–20: 17–48 (Hebrew).

Lifshitz, G. (1990) 'Aliya, Internal Immigration and the creation of inter-regional Gaps', in Gonen A. (ed.) *Geography of Immigrant Absorption: Lessons from the Past and a Glance toward the Future*, Jerusalem: Department of Geography, The Hebrew University in Jerusalem (Hebrew).

Megbolugbe, I.F. and Linneman, P.D. (1993) 'Home Ownership', *Urban Studies* 30(4/5): 659–682.

Mikonovski, Y. and Caspi, S. (1991) *Direct Absorption Course as a Prime Objective of Ministry of Immigration Absorption Preparation for the Mass Immigration of the 90s* (MA Thesis), Tel-Aviv: Tel-Aviv University (Hebrew).

Namir, M. (1972) *In the Face of the Transit Camps* ('Ma'abarot'), Tel-Aviv: Orpaz.

Rubinstein, A. (1996). *The Constitutional Law of the State of Israel*, Tel Aviv: Schocken Publishing House.

Sasson, H. (1992) *Privatization Processes at the Ministry of Housing: Trends and Prospects* (MA Thesis), Tel Aviv: Program of Public Policy, Tel-Aviv University (Hebrew).

Soen, D. and Kipnis, B. (1971) 'Afula, Nazareth Illit and Migdal Ha'emek: Analysis of the Development Towns Cluster', *Environmental Planning Quarterly* 1–10 (Hebrew).

Swirski, S. and Bernstein, D. (1980) 'Who worked, in what, for whom and for what?', *Notebooks for Research and Criticism* 5: 5–66, Haifa (Hebrew).

Swirski, S. and Katzir, S. (1978) 'Ashkenazi and Mizrahi Jews: Dependency Relationship Created', *Notebooks for Research and Criticism* 1: 21–59, Haifa (Hebrew).

Tanne, D. (1959) 'The Public Building in Israel: Problems and Prospects' in Darin-Drabkin, H. (ed.) *Public Housing in Israel: Surveys and Evaluations of Activities in Israel's First Decade (1948–1958)*, Tel-Aviv: Gadish.

CHAPTER 10

Israeli settlements and the Palestinian refugee question: Evaluating the prospects and implications of settlement evacuation in the West Bank and Gaza – a preliminary analysis

Geoffrey Aronson and Jan de Jong, Foundation for Middle East Peace, Washington, DC

PALESTINIAN SPATIAL DEVELOPMENT in the Israeli-occupied West Bank, East Jerusalem and Gaza Strip is characterized by a number of factors. Some of these are expressions of an authentic Palestinian response to population growth and economic and social development. Others are the product of Jordan's rule or the endemic conflict with Israel and the massive dislocations that result from prolonged occupation, Israeli settlement expansion, and the lack of sovereign control over the allocation of national resources. The resulting system of towns and villages in this Palestinian region reflects its organic, haphazard, unplanned, pre-industrial antecedents.

Israeli settlements and their associated infrastructure, in contrast, are modern, purpose-built communities planned to consolidate a national political strategy. They are not merely bricks and mortar to be integrated seamlessly into this troubled Palestinian reality. Their existence is the product of a set of assumptions, objectives, and circumstances, certainly different from, if not antithetical to premises that animate Palestinian society. It need only be said that settlements were fashioned as part of a zero-sum contest to conquer and control space, and thereby stifle rather than cultivate and nurture the development of Palestinian life, to suggest the depth of the potential antagonisms to Palestinian development that they represent.

Settlements were consciously constructed in order to offer their Israeli residents a marginally better living and communal environment than comparable locations in Israel. The standard of services made available to settlers, from housing size to education and public amenities, has proved to be a costly investment counted in billions of dollars. Per capita operation and maintenance costs in settlements, reflected in capital transfers from the national government to settlements, are far higher than the average within Israel, let alone those in Palestinian cities and towns of the West Bank and Gaza Strip. The entire municipal budget of Bethlehem, according to the city's mayor, is only US $3.5 million, a sum that pales before the budget of Ma'ale Adumim, a nearby settlement. This extraordinary expenditure is responsible for the present high standards maintained in most settlements, but this level of expenditure would be unsustainable if such areas were to be evacuated by Israel and come under Palestinian rule.

Notwithstanding the antipathetic objectives that inspired Israel's construction of settlements and their high operating costs, and regardless of whether settlements are evacuated in the context of a final status or interim agreement, or indeed as a unilateral measure, Palestinians will be presented with the challenge of integrating the evacuated sites into the existing Palestinian social, economic, and national-political structures, either by utilizing the resources which come into their possession or by destroying them as uneconomical or inconsistent with Palestinian interests.

The tabulation of settlement assets is a straightforward if time-consuming exercise and the task lends itself to quantification and assembly in database form. Assessing the value – and not only in strict monetary terms – of these assets for the Palestinian community is a far more prosaic exercise.

The limited discussion of this matter to date has been framed by three widely shared assumptions: first, that evacuated settlements represent a natural and self-evident value to the Palestinian community; second, that the transition from Israeli to Palestinian use would be a natural and seamless one; and third, that refugees are the most logical inheritors of housing vacated by settlers. Our assessment of the potential utility to the Palestinian community of settlement assets evacuated by Israel, a study funded by Canada's International Development Research Centre, was in large part the product of such assumptions. However, we do not see such assumptions as self-evident, nor indeed as necessarily accurate, and our inquiry has not been guided by them.

Our efforts represent the first attempt to create a comprehensive settlement database and to investigate the question of what value, if any, these assets represent for Palestinians. We assume that these assets will be left intact by Israel as they withdraw and that they will be secured for Palestinian use by Palestinians or others in the aftermath of withdrawal. Our analysis on the utility of settlements for Palestinians is based, as it should be, on principles and plans generated by the Palestinians themselves. The context in which these assets will be used, and the social and political priorities that fashion the world in which the settlements and their assets will be exploited, is a Palestinian one. As a consequence, we have not sought to create new paradigms but rather, insofar as is possible, to use existing Palestinian plans as informative baselines from which to assess the utility, or lack thereof, of settlements evacuated in a variety of possible scenarios.

DEVELOPMENT AND URBANIZATION

Palestinian habitation is characterized by the Palestinian Authority's Ministry of Planning (MOP) as

> a system of built-up areas developed more or less randomly, scattered by man-made interference, with the topography lacking the essential inter-linking infrastructure in terms of network facilities that characterize a mature and well-developed settlement system. ... The main challenge for the future is to achieve a balanced development, one that accommodates socio-economic needs generated through population growth, and development towards economic and environmental sustainablility.
>
> (MOPIC 1998: 6–7)

THE GAZA STRIP

The Gaza Strip has an area of 365 km^2 with a built-up area of 15 per cent of the total, and a population of approximately

1.2 million, a number which will double by 2015. As the Gaza Governorates Regional Plan (MOPIC 1997) notes, one large core city, Gaza City, contains one third of the entire population and dominates the road network, which runs in a north–south direction. Refugee camps and urban villages dominate the middle region, while small cities and towns characterize both northern and southern extremities.

The Gaza Governorates Regional Plan anticipates the repatriation to Gaza of 590,000 returnees by 2015. It supports the development model 'Two Core Cities', which proposes that Gaza City and Khan Yunis will absorb more than one half of the area's projected population growth, including 30 per cent and 70 per cent of returnees respectively, with numerous local centres located throughout the area absorbing the remainder and providing local services. This 'compact pattern of development' with accompanying high population densities best suits the dual requirements of providing housing and maximal utilization of land for agricultural use and environmental protection. The plan also calls for the protection of most of the lands associated with the settlements in the Katif bloc and in the northwestern corner of Gaza. This is necessary in order to preserve land for recreation and agriculture, and to protect aquifers.

Housing densities are an average of 17 persons/dunam (pd), increasing to 90 pd in Shati camp (10 dunams = 1 hectare). The plan calls for an increase in density in already built-up areas to 37 pd and the resettlement of 70 per cent of refugee camp residents to new areas by 2015. This ratio suggests that a neighbourhood of 5,000 residents requires 130 dunams, including 65 dunams for housing (5.5 housing units/dunam), 32.5 dunams for services and open space, and 32.5 dunams for transportation. These standards translate into 3,925 dunams required to support a population of 100,000, at a density of 3.6 housing units/dunam.

Based upon these standards, and given the need to rehabilitate run-down housing and provide housing for refugees resettling from camps, there is a need to create 266,000 new residential units by 2015. This figure may be broken down as follows: 186,000 units for population increase; 51,000 units for resettled refugees; and 29,000 new units for urban renewal.

WEST BANK

According to the 1998 Ministry of Planning Regional Plan for the West Bank Governorates, by 2020, the Palestinian population of 2.3 million in the West Bank, including East Jerusalem, is estimated to increase to 3.8 million, including 780,000 immigrants, with an economically active population of almost 2.5 million aged 15 to retirement (currently 890,000, of whom only 42.5 per cent are in the labour force).

The existing built-up areas of the West Bank – living space characterized by scattered, decentralized low-density development which is almost the exact opposite of development in settlements – will need to be doubled by 2010 in order to accommodate the projected population increase (MOPIC 1997: 25).

The existing housing infrastructure in the West Bank is 238,000 units, of which 18,000 are located in refugee camps. The average housing density is 2.2 persons/room, increasing to 2.5 in camps. During the 1997–2010 period, 280,000 units will need to be constructed, including 30,000 units in existing built-up areas, for a net total of 250,000 units.

The total area required for new developments is 258 km². There are three options for residential development at varying densities:

(A) 168 km² is required for residential use for construction of 250,000 units at a density of 670m² land/unit, and 1.5 units/dunam

(B) 92 km² is required for residential use for construction of 250,000 units at a density of 365 m² land/unit, and 2.7 units/dunam

(C) 64 km² is required for residential use for construction of 250,000 units at a density of 257 m² land/unit, and 3.9 units/dunam

The Palestinian Authority (PA) Ministry of Planning (MOP) targets the low density Option A as the realistic scenario, which suggests an approximate figure of 1.5 hu/dunam or 1,500 housing units (hu) per km².

UTILITY OF SETTLEMENT HOUSING

Roughly speaking, if the 168 km² of land noted in Option A is related to the more than 100 km² area of civilian Israeli settlement in the

West Bank and East Jerusalem, and the approximately 100,000 housing units therein, the simple conclusion is that if all settlement housing stock were evacuated, that is, if Israel withdrew from all
territories occupied in June 1967, the remaining housing infrastructure would numerically satisfy 40 per cent (100,000 of 250,000) of
the MOP-projected West Bank housing needs. Furthermore, the
45,000 urban settlement housing units in East Jerusalem occupy
12.5 km². This density rate of 3,600 hu/km² is more than double the
targeted Palestinian (low) housing density, but only slightly higher
than the Palestinian high density figure.

According to this simple analysis, in a best-case scenario, all settlement housing stock available in all West Bank settlements would provide for 20 per cent of projected Palestinian housing requirements in
the period to 2010. Housing in all East Jerusalem settlement areas
would equally support an additional 20 per cent of projected housing
needs.

The rates for the Gaza Strip are far less significant. The 1,200 Gaza
settlement units, which supported a population of 7,500 on the eve
of their evacuation and subsequent destruction in mid-2005, represented less than 1 per cent (1,200 of 237,000 new units required).

The Palestinian development plan explores four models for the
distribution of the projected population increase (natural increase
plus immigration). Model 1 postulates proportionally equal growth
for every locality, roughly doubling the population of each by 2020.
Model 2 projects all growth will be channelled to 35 main towns and
large villages. Model 3 divides this growth as follows: 60 per cent to
Nablus, Metropolitan Jerusalem and Hebron, and 40 per cent to the
remaining towns in the previous group of 35. Model 4 restricts all
growth to the West Bank's central ridge locales along Route 60.

The Ministry of Planning selected Model 4 as the preferred option.
We will assess the potential contribution settlement housing could
make to satisfying Palestinian housing needs defined by this model.

The Palestinian plan favours urban 'growth-poles' growing out of
existing towns and villages. This is a sound and fruitful concept.
MOP projects that the biggest demand for land for residential expansion will focus on the ridge corridor along Route 60, especially
between Ramallah and Bethlehem (MOPIC 1998). Models 3 and 4
channel much population growth to Metropolitan Jerusalem,

doubling today's population in this area by the year 2020. The 60,000 settlement housing units in metropolitan Jerusalem – using an average occupancy ratio of 8 persons per housing unit – would largely accommodate the projected need of Model 3 or 4. The built-up areas of these settlements, however, are least likely to be evacuated. Such an analysis raises the question of whether the remaining 40,000 settler housing units in the rest of the West Bank would be equally suited to meet MOP targets.

In this analysis, optimal housing and productivity zones (cultivation, commerce, industry) will be measured in terms of the most vital constraints to housing and urban development. In particular, the analysis focuses on the effect of the different strategies on agriculturally significant lands, determined by use of the Palestinian Economic Council for Development and Reconstruction (PECDAR) Strategic Water Plan, including those that come into Palestinian possession as a consequence of settlement evacuation; ecologically significant areas; and areas with high water sensitivity and landscape quality.

Gross indicators offer a basic and often not very helpful way of assessing the suitability of settlement housing for Palestinian needs. At one end of the spectrum considerations related to suitability may not be decisive, as price differentials will reflect the marketplace's assessment of each location's strengths and weaknesses. In other words, if the price is right, there is a buyer for everything. However, the situation in the occupied territories reflects considerations other than those of the marketplace, which may require Palestinian representatives and others to make judgements about the suitability and perhaps the monetary value of settlement assets.

Suitability is a function of numerous factors and considerations. Some of these have been noted above. Other issues impacting upon suitability include considerations related to land use and transportation. Settlements might be far away from suitable transportation networks or places of possible employment. As far as possible, our analysis attempts to evaluate the suitability of settlement assets, using benchmarks relating to ecology, water, and landscape preferences devised by Palestinian planners.

As much as we endeavour to assess the utility of settlement assets, there are also areas of evaluation that we do not address. We have not considered questions relating to the establishment of mechanisms for the transfer of assets from Israeli to Palestinian control, including the broad issue of securing assets against theft or appropriation. We do not address the question of land ownership, or mechanisms for determining or adjudicating ownership claims by Palestinians against lands or assets formerly held by Israeli individuals or institutions. We do not suggest ways in which to manage the disposition or distribution of settlement assets.

We do not hazard a dollar value for settlement assets, and for good reason. Settlement assets can be valued according to relative value in Israel's national market. In formal economic terms, this value decreases to zero as Israel implements a decision to evacuate. That is, in the aftermath of a decision to evacuate, there is no Israeli market for fixed settlement assets, other than one regarding compensation, which would be granted at prices determined by the government of Israel, which do not reflect economic criteria. At this stage the settlements – in classic economic terms – are worthless.

The transfer of settlement assets from Israeli to Palestinian control would establish new criteria for their valuation. In the West Bank today, the construction of a dwelling of 120 m², a size typical of housing in the region, costs approximately US $41,400 and US $37,260 in the Gaza Strip (Elwan 2003). From this simple benchmark, which makes no provision for the varying cost of services and land (remember the three rules of real estate valuation: location, location, location) a rough valuation of residential assets in settlements could be made.

Finally, we do not explicitly match specific Palestinian populations such as refugees with settlement housing, beyond observations about the type and size of housing available to Palestinians as a consequence of Israeli evacuation.

As the Palestinian Authority develops standards for the eventual reintegration of territories evacuated by Israel, certain basic assumptions have been formulated. The Ministry of Planning's report on Reintegration and Development of Evacuated Areas, prepared in late 2004 in the context of the impending evacuation of all settlements in the Gaza Strip and four in the Jenin area of the West Bank, notes that:

> The reintegration of the evacuated areas into the Palestinian system is one of the most critical components for ensuring the political, social, economic, cultural, physical, environmental benefits associated with the return of colonies' areas into the Palestinian domain. The

evacuated areas should not be treated as separate islands, but should be incorporated as parts of the Palestinian environment and accordingly integrated within the overall existing Palestinian infrastructure and spatial patterns.

Any future use of evacuated areas and/or installations should be assessed against the long term developmental vision and objectives, and strategies leading to a viable, contiguous, prosperous and independent Palestinian state. In this respect, the Gaza Strip cannot be seen as an isolated or semi-independent territorial or political entity. ... It cannot be assumed that structures installed for the purpose of occupation, colonization and annexation of Palestinian land would be of value for independent Palestinian development. From the perspective of the occupied people, one would assume that the opposite is the case. That is, these installations would be detrimental rather than beneficial to Palestinian development.

(MOPIC 2004: pp. 3, 7)

To the extent that our inquiry was guided by an assumption of the self-evident value of evacuated settlement assets to the Palestinian community, the process of evaluation accompanying Israel's anticipated redeployment from the Gaza Strip and four settlements in the Jenin area of the West Bank has been a sobering experience. Our analysis of the utility of settlement areas to be evacuated supports the overall assessments made by MOP, that is, that while the basic infrastructure created by Israel, including roads, telecommunications, water, and electricity networks, can be useful to and complement Palestinian development plans, particularly in the Gaza Strip, the location and nature of the dwelling units and the limited communal, commercial, and industrial facilities (with the possible exception of the Erez industrial zone in north Gaza) represent, at best, marginal additions to Palestinian development efforts. Indeed, the Palestinian Authority concluded that the destruction of the entire infrastructure of housing in the Gaza Strip of approximately 1,200 units would enhance rather than complicate Palestinian development assessments and goals, which include, *inter alia*, the provision of suitable housing for Gaza's existing refugee population and an anticipated influx of Palestinians, many of them refugees, in coming years.

The destruction of the visible superstructure (as opposed to the infrastructure) of settlement assets associated with the Gaza disengagement plan establishes a precedent for future Israeli evacuations of occupied territories. It is important to note that the decision-making dynamic that produced the policy of settlement destruction was led by the government of Israel. Israel's conclusions at first were tacitly supported by the PA, a view that was later articulated with greater clarity as the disengagement period approached.

However, there is no reason to believe that the infrastructure left by Israel will be as inconsequential, if not deleterious, to Palestinian requirements as is the housing stock included in the Gaza disengagement plan. Indeed, while for Israel the precedent of destroying settlement housing upon evacuation was established in the retreat from Sinai (in Yamit if not in the small Red Sea settlements) and in the current disengagement plan, for Palestinians, opposition to retaining settlement housing assets is tied, not to issues of principle, but to an assessment of their utility. While these assessments appear to complement each other in the Gaza plan, there is no guarantee that this will be the case in future Israeli withdrawals.

Our research suggests however that the settlement housing in the West Bank and East Jerusalem that will be most helpful to Palestinians is indeed unlikely to be evacuated by Israel in any of the settlement evacuation scenarios that we have postulated. Built-up urban settlement areas in and around Jerusalem in particular that could easily complement Palestinian development strategies are unlikely candidates for evacuation. Settlements like Kiryat Arba, with 1,200 units could provide useful housing and limited industrial space for Hebron, which it abuts. Ariel, with a current settler population of 18,000, offers some attractive ingredients necessary for successful integration, such as an integrated housing and transportation network of sufficient scale and proximity to existing Palestinian employment and commercial poles, which would make the settlement useful in its current configuration. There are also other smaller settlements that offer more attractive assets, including Itamar near Nablus, Ofra near Silwad, Bet El near Ramallah, the Jordan Valley settlement of Masua near the proposed new city of Jiftlik, the Etzion Bloc settlements, with the prominent exception of Betar Ilit, and Bet Haggai near Hebron.

Overall, however, these locations are exceptions to the rule we have seen established in the Gaza disengagement plan. The settlements to be evacuated by Israel under most plausible withdrawal scenarios will provide important assets, such as transportation, water, and communications networks that can facilitate Palestinian development and thus contribute indirectly to housing anticipated increases in Palestinian population, including refugees. However, in terms of housing stock for refugees or other Palestinians, evacuated settlements can be expected to be of only isolated and marginal value.

BIBLIOGRAPHY

Elwan, A. (2003) *Housing and Infrastructure Scenarios for Refugees and Displaced Persons*, Washington, DC: World Bank.

Palestinian National Authority Ministry of Planning (MOPIC) (1997) *Draft Regional Plan – Gaza Governorates*, Gaza: MOPIC.

—— (1998) *The Regional Plan for the West Bank Governorates*, Ramallah: MOPIC.

—— (2004) *Reintegration and Development of Evacuated Areas*, Gaza: MOPIC.

Notes

2 STATISTICAL DATA ON PALESTINIAN REFUGEES: WHAT WE KNOW AND WHAT WE DON'T

1 PLO established this bureau in 1979. It used to compile statistics from secondary sources on the Palestinian people, in addition to carrying out infrequent surveys targeting Palestinian refugees living in Lebanon and Syria. Currently, this office is part of PCBS and provides limited statistical services on Palestinian refugees in these two countries. These statistics are usually published in Ramallah by PCBS. Moreover, the bureau has collected data on living conditions of refugees in the two countries on behalf of Fafo upon agreement and permission granted to Fafo by PCBS in Ramallah.

2 While international recommendations suggest that a census should be carried out in 2007, we recommend that a census is carried out exactly one year after the establishment of a Palestinian State. This census will capture socio-demographic changes in the Palestinian society of the emerging state as a result of the expected return of some Palestinians to the independent Palestinian state.

3 This survey was conducted in partnership with Fafo. It was designed to serve as a pilot for the upcoming Palestinian census. The sample size was 15,000 households.

4 In fact, this survey was designed to be conducted on an annual basis. Three rounds were implemented. Financing problems led to cessation of this survey until 2001. PCBS recommends that a three-year cycle is put together starting 2005.

5 This survey was designed to measure the impact of Israeli military field activities on the psychosocial conditions of these two vulnerable groups within Palestinian society.

6 This survey targets the Palestinian population of Jerusalem. While all PCBS statistical activities cover Jerusalem, this survey is supposed to provide extensive coverage of this part of the country due to the special conditions of Jerusalem.

7 The poverty line for a household of two adults and four children was estimated for 2002 to be almost $360. This represents almost $1.97 a day/person.

8 The full details of this survey can be obtained from PCBS (email: diwan@pcbs.pna.org).

4 SOCIAL CAPITAL, TRANSNATIONAL KINSHIP AND REFUGEE REPATRIATION PROCESS: SOME ELEMENTS FOR A PALESTINIAN SOCIOLOGY OF RETURN

1 Although Sari Hanafi was the Director of the Palestinian Diaspora and Refugee Center, Shaml, at the time of writing this paper, this work reflects only his views. He expresses his gratitude to Ann Lesch for her editing of this chapter. He thanks the many researchers who critiqued the first draft, including Roula El Rifai, Pamela Scholey, Riina Isotalo, Cedric Parizot and Nadim Rouhana.

2 This survey encompassed 2,254 Palestinian households in 19 communities in the Palestinian territories in the summer of 1999. (See Giacaman and Johnson 2002.)

3 Fafo is the Norwegian Institute for Applied Social Science. The Fafo survey is about the living conditions of Palestinian refugees in Lebanon and Jordan. In Lebanon it covers a sample of 4,000 households in refugee camps and relatively homogeneous refugee areas (Ugland 2003). In Jordan, the survey employed two methods: a survey of stratified probability sample of about 3,100 households selected from 12 camps; and 13 focus groups. The primary purpose of the focus group discussions was to learn how camp dwellers perceive economic hardship, unemployment, and work opportunities (Khawaja and Tiltes 2002).

4 PSR's survey was conducted between 16 January and 5 February 2003, targeting 1,498 Palestinian refugee households distributed among 150 localities in the West Bank and Gaza Strip.

5 Here much criticism can be levelled at many surveys conducted in the Palestinian territories that have relied on emotionally based questions.

6 The Public Health Institute of Birzeit University is currently examining this issue.

7 Close relatives are defined as parents, spouses, children or siblings.

8 Second degree relatives are defined as matrimonial and patrimonial aunts and uncles and their families.

9 Some 82 per cent of those surveyed said they received the same assistance as before the *intifada*.

10 See for example the European Union report commissioned in 1999, *Prospects for Absorption of Returning Refugees in the West Bank and the Gaza Strip*, the Institute of International Economic Relations (Charalambos and Huliaras 1999).

11 See the critique by Grillo, Riccio and Salih (2000: 19).

12 Transfer of Knowledge Through Expatriate Nationals (TOKTEN) is an interesting mechanism for tapping into national expatriate human resources and mobilizing them to undertake short-term consultancy work in their countries of origin. The United Nations Development Programme (UNDP), which founded TOKTEN, demonstrated that specialists who had migrated to other countries and achieved professional success abroad were enthusiastic about providing short-term technical assistance to their country of origin.

13 More precisely we can define entrepreneurship as 'an attempt at new business or new venture creation, such as self-employment, a new business organization, or the expansion of an existing business, by an individual, a group of individuals, or an established business' (Reynolds, Hay and Camp 1999: 23).

14 Here we use the ILO classification and the definition of the entrepreneur (ILO 1998).

15 Personal communication with the author.

16 I believe that the right of return is the key to any durable solution to the Palestinian–Israeli conflict including the end of the occupation and the resolution of the land issue, because the right of return requires Israelis to acknowledge their moral responsibility and to be held accountable for the birth of the Palestinian refugee problem and the colonial practices deployed during the war of 1948.

17 Palestinians residing in Lebanon may not be able to determine their intention to return if the Lebanese position remains unclear. Will the Palestinians be thrown across the border, as happened in Libya, or will they be given the right to choose?

18 This figure is too high for Palestinians actually resident in Lebanon. It includes Palestinians with Lebanese travel documents or passports. We think the number cannot exceed 300,000.

6 REFUGEES, REPATRIATION, AND DEVELOPMENT: SOME LESSONS FROM RECENT WORK

1 See, for example, Abu Sitta, S. (1997) 'The Feasability of the Right of Return', at <http://www.arts.mcgill.ca/MEPP/PRRN/papers/abusitta.html>; Abu Sitta, S. (2001) 'The Return of the Refugees: The Key to Peace', *Middle East Insight* 26 (2), available online at <http://www.mideastinsight.org/3_01/abu.html>.

2 Initial World Bank work focused on general, order-of-magnitude costs, and was not specific to any particular geographic area. Later work, in conjunction with the Palestinian Authority, focused largely on refugee absorption in the West Bank and Gaza, but developed methodologies that could be applied to other areas. Needless to say, as an international organization the World Bank works in partnership with host countries, and its ability to examine refugee absorption in Israel or current host countries is determined by the (un)willingness of local authorities to undertake such studies.

3 UNRWA registration data shows some 389,233 refugees registered in Lebanon in December 2002. It is generally accepted, however, that a large proportion of these registrants do not currently reside in Lebanon (UNRWA 2003).

4 Calculation based on data presented in World Bank (2003) *Housing and Infrastructure Scenarios for Refugees and Displaced Persons*, Table 11.

5 The areas studied were Jenin, Jericho, Nablus, Taqumia, Tubas.

7 PLANNING IN SUPPORT OF NEGOTIATIONS: THE REFUGEE ISSUE

The findings, interpretations, and conclusions expressed in this chapter are those of the author(s) and do not necessarily reflect the views of the Board of Executive Directors of the World Bank or the governments they represent. The World Bank does not guarantee the accuracy of the data included in this work. The boundaries, colors, denominations, and other information shown on any map in this work do not imply any judgment on the part of the World Bank concerning the legal status of any territory or the endorsement or acceptance of such boundaries.

1 *Waqf* or endowment land is public or private land that has been donated, usually to religious institutions, to be used for charitable purposes. All lands owned by religious institutions are considered to be *waqf* land.

2 A dunum is a unit of land area enclosing 1,000 square metres.

3 Source: Foundation for Middle East Peace, 1999.

8 INFRASTRUCTURE SCENARIOS FOR REFUGEES AND DISPLACED PERSONS

1 The reports referenced here are just three of several studies and analyses carried out by the World Bank and by independent consultants on topics related to the needs of refugees and displaced people following an eventual peace agreement.

2 *Waqf* or endowment land is public or private land that has been donated, usually to religious institutions, to be used for charitable purposes All lands owned by religious institutions are considered to be *waqf* land.

3 Many Palestinian refugees and displaced people live in formal housing stock of good quality, which is indistinguishable from other formal housing stock, visually and statistically.

4 Report (A) presents details on the assumptions underlying the options (Annexes 4 and 5), as well as schematic diagrams of the various upgrading and redevelopment types (Appendix 3).

5 These issues are discussed to some extent in Annex 8 of the Phase I paper.

6 The costs of temporary relocation, as for example in the redevelopment options, is not included in the estimates.

7 The figures are as in Report (A), Table 2.1, except that costs of bulk water for new towns and cities are excluded.

8 Unit construction costs allow estimates to be made of various housing solutions – including upgrading, serviced plots, and adding rooms incrementally, etc., and thereby inform estimates of the amounts of financing that may be needed by households. Some of the issues and options in housing finance are summarized in this chapter. However, the authors do not advocate any particular model, but only provide basic information.

9 Costs are based on prices in 2000. No contingencies are included.

10 The focus of this study was on public and *waqf* land, since donors are generally reluctant to pay for land purchase. However, another option could be the acquisition of private land. Future analysis could, for example, look at availability and purchase of less expensive rural land, and/or pinpoint privately owned land in areas where there is economic potential for residential development. The consultant's study on land

therefore also briefly reviewed and outlined information on building codes, zoning, urban structures, densities, etc., and on provisions for changing land use, for example, changing public ownership to private.

11 For example, costs of additional electricity infrastructure and various types of public services, are not included.

12 International access is controlled by Israel. There is no operational railway system, and the seaport has not yet been constructed in Gaza.

13 This figure does not include the Israeli built roads, which only serve Israeli settlements, bypassing Palestinian population centres.

14 Under Oslo and subsequent accords between the Palestine Liberation Organization (PLO) and Israel, the Palestinians will be allowed three safe passages between the West Bank and Gaza through Israel. To date only one such passage has been agreed by Israel, connecting the northern part of Gaza with the southern part of the West Bank in the Hebron area, but it is rarely open.

15 This limitation reflects the direct public investment perspective of this particular study, and the assumption that serviced land (with or without housing), may need to be made available quickly, for example, to assist families who do not have the option to remain in current host countries. Public funds for land acquisition are assumed to be extremely limited, and donor agency funding guidelines tend to preclude land acquisition. However, as pointed out in Report (C) on Housing Finance – where the focus is on options for financing a variety of housing solutions – many new residents are likely to find housing solutions through traditional housing markets, involving the acquisition of private land and housing.

16 Available public land within municipal boundaries, for the purposes of this study, refers to parcels of land greater than 2,000 square metres – the minimum land area for high-rise residential housing under prevailing regulations.

17 Maps are shown in Annex 1 of the Phase II paper *Absorption of Refugees in the West Bank and Gaza: Potential for Housing Accommodation on Public Land in Selected Study Areas.*

18 The absorption capacity of the new town sites included in the study is potentially much larger (more than 300,000 at low density levels) if all the available public land in the Gaza site east of Rafah is taken into consideration, rather than the limiting number of 50,000 used for that site (see note to Table 7.8).

19 Annex 7 of Report (B) gives details on how the cost estimates from Report (A) were adjusted for these aggregated estimates.

20 As noted earlier, however, the inclusion of housing and land in the cost analysis should not be taken as an endorsement of full-scale public

construction of housing, nor is there an expectation that donors or other parties would be willing or able to pay for housing construction. Housing cost estimates may be used for models of various housing solutions and their overall costs (for example, core units or incrementally built houses), and for analysing housing finance needs, for example.

21 According to the Jordan Living Conditions Survey, 79 per cent of all *dars* (traditional houses) and 82 per cent of all apartments have between two and four rooms, not counting kitchen, bathroom and hallways. According to the 1994 census, the median size of dwelling unit is about 100 square metres, including kitchen, hallways, toilets, and storage areas.

22 This cost of construction covers basic low-income-type provision, including only rendered walls, concrete floors, the minimum of simple fittings, and no heating.

23 Including design and supervision, but not contingencies.

24 That is, 75 per cent of the construction cost, but without the 15 per cent design and supervision included in the new housing cost.

25 There is significant research showing, for example, that, under favorable conditions, even poor families will borrow at market rates to improve their housing.

26 Such a programme should, ideally, offset the economic cost of relocation without creating any particular financial incentive to relocate.

27 In an ideal situation, such a programme should offset the economic cost of relocation without creating any particular financial incentive to relocate.

28 The consultants identified several locations, not included in the original study, which have relatively large public lands.

9 LAND AND HOUSING STRATEGIES FOR IMMIGRANT ABSORPTION: LESSONS FROM THE ISRAELI EXPERIENCE

1 The most prominent expression for this approach were two national comprehensive plans, the 'Sharon Plan' and National Outline Plan no. 31. They were prepared to direct the new development required for Israel's two mass immigration waves: the first, in the early 1950s and the second in the early 1990s. (See Brutzkus 1964).

2 Until recent years, single young adults had hardly any rights to subsidized mortgages for regular housing.

3 During Israel's first decades this sector was large and included various groups based on place of employment, party affiliation or ideology.

4 Current terms of entitlement for housing are presented at the Ministry of Housing Internet site, at: <http://www.moch.gov.il/Moch/HousingSupport/VatikimInfo.htm> (in Hebrew).

5 Terms of Additional support for Immigrants are presented at the Ministry of Housing Internet site, at: <http://www.moch.gov.il/Moch/HousingSupport/OlimInfo.htm> (in Hebrew).

6 However, take into account that Israeli families tend to be larger than the average for the advanced-economy world today.

7 The Hebrew term for immigrant absorption used in most Hebrew publications is '*klitat aliya*'. This is a unique term that literally means 'ascent to the Holy Land'. For simplicity I have translated it simply as 'immigrant absorption'.

Index